Jesus First For Men

365 Devotions To Start Your Day

BroadStreet Publishing Group LLC

16pt

Copyright Page from the Original Book

BroadStreet Publishing Group, LLC.
Savage, Minnesota, USA
Broadstreetpublishing.com

Jesus First for Men
© 2023 by BroadStreet Publishing®

Devotional entries composed by Eoghan Holdahl

All rights reserved. No part of this publication may be reproduced, distributed, or transmitted in any form or by any means, including photocopying, recording, or other electronic or mechanical methods, without the prior written permission of the publisher, except in the case of brief quotations embodied in critical reviews and certain other noncommercial uses permitted by copyright law.

Scripture quotations marked niv are taken from the Holy Bible, New International Version®, NIV®. Copyright © 1973, 1978, 1984, 2011 by Biblica, Inc.™ Used by permission of Zondervan. All rights reserved worldwide. www.zondervan.com. The "NIV" and "New International Version" are trademarks registered in the United States Patent and Trademark Office by Biblica, Inc.™ Scripture quotations marked nlt are taken from the Holy Bible, New Living Translation, copyright © 1996, 2004, 2015 by Tyndale House Foundation. Used by permission of Tyndale House Publishers, Carol Stream, Illinois 60188. All rights reserved. Scripture quotations marked esv are taken from the ESV® Bible (The Holy Bible, English Standard Version®), Copyright © 2001 by Crossway, a publishing ministry of Good News Publishers. Used by permission. All rights reserved. Scripture quotations marked csb are taken from the Christian Standard Bible®, Copyright © 2017 by Holman Bible Publishers. Used by permission. Christian Standard Bible® and CSB® are federally registered trademarks of Holman Bible Publishers. Scripture quotations marked nasb are taken from the New American Standard Bible, Copyright 2020 by The Lockman Foundation. Used by permission. All rights reserved. Scripture quotations marked nkjv are taken from the New King James Version®. Copyright © 1982 by Thomas Nelson. Used by permission. All rights reserved. Scripture quotations marked ncv are taken from the New Century Version®. Copyright © 2005 by Thomas Nelson. Used by permission. All rights reserved. Scripture quotations marked tpt are taken from The Passion Translation® of the Holy Bible. Copyright © 2020 by Passion & Fire Ministries, Inc. Used by permission of BroadStreet Publishing®. All rights reserved.

Editorial services by Sarah Eral and by Michelle Winger | literallyprecise.com

TABLE OF CONTENTS

INTRODUCTION	ii
JANUARY	1
JANUARY 1: DO THE WORK	2
JANUARY 2: BROKEN STRENGTH	4
JANUARY 3: OUR THOUGHTS	5
JANUARY 4: UNSHAKEABLE FOUNDATIONS	7
JANUARY 5: PRAISE	9
JANUARY 6: PLANNED	11
JANUARY 7: LAVISH GOODNESS	13
JANUARY 8: BEING A BLESSING	15
JANUARY 9: ONE THIRD	17
JANUARY 10: EXALTED	18
JANUARY 11: SOBER JUDGMENT	20
JANUARY 12: PROCLAIMING POWER	22
JANUARY 13: COMPLEX	24
JANUARY 14: SOLITARY	26
JANUARY 15: FAITHFUL	28
JANUARY 16: A CONSUMING PEACE	30
JANUARY 17: WAITING	32
JANUARY 18: MEEK STRENGTH	34
JANUARY 19: HEARTS IN TUNE	36
JANUARY 20: RESTING AT LAST	38
JANUARY 21: WORKING AND DESIRING	39
JANUARY 22: THE GREATEST GIFT	41
JANUARY 23: FROM THE GRAVE	43
JANUARY 24: HIDDEN IN FAITHFULNESS	45
JANUARY 25: ENTHUSIASTIC WORK	47
JANUARY 26: PRACTICING AND PREACHING	49
JANUARY 27: LIVING FOR SELF	51
JANUARY 28: CHILD OF GOD	53
JANUARY 29: WATCHING OVER US	55
JANUARY 30: THANKFUL IN LOVE	57

JANUARY 31: FEAR AND SERVE	59
FEBRUARY	**61**
FEBRUARY 1: FALSE HOPE	62
FEBRUARY 2: ROOTING DOWN	64
FEBRUARY 3: KNOWLEDGE'S EXCELLENCE	66
FEBRUARY 4: STONY HEARTS	68
FEBRUARY 5: TEMPTED EVERY WAY	70
FEBRUARY 6: EXALT AND PRAISE	72
FEBRUARY 7: UNKILLABLE	74
FEBRUARY 8: TRANSCENDENT	76
FEBRUARY 9: GREATEST CONFIDENCE	78
FEBRUARY 10: YOUR TREASURE	80
FEBRUARY 11: GOD OF REST	81
FEBRUARY 12: HEART WISDOM	83
FEBRUARY 13: WRAPPED IN GOD	84
FEBRUARY 14: HELPLESS	86
FEBRUARY 15: NEEDLESS ANGER	88
FEBRUARY 16: CELEBRATION	89
FEBRUARY 17: DELIGHTED IN RIGHTEOUSNESS	91
FEBRUARY 18: BETTER ONE DAY	93
FEBRUARY 19: GOD'S ULTIMATE PLAN	95
FEBRUARY 20: WORRY ENTERS	96
FEBRUARY 21: UNTROUBLED AND UNAFRAID	98
FEBRUARY 22: DRAWN BY KINDNESS	100
FEBRUARY 23: UNTOLD BLESSINGS	102
FEBRUARY 24: GENTLE AND LOWLY	104
FEBRUARY 25: SLOWED DOWN	106
FEBRUARY 26: ACHIEVING STABILITY	108
FEBRUARY 27: BROTHERLY CARE	110
FEBRUARY 28: DWELLING IN FAITH	112
MARCH	**113**
MARCH 1: BEFORE ALL	114
MARCH 2: GIFT OF VIRTUE	116
MARCH 3: CREATOR AND REVEALER	117

MARCH 4: EMPOWERED THROUGH WISDOM	119
MARCH 5: NEW LIFE	121
MARCH 6: IN HIS PRESENCE	123
MARCH 7: CRAVING	125
MARCH 8: PUREST FAITHFULNESS	127
MARCH 9: MINDSET	129
MARCH 10: STRENGTHENED	131
MARCH 11: BROKEN WALLS	133
MARCH 12: SLAVES AND HEIRS	135
MARCH 13: NEVER PASSED OVER	137
MARCH 14: JOYFUL HEART	139
MARCH 15: MAN'S PURPOSE	140
MARCH 16: BROTHERLY AFFECTION	142
MARCH 17: PASSING SHADOWS	144
MARCH 18: BECAME HUMAN	146
MARCH 19: FAVOR OF GOD	148
MARCH 20: IN RETURN	150
MARCH 21: HIDING GOD'S PRESENCE	152
MARCH 22: WHAT WE KNOW	154
MARCH 23: A SELFLESS LIFE	156
MARCH 24: SWEET REST	158
MARCH 25: UNDERSTAND AND EXPRESS	159
MARCH 26: RELIABLE DEFENDER	161
MARCH 27: PURSUING WHAT MATTERS	163
MARCH 28: GOD OF LIGHT	165
MARCH 29: AS WE ARE	167
MARCH 30: GLORIOUS SPLENDOR	169
MARCH 31: FINALLY HEALED	171
APRIL	**173**
APRIL 1: TENDER LEADER	174
APRIL 2: LOVE'S WORTH	176
APRIL 3: FALSE HOPES	178
APRIL 4: IDLE LIVES	179
APRIL 5: LIVING WITH FAITH	181

APRIL 6: EVENTUAL REST	183
APRIL 7: ADMITTED WEAKNESS	185
APRIL 8: BROTHERLY FRIENDSHIP	187
APRIL 9: THANKFUL FOR EVERYTHING	189
APRIL 10: SOFTENED THROUGH WISDOM	191
APRIL 11: WALKING ALONGSIDE	193
APRIL 12: SUFFERING PATIENTLY	195
APRIL 13: WEIGHT OF GLORY	197
APRIL 14: HUMILITY HIDING	199
APRIL 15: FEARING THE SITUATION	201
APRIL 16: NEWNESS	203
APRIL 17: FOUNTAIN OF GOOD	205
APRIL 18: COVERED BY LOVE	207
APRIL 19: NOTHING REJECTED	209
APRIL 20: PERFECT PROVIDER	211
APRIL 21: TRUE COMPETENCE	213
APRIL 22: FAITHFULLY STRENGTHENED	215
APRIL 23: CAPTURED BY IGNORANCE	217
APRIL 24: STEADFAST ROCK	219
APRIL 25: THE HUMAN PROBLEM	221
APRIL 26: FREE OF BONDAGE	223
APRIL 27: MAGNIFICENT DESTINY	225
APRIL 28: FRUITLESS PAIN	227
APRIL 29: CRUSHED BY SIN	229
APRIL 30: ALIVE AND ACTIVE	231
MAY	**233**
MAY 1: CALLED TO PEACE	234
MAY 2: PEACE AND RIGHT-LIVING	236
MAY 3: DIVIDED HEART	238
MAY 4: HOLY CAREGIVER	240
MAY 5: PROOF	242
MAY 6: DIRTY SECRETS	244
MAY 7: CONSTANT FAITH	246
MAY 8: IDENTITY	248

MAY 9: WAITING AND READY	250
MAY 10: WISDOM AND WORK	252
MAY 11: FILLED WITH JOY	254
MAY 12: NO EXCUSES	256
MAY 13: DANGEROUS LOVE	258
MAY 14: REST IN ADVERSITY	260
MAY 15: PROMISE	261
MAY 16: ACTIONS SPEAK VOLUMES	262
MAY 17: LOVABLE	264
MAY 18: BE LIFTED UP	266
MAY 19: RIVER FROM GOD	267
MAY 20: PASSIONATE LOVE	269
MAY 21: BY OUR SIDE	270
MAY 22: PURPOSEFUL PEACE	272
MAY 23: EVIDENCE	273
MAY 24: DIFFERENT WEALTH	275
MAY 25: WHOLE BEING	277
MAY 26: ONE ANSWER	279
MAY 27: STRONG IN WEAKNESS	281
MAY 28: WEALTH IN WAITING	283
MAY 29: BACK TO LIFE	285
MAY 30: IMMOVABLE AND GENTLE	287
MAY 31: MARKED BY JESUS	289

JUNE   291

JUNE 1: SPIRIT AND BODY	292
JUNE 2: POWER BEYOND MEASURE	294
JUNE 3: LETTING GO	296
JUNE 4: FAMILIES	298
JUNE 5: HOLY REST	300
JUNE 6: LAW OF LOVE	302
JUNE 7: GETTING STUCK	304
JUNE 8: ONLY THE PATIENT	306
JUNE 9: DRAW NEAR	308
JUNE 10: CONFIDENCE	309

- JUNE 11: LEFT WANTING — 311
- JUNE 12: THE LORD IS ALWAYS — 313
- JUNE 13: ENDLESS GRACE — 315
- JUNE 14: HIGHEST STANDARD — 317
- JUNE 15: TEACHABLE NATURE — 319
- JUNE 16: ALWAYS FILLED — 320
- JUNE 17: FIX YOUR GAZE — 322
- JUNE 18: REFUGE — 324
- JUNE 19: WELL PLANNED — 325
- JUNE 20: OUR PRIDE — 327
- JUNE 21: CONSTANT IN PRAYER — 328
- JUNE 22: PURPOSE — 330
- JUNE 23: DIFFICULT PROGRESS — 332
- JUNE 24: FEEBLE EXISTENCE — 334
- JUNE 25: HIS BLESSED PRESENCE — 336
- JUNE 26: GOD'S PASSIONATE LOVE — 338
- JUNE 27: LABOR IN VAIN — 340
- JUNE 28: WHAT'S WITHIN — 342
- JUNE 29: OVERCOMING DEMONS — 344
- JUNE 30: JUST CALL HIM — 346

JULY — 348

- JULY 1: OUR POWER — 349
- JULY 2: IMMORTAL INHERITANCE — 351
- JULY 3: ETERNAL COMFORT — 353
- JULY 4: FAITH IN THE GOOD — 355
- JULY 5: MEN WHO FALL — 356
- JULY 6: EVERYTHING — 358
- JULY 7: VERY GOOD — 359
- JULY 8: APPROACH BOLDLY — 361
- JULY 9: RUN WITHOUT BREAKS — 363
- JULY 10: GOOD WISDOM — 365
- JULY 11: UNOFFENDED — 367
- JULY 12: MEN OF CONFIDENCE — 369
- JULY 13: IN ALL THINGS — 371

JULY 14: PROTECTION AND COURAGE ... 373
JULY 15: LIVES OF STRENGTH ... 375
JULY 16: TRUE WITNESS ... 377
JULY 17: STEADFAST ... 378
JULY 18: MAN OF MOTIVATION ... 380
JULY 19: FREE TO SUCCEED ... 382
JULY 20: GIVEN A GIFT ... 384
JULY 21: CHANGE ALL AROUND ... 386
JULY 22: BOASTING IN WEAKNESS ... 388
JULY 23: BECOMING A MAN ... 390
JULY 24: GOD REPLIES ... 392
JULY 25: LOOKING BACK ... 394
JULY 26: EYES ON HEAVEN ... 396
JULY 27: HEART OF WORSHIP ... 398
JULY 28: INDEPENDENT IN VIRTUE ... 400
JULY 29: SINGING TRUTH ... 402
JULY 30: LIVING EMPOWERED ... 404
JULY 31: FORGIVING ONE ANOTHER ... 406

AUGUST ... 408

AUGUST 1: ULTIMATE ACCOUNTABILITY ... 409
AUGUST 2: WORK AND REST ... 411
AUGUST 3: HOLY CALLING ... 413
AUGUST 4: OPEN TESTIMONIES ... 415
AUGUST 5: SET FOR SUCCESS ... 417
AUGUST 6: DRINK DEEPLY ... 418
AUGUST 7: DARK TIMES ... 420
AUGUST 8: BEYOND THE VISIBLE ... 422
AUGUST 9: RESPONDING LIKEWISE ... 424
AUGUST 10: STUDY HIS THOUGHTS ... 426
AUGUST 11: CONFIDENT PATIENCE ... 428
AUGUST 12: GOD OF POWER ... 429
AUGUST 13: PRUDENT WORDS ... 431
AUGUST 14: HE HAS TOLD ... 433
AUGUST 15: TRACK RECORD ... 435

- AUGUST 16: MINDFUL OF GOD — 437
- AUGUST 17: ONE WAY — 439
- AUGUST 18: MERCY AND COMPASSION — 441
- AUGUST 19: GOOD LEADERSHIP — 443
- AUGUST 20: HOLY DESIRES — 445
- AUGUST 21: LIVING IN FEAR — 447
- AUGUST 22: OUR FIRST GOAL — 449
- AUGUST 23: ACCEPTANCE — 451
- AUGUST 24: SACRIFICIAL LOVE — 453
- AUGUST 25: LETTING GO — 455
- AUGUST 26: CONTINUING — 457
- AUGUST 27: HOPE IN TRIALS — 459
- AUGUST 28: ALREADY PERFECT — 461
- AUGUST 29: SURRENDERED — 463
- AUGUST 30: UNCONTROLLED SPIRIT — 465
- AUGUST 31: OUR FINAL TRIUMPH — 467

SEPTEMBER — 469

- SEPTEMBER 1: MEN OF VIGILANCE — 470
- SEPTEMBER 2: HOLY GUARD — 472
- SEPTEMBER 3: MEN OF WISDOM — 473
- SEPTEMBER 4: VICTORIOUS — 475
- SEPTEMBER 5: PERFECTION MINDSET — 477
- SEPTEMBER 6: COST OF SIN — 479
- SEPTEMBER 7: BEING CONSCIOUS — 481
- SEPTEMBER 8: NOT FOREVER — 483
- SEPTEMBER 9: THE GREATEST MAN — 485
- SEPTEMBER 10: SUSTAINED IN CHRIST — 487
- SEPTEMBER 11: WITHOUT SHAME — 488
- SEPTEMBER 12: REMEMBRANCE — 490
- SEPTEMBER 13: MERE PEOPLE — 492
- SEPTEMBER 14: MAKING ALLOWANCE — 494
- SEPTEMBER 15: EVERY SORROW — 496
- SEPTEMBER 16: LIVING IN DARKNESS — 498
- SEPTEMBER 17: EVER-WAKING FRIEND — 499

SEPTEMBER 18: OUTSIDE OPINIONS	501
SEPTEMBER 19: PROMISE OF DISCIPLINE	503
SEPTEMBER 20: SURROUNDED IN VICTORY	504
SEPTEMBER 21: WORK HAS MEANING	506
SEPTEMBER 22: UNTOLD GLORIES	508
SEPTEMBER 23: GOD OF EMPATHY	510
SEPTEMBER 24: UNFATHOMABLE DEPTHS	512
SEPTEMBER 25: GOD OF GOODNESS	514
SEPTEMBER 26: GIVING IN POVERTY	516
SEPTEMBER 27: LEAVE THEM	518
SEPTEMBER 28: OUR PUREST FAITH	520
SEPTEMBER 29: TRUE WORK	522
SEPTEMBER 30: SHINING FRAGILITY	524
OCTOBER	**526**
OCTOBER 1: TO KNOW GOD	527
OCTOBER 2: SOLE DESIRE	529
OCTOBER 3: CHAINED DOWN	531
OCTOBER 4: FULLNESS OF JOY	533
OCTOBER 5: JOY HOPE PATIENCE	535
OCTOBER 6: BURDENED BEYOND MEASURE	537
OCTOBER 7: FOLLOWING JESUS	539
OCTOBER 8: APART FROM CHRIST	541
OCTOBER 9: DISPLAYING WISDOM	543
OCTOBER 10: FEARLESS GLORY	545
OCTOBER 11: CHOOSE THE UNSEEN	547
OCTOBER 12: MEN OF CARE	549
OCTOBER 13: EMPTY DARKNESS	551
OCTOBER 14: IN AND OUT	553
OCTOBER 15: EYES OF FAITH	555
OCTOBER 16: BE STILL	557
OCTOBER 17: PRAYING OPENLY	558
OCTOBER 18: EACH OF US	560
OCTOBER 19: TIRELESS HEART	562
OCTOBER 20: PATH OF THE LORD	563

OCTOBER 21: FEAR	565
OCTOBER 22: ALMIGHTY HELP	566
OCTOBER 23: FLESH OR SPIRIT	568
OCTOBER 24: LOVE INCOMPREHENSIBLE	570
OCTOBER 25: BEYOND FALSEHOOD	572
OCTOBER 26: RUNNING FOREVER	574
OCTOBER 27: WHY TRY	576
OCTOBER 28: FLEEING AND FIGHTING	578
OCTOBER 29: IT MAKES SENSE	580
OCTOBER 30: SINCERE LOVE	582
OCTOBER 31: BEAUTIFUL PRAYER	583
NOVEMBER	**584**
NOVEMBER 1: PRIVATE CONDUCT	585
NOVEMBER 2: FIGHTING SURRENDER	587
NOVEMBER 3: BROTHERS AND SISTERS	589
NOVEMBER 4: PROTECTED IN WAR	591
NOVEMBER 5: GOOD AS DONE	593
NOVEMBER 6: IT IS DONE	594
NOVEMBER 7: INCOMPARABLE LIFE	595
NOVEMBER 8: LITTLE WHILE	597
NOVEMBER 9: MEANINGFUL WORK	598
NOVEMBER 10: COMMON NEED	600
NOVEMBER 11: STEADFAST IN THE STORM	602
NOVEMBER 12: HIS MIND FOR US	604
NOVEMBER 13: UNSHAKEABLE FAITH	606
NOVEMBER 14: STRENGTH AND SHIELD	608
NOVEMBER 15: BROTHERLY ACCOUNTABILITY	610
NOVEMBER 16: FAITH AND BOLDNESS	612
NOVEMBER 17: STRONG AND BRAVE	614
NOVEMBER 18: EQUAL MEASURES	616
NOVEMBER 19: GENEROSITY AND FAITH	618
NOVEMBER 20: PRIESTS OF LIGHT	620
NOVEMBER 21: INNER DRIVE	622
NOVEMBER 22: ONCE AND FOREVER	623

NOVEMBER 23: ARE WE WILLING	625
NOVEMBER 24: WITHOUT COMPULSION	627
NOVEMBER 25: MEN OF CONFIDENCE	629
NOVEMBER 26: OUT OF SIGHT	631
NOVEMBER 27: WILLINGLY FOOLISH	633
NOVEMBER 28: HEART CONTENTS	635
NOVEMBER 29: SURROUNDED BY POWER	636
NOVEMBER 30: BETTER THAN LIVING	638
DECEMBER	**639**
DECEMBER 1: ANCHORED	640
DECEMBER 2: WITHOUT FATIGUE	642
DECEMBER 3: HIDDEN PERSON	643
DECEMBER 4: TRUE OVERSEER	645
DECEMBER 5: CONTINUING	647
DECEMBER 6: BELONG TO HIM	649
DECEMBER 7: BELIEF STRUGGLE	651
DECEMBER 8: HOPE IN	653
DECEMBER 9: CONFLICTING DESIRES	655
DECEMBER 10: CLOTHED IN LOVE	657
DECEMBER 11: HOLY DESIRE	658
DECEMBER 12: CONVICTED LIFE	659
DECEMBER 13: STRONG PEACE	661
DECEMBER 14: RECONCILING LIFE	663
DECEMBER 15: MAN'S GOOD PRAYER	665
DECEMBER 16: MANLY GENTLENESS	667
DECEMBER 17: ALWAYS AN ESCAPE	669
DECEMBER 18: CRUSHED IN GOD	671
DECEMBER 19: UNIQUELY EQUIPPED	672
DECEMBER 20: GLORY TO HIS NAME	674
DECEMBER 21: GOD OF DELIVERANCE	676
DECEMBER 22: IN HIS TIME	678
DECEMBER 23: OUR GREATEST SATISFACTION	680
DECEMBER 24: COUNTERFEIT LOVE	682
DECEMBER 25: CHRIST IS HERALDED	684

DECEMBER 26: HARMONY AND PEACE	686
DECEMBER 27: LONGING FOR DELIVERANCE	687
DECEMBER 28: APPROVED WORKER	689
DECEMBER 29: MIMICKING CHRIST'S KINGDOM	691
DECEMBER 30: OUR DIFFERENCES	693
DECEMBER 31: ALWAYS	695

Seek first God's kingdom and what God wants. Then all your other needs will be met as well.
MATTHEW 6:33 NCV

INTRODUCTION

When do you find time to connect with God? Even if we try to be intentional about it, everyday activities and responsibilities often find a way to take priority over our time with Jesus. Prayer can happen at any time, and of course it does, but there is value in setting aside a specific time to communicate with the Lord. The notion of getting alone with God to start the day was an example set by Jesus himself! He got up before daylight to pray in a solitary place. We don't know what about or who for, we just know it was his way of connecting with the Father before doing anything else.

As you quiet yourself before him and meditate on these Scriptures, devotions, and prayers, experience the goodness of his presence, and be refreshed with his perfect peace. When you prioritize Jesus above everything, other concerns fade. Hope dawns with the new day. Tender mercies fall fresh. Boundless joy springs up from a well within. And you find the strength to walk through each day with grace for others and for yourself.

JANUARY

With the loving mercy of our God, a new day from heaven will dawn upon us.
LUKE 1:78 NCV

JANUARY 1

DO THE WORK

"Be strong and courageous, and do the work. Don't be afraid or discouraged, for the LORD God, my God, is with you. He will not fail you or forsake you. He will see to it that all the work related to the Temple of the LORD is finished."
1 CHRONICLES 28:20 NLT

Having courage and taking action often go hand in hand. In today's verse, David tells Solomon to "do the work." He has to live the virtues of strength and courage in order to gain them. The greater the measure of possible failure, the greater the measure of courage required. This is why David promises his son, "He will not fail you or forsake you." We need not fear failure as long as God is doing the work through us; he will uplift us if we fail.

All God asks is that we do the work. We take initiative, listen for the Lord's plan, and do what he asks. As long as we have his strength, we need not fear being crushed by our failures. God's plan remains in place. He planned to build the temple, and he did. He plans to work mightily in our lives, and he will.

God, please give me strength and courage to meet this day. Give me the heart to do the work with great faith in what you can do.

JANUARY 2

BROKEN STRENGTH

In repentance and rest is your salvation,
in quietness and trust is your strength.
ISAIAH 30:15 NIV

The road to Christ is a narrow, steep one. It is a path of humility that crafts into us the qualities of our Savior. It teaches us to acknowledge God through repentance of our sins and to trust in his plans. We can't repent if we believe ourselves to be right, and we can't rest if we rely on ourselves to provide. Repentance, rest, quietness, and trust teach us dependance on Christ.

These virtues teach us to acknowledge God as our source of strength instead of ourselves. According to Isaiah, these meek virtues are our salvation as well; God rejects a proud heart but exalts the humble (James 6:4). Culture pushes men to desire posterity, strength, and respect. These are good things to desire, but God wants us to desire them as gifts from him for his glory.

Dear Lord, give me your strength for this day. Teach me to depend on you for my provision, salvation, and peace.

JANUARY 3

OUR THOUGHTS

On the glorious splendor of your majesty, and on your wondrous works, I will meditate.
PSALM 145:5 NLT

This psalm is a beautiful picture of devotion. The psalmist's mind is where God desires it to be: centered on him. He gives his Lord glory through adoration and meditation. What our minds focus on often dictates our spiritual health. If we focus on God's "glorious splendor" and all we can be thankful for, our souls and hearts fill with light. If we focus on sexual satisfaction, earthly gratification, or anything that is not God, our minds and spirits darken.

We might drift away from the image of God and his purpose for us. We are made for heaven, but the distractions of this life try to convince us that our focus should be on earth. However, the things around us only find their significance in Christ. Our career goals, physical health, relationships, and everything in between are fruitless if not seen through the eyes of heaven. Even while on earth, our meditation is on the eternal.

God, focus my mind on your glory and wondrous works. Remind me why I breathe; give me your perspective for the day.

JANUARY 4

UNSHAKEABLE FOUNDATIONS

Let us be thankful, because we have a kingdom that cannot be shaken. We should worship God in a way that pleases him with respect and fear.
HEBREWS 12:28 NCV

How often do we truly consider the omnipotence of God? Can any fear, anxiety, or failure stand in the face of God's unshakeable nature? We meet disappointments every day and sometimes every hour. God has planned it. We confront difficulties and heartbreak; we are pushed beyond our limits. God has planned it.

No experience can shake the kingdom of God. We are members of this kingdom, and as members, we have access to the promise of security. With this in mind, the writer of Hebrews cries out, "Let us be thankful." Those who control earthly kingdoms and nations question whether they will live to fight another year, but it is not so with God. Out of this deep well of security, this appreciation for an unshakeable kingdom, we have no other recourse but to worship God with respect and reverence.

Lord, you stand strong in the heavens, and you founded a kingdom to last beyond every generation. Give me a heart of praise for what you have done.

JANUARY 5

PRAISE

Praise him for his mighty works;
praise his unequaled greatness!
PSALM 150:2 NLT

As men, we often catch ourselves comparing our "greatness" and "mighty works" to others' deeds and stature. The moment we achieve something, we are tempted to compare our success. Two traps present themselves. One, we might compare to those below us and consider ourselves greater than we are. Two, we can compare ourselves to those greater than us and be filled with unneeded shame and frustration. There is always the possibility of meeting someone greater. There will always be someone smarter, stronger, or further along in life.

God is the answer to the temptation of comparison. *Unequaled* is the word the psalmist uses to describe God's greatness. He is the greatest one, and his mighty works are the mightiest. There is no use doing anything for the sake of comparison; God will always have unequaled greatness. For this, we praise him. It is his right.

Dear Lord, I praise you because you are the greatest in all you do. You are the humblest and the most righteous. You have removed my temptation to compare because you are unequaled.

JANUARY 6

PLANNED

"Before I formed you in the womb I knew you, before you were born I set you apart."
JEREMIAH 1:5 NIV

God desires his children to be prudent and wise, but he also wants them to remember he is the one planning. His plans have existed longer than us and will continue after our time on earth is done. In this passage, God says through the prophet Jeremiah, "Before I formed you in the womb, I knew you." He knows us better than we know ourselves. He sees us without the blinding effects of human emotion, bias, and idealization.

God also says he "set you apart." He decided our purpose far before we could think. Rather than including God in our plans, we have the honor of being included in God's plans. In light of God's surpassing knowledge and foresight, what is our anxiety? How can we worry in light of his steadfast purpose for us? Even if we question it, God still has a plan for our lives that transcends our ability to understand it.

Lord, may my every care and worry be banished by the thought of your knowledge

and purpose for me. Help me trust in the plan you have founded.

JANUARY 7

LAVISH GOODNESS

How great is the goodness you have stored up
for those who fear you.
You lavish it on those who come to you for
protection, blessing them before the watching
world.
PSALM 31:19 NLT

It is within God's rights to withhold comfort and blessing from us. Many of God's children experience lives of continuous hardship and persecution, but to them, lavish goodness is no foreign concept. We are blessed "before the watching world" and not just in the ways people assume. We are given eternal blessings. We rest in the spiritual protection of the Lord knowing he will guard us from all evil and earthly destruction as long as he has something left for us to do. The greatest blessing is looking forward to eternity with God. No one can earn a fraction of such a blessing.

We can truly say to God, "How great is the goodness you have stored up for those who fear you." Upon our devotion and faith, God gives us peace while on earth and peace for eternity. He gives us the fruit of the Spirit to set us apart from the watching world, and he transforms us into our best selves.

Lord, thank you for your great goodness. Thank you for all the blessings, both eternal and temporary, you have given me. I praise your name!

JANUARY 8

BEING A BLESSING

Take advantage of every opportunity to be a blessing to others, especially to our brothers and sisters in the family of faith!
GALATIANS 6:10 TPT

The difficulty in following Paul's advice in this verse has less to do with willingness and more to do with creativity. Between working and sleeping, it's difficult to find time and ways to bless others. We may be willing, but we don't always see the opportunities around us. We have to be creative like the people who delivered the paraplegic to Jesus through the roof.

Being a blessing is more than giving; it's serving. Letting others go before us in line, sharing our meals, mowing lawns, and doing things we would not do by default are all manifestations of being a blessing. According to Paul, these opportunities are especially valuable when they bless our brothers and sisters in Christ. Our fellow Christians understand the meaning of our actions and are often persecuted by the world.

Lord, make me a blessing today. Open my eyes to the needs around me and especially within your church.

JANUARY 9

ONE THIRD

Good comes to those who lend money generously and conduct their business fairly.
PSALM 112:5 NLT

For most people, the work week is forty hours long. One third of each day, Monday through Friday, is spent working. Since this takes up such a large percentage of our existence, how we conduct ourselves at work is important. Is our moral life at home in contrast to our moral life at work?

Fairness and generosity are touchy subjects in today's culture. Most people feel they deserve more from the world than what they are getting; everybody would agree that the world is unfair in many ways. Godly satisfaction does not come from receiving but giving. Today's psalm says, "Good comes to those who lend money generously." If we find ourselves wanting what we think we deserve, we should instead search for the generosity to give others what they need. Then we will have the greatest satisfaction.

Lord, give me a generous heart today. Teach me to conduct my business fairly and to show your light through my actions.

JANUARY 10

EXALTED

He brought me to the banqueting house, and his banner over me was love.
SONG OF SOLOMON 2:4 ESV

In this picture painted by the bride of Solomon, Solomon blesses his most beloved by personally bringing her to a place of food and relaxation. He gives her a place of honor and heralds her with a banner of love. This picture also depicts Christ's relationship to us. While we were still sinners, Christ took us from our lowly station and brought us to his table. He gave us honor when we deserved shame and blessed us when we deserved curses.

The greatest way we can experience God's favor for us is by showing godly favor to others. When we open up our hearts in generosity, exalting those dismissed by society, we experience the feelings Christ has toward us. This is a great blessing. May we, like Solomon, raise the lowly up. May we bring them to a place of feasting and hold our banner of love over them proudly for all to see.

Lord, please give me grace for the world. May I treat the lowly as Solomon treated his bride: with love and generosity.

JANUARY 11

SOBER JUDGMENT

By the grace given to me I say to everyone among you not to think of himself more highly than he ought to think, but to think with sober judgment, each according to the measure of faith that God has assigned.
ROMANS 12:3 ESV

Pride is dangerous. When we evaluate our worth as higher than it is, we can ruin our relationships by exalting ourselves to a place we don't deserve. People are our equals. Their judgment matters just as much, their opinions are equally valid, and they are just as likely to be right. Once we sever our identity from our strength, achievements, and stature, we can do the work Jesus expects of us.

Paul asks us to consider ourselves with "sober judgment." This doesn't mean we should think of ourselves as worthless and terrible at anything we try; that's an inaccurate and dangerous picture of who we are. Christ wants us to think of ourselves accurately and sparingly. Our judgment should not be impaired by pride or desire but accurate with the facts. Simultaneously, our spiritual health depends on us not thinking about ourselves too often and instead giving our focus to those around us.

Lord, please make me a man of humility. Give me the sober judgment of Christ and help me view others with respect and kindness.

JANUARY 12

PROCLAIMING POWER

Let each generation tell its children of your mighty acts; let them proclaim your power.
PSALM 145:4 NLT

How we live is a proclamation of what we believe. When we live with passion, we proclaim a source of that passion. When we live with weakness, we do the same. We can't live lives of weakness and expect people to believe our gospel of power. Our words and actions must proclaim the God of passion, life, and hope. This testimony has been carried by every generation of Christ's church, and now it's our turn to carry it.

The apostle Paul echoes the psalmist when he tells his understudy, Timothy, "God has not given us a spirit of timidity, but of power" (2 Tim 1:7, NASB). God wants our pride and selfishness broken so we can be perfected in his power. He wants us to put on him and take off our identity so we may be equipped to proclaim to each generation the source of our strength and new identity.

Lord, please give me the faith to take each day with optimism. Give me words to

proclaim your power and actions to agree with my words.

JANUARY 13

COMPLEX

> Thank you for making me so wonderfully complex! Your workmanship is marvelous—how well I know it.
> PSALM 139:14 NLT

Every man is a complex being. God created us at the intersection of the physical and the spiritual, so figuring out who we are is confusing even to ourselves. Add our unique experiences and the forces that act on us, and we truly are "wonderfully complex." God delights in this complexity. He is the architect of it, and he purposefully made us unique. Nothing about who we are and what we have gone through is random.

When misunderstood, our God-given complexity can be a burden. We wonder why we are the way we are, and we wish we could be anyone but ourselves. This is not the perspective of the psalmist. "Your workmanship is marvelous—how well I know it," he says. Despite the flaws and the trouble of pride, our identity is God's workmanship, and every day we live for him, we grow closer to the men he created us to be.

Lord, please give me faith in who you have made me to be. Remind me that my struggles and my identity have a purpose, and you will use them.

JANUARY 14

SOLITARY

Very early in the morning, while it was still dark, Jesus got up, left the house and went off to a solitary place, where he prayed.
MARK 1:35 NIV

Jesus set us the greatest precedent for how Christians should walk through life. In this passage, even the perfect son of God went off to pray and be alone. There are different terms for this, but at its heart, it is communion with God. It is a repeated renewal of relationship, so the child of God stays close to the heart and presence of the Father. This can take dedication and planning as Jesus showed by rising "very early in the morning."

Beyond requests, praying means listening to God and reshaping our minds and hearts. Praying is the most active way we can listen for God's will in our lives; praying in solitude as Jesus did reshapes our focus and gives us peace. It is a way for us to slow down and regain control of ourselves lest the world take control of us through our desires and physical needs.

Lord, give me the passion to rise early in the morning to be with you. Give me an

overwhelming desire for your presence that reshapes my habits.

JANUARY 15

FAITHFUL

I will not break my agreement nor change what I have said.
PSALM 89:34 NCV

Our faithfulness to God flows from his faithfulness to us. Faithfulness is a key aspect of who God is, and throughout Scripture, we see God affirming his faithfulness through numerous covenants. In this psalm, the writer records God affirming his faithfulness to David. This faithfulness was not reciprocated perfectly. David betrayed the Lord on multiple occasions with murder and adultery, yet the Lord remained faithful to him.

As men, are we willing to be bigger than our pain? The pain of betrayal cuts deeper than many physical wounds. Are we willing to continue in faithfulness and commitment when situations and people don't live up to our expectations? Are we willing to show the love of God to those who don't deserve it? We didn't deserve it either, yet God chose to love us anyway. Our calling is to act as he acted in loving faithfulness to a faithless and adulterous world that continually lets us down.

Lord, give me the wisdom and strength to know when to continue in faithfulness. Show me how to be loving when unloved by those around me.

JANUARY 16

A CONSUMING PEACE

Perfect, absolute peace surrounds those whose imaginations are consumed with you; they confidently trust in you.
ISAIAH 26:3 TPT

The imagery used by Isaiah is intense. He describes a people "whose imaginations are consumed with you." When was the last time we could accurately describe our imaginations as being "consumed" by another in a way that wasn't sexual? When was the last time we tasted such pure and holy fire? May our minds again know the absolute peace of being consumed by the thought of the Lord. A "perfect, absolute peace" floods our minds when we yield to the Lord.

The last line says, "they confidently trust in you." The mind consumed by the Lord has known the troubles and the cares of this world but is nevertheless impervious to them. This mind trusts the Lord because the Lord holds the whole world in his hand and has never seen an event he didn't plan. Why would we not confidently trust such a God of consuming peace?

Lord, let the thought of you be my holy obsession. Let my mind continually dwell on you and thus dwell in peace.

JANUARY 17

WAITING

Wait for the LORD;
be strong, and let your heart be courageous.
Wait for the LORD.
PSALM 27:14 CSB

Waiting is not easy. It is a soul-refining task created to grow our patience and sabotage our pride. In pride, we want to act. We want to see our actions accomplish things, but God would have us wait in patience. We are small-minded to think we can do anything apart from the hand of the Almighty. The psalmist says, "Be strong, and let your heart take courage." Our hearts should not be weakened through waiting; they should grow strong in holy dependence on the Lord.

Twice the psalmist demands, "Wait for the Lord." This is no passive task but an active watching and waiting for the plan God has set to unfold. This doesn't mean we should forget about God's working. We are tasked with a difficult job which requires our full attention. Yes, wait for the Lord!

God, give me patience when I would rather act apart from you. Remind me of your power and your plan held since the foundations of the world.

JANUARY 18

MEEK STRENGTH

> Put on then, as God's chosen ones, holy and beloved, compassionate hearts, kindness, humility, meekness, and patience.
> COLOSSIANS 3:12 ESV

Jesus is both the Lion of Judah and the Lamb who was slain. He is perfect because he has virtues that seem to be opposites but are consummated in him. He is meek but mighty. He is compassionate and also strong in his judgment. Jesus wants us to be the same. He wants us to grow as beautiful image bearers of both mightiness and meekness.

The virtues in this Colossians verse all have their root in self-control. God did not promise us control of our lives, but he does want us to have control over our hearts and minds. He desires for us, as his "holy and beloved," to manifest our passion as compassion, our hurt turned into kindness, and our pride brought low to raise humility. If we are bringers of light to a world drenched in darkness, we need the virtues God has stored up for us.

Lord, please grow in me a heart that feels what you feel. Give me compassion, kindness, humility, meekness, and patience.

JANUARY 19

HEARTS IN TUNE

O LORD, do good to those who are good,
whose hearts are in tune with you.
PSALM 125:4 NLT

The psalmist leans on his musical knowledge as he prays for those "whose hearts are in tune with" the Lord. He prays for God's grace and favor to be given to those who act as God acts: in goodness. He prays for people's actions to mirror the way God treats them and that wickedness would not befall the good. This is a deep and passionate cry to the Lord for justice to be seen on the earth.

Some might assume that in being consumed in goodness and following God, our identities would be lost like droplets in an ocean. Instead, attuning our hearts to the Lord is more like a note finding its place in a symphony. Each of us has a unique goodness from the Lord distinct from anybody else's though similar in quality. We receive our true selves through attuning our hearts to the Lord's song.

God, may I see justice done on behalf of the goodhearted. May I see the righteous

treated fairly and not persecuted for their virtue.

JANUARY 20

RESTING AT LAST

In peace I will lie down and sleep,
for you alone, O LORD, will keep me safe.
PSALM 4:8 NLT

Without trust in the Lord, our sleep is imperfect. Our minds worry about our safety, what we have not done, and what we should be doing rather than let ourselves rest. With the Lord, we can rest assured in the knowledge that God does the work, and we are his instruments. God keeps us safe, and we can sleep knowing he is the one who watches over our souls and bodies. Whatever may come, he is there to meet it with us.

"You alone, O LORD," says the psalmist. There is no other source of safety. Even the rich who sleep behind many locked doors owe their ultimate security to God. He gives security, and he can take it away at a moment's notice. Nothing we can do can assure our safety, but we can work to be better assured of God's promises of providence and care. He is faithful to his beloved children and has reserved holy and perfect rest for us.

God, give me rest in you.

JANUARY 21

WORKING AND DESIRING

God is working in you, giving you the desire and the power to do what pleases him.
PHILIPPIANS 2:13 NLT

In our Bible studies, spiritual disciplines, and strategies, God is at work. He crafts and shapes us. He is the one working because he saw us first and decided to take our poor, forgotten souls from the mire and breathe new life into us. However, God doesn't want soldiers who just follow orders. He wants souls with holy desire. The work of the Lord in us is the perfection of our desire and power for the sake of his pleasure.

As children, we are born powerless and with little influence. We have innocent, unconstrained desires. By growing up and walking with God, our desires are shaped and directed toward what is holy: worship, service, love, good, and relationships with other souls. Often what seems like weakness is actually the perfection of power in us. By breaking us, he makes us desire wholeness all the more, and he gives us the power of will we didn't have before.

God of glory and desire, sanctify me and make me righteous in you. Give me a holy desire to do your will.

JANUARY 22

THE GREATEST GIFT

"This is how much God loved the world—he gave his one and only, unique Son as a gift. So now everyone who believes in him will never perish but experience everlasting life."
JOHN 3:16 TPT

When God sent his Son to die for us, he gave us a gift beyond comparison. God has only one Son, one person to bear the divine image of God in human flesh. There is none like him, and when God sent him to die for our sins, his life and death brought him great pain. The salvation extended to us through his death, however, was counted by God to be worth the sacrifice.

How this verse starts is important. It says, "*This* is how much God loved the world." It was to *this* measure, to *this* extent, that God extended his love for all of us. He died for us, so the question now is whether we are willing to die for him. Are we willing to give up our lives as an act of love to God and surrender ourselves to him? This is the measure of devotion that God extended to us and the measure he asks of us.

Lord, I give you my heart and life. Use it as you will and make me rejoice in your love and salvation.

JANUARY 23

FROM THE GRAVE

He saves my life from the grave and loads me
with love and mercy.
PSALM 103:4 NCV

Dead people can't choose anything or make decisions. When the psalmist says, "He saves my life from the grave," he is speaking into the fact that when Christ saves us, it has nothing to do with our desires or choices. We are enemies of the cross redeemed by a merciful savior who chooses for us what we can't choose ourselves. He attained this salvation through the grave by dying and becoming the first and only person to die and rise again of their own choice.

Our salvation is at the heart of our relationship to Christ. Every moment of every day is changed by the fact that we are in a relationship with God and no longer opposed to his gospel. We are loaded, as the verse says, with love and mercy like a pack animal ready for a long journey. May this salvation be seen in every facet of our lives.

Lord God, thank you for saving me while I was yet dead. Thank you for redeeming me

while I was still your enemy, Your love and your mercy have renewed me.

JANUARY 24

HIDDEN IN FAITHFULNESS

It is impossible for God to lie for we know that his promise and his vow will never change! And now we have run into his heart to hide ourselves in his faithfulness. This is where we find his strength and comfort, for he empowers us to seize what has already been established ahead of time – an unshakable hope!
HEBREWS 6:18 TPT

We are called to be bold. We are called to push beyond constraints, latch our hope to the glorious future, and let go of the past's hold on us. We are also called to be bold in the right ways. When it comes to evil, we are told to flee. Yes, to run away! This verse from Hebrews tells us, "Now we have run into his heart to hide ourselves." Our boldness and strength in the Lord do not extend to impurity and faithlessness. Into these things, we do not go boldly.

Hiding in Christ, we have both comfort and strength. When every earthly comfort is taken away and those we love are lost, we have the privilege of digging deeper into the comfort of the Lord. He is our refuge in every storm and our strength in every moment of weakness. There is no one like him, perfect in faithfulness and a sure hope. We can't change his character, and in this we rejoice.

Dear God, today I hide myself in you. Fill my soul with the comfort and strength of the Lord and make me trustful in you.

JANUARY 25

ENTHUSIASTIC WORK

> Work with enthusiasm, as though you were working for the Lord rather than for people.
> EPHESIANS 6:7 NLT

How many men would say that they "work with enthusiasm?" This is a tall order for anyone to fill. Often, it's all we can do to keep working let alone do so with great energy and purpose. The lie we lead ourselves to believe is that as long as we show up, it's enough. As long as we are present, our duty is fulfilled. However, few things are more repulsive to God than a lukewarm believer. He wants passionate men who act with purpose and deep humility. He does not want a kingdom of believers drowning in stagnant apathy.

The solution to apathy is living before the face of God and remembering that every action we take has the potential for eternal impact. Once we remember we are in the presence of the almighty, our work feels more significant. No matter the job, no matter the work, it is all made significant by doing it "for the Lord rather than for people."

Oh God, remind me today of the importance of my work. Remind me how important it is to work with you rather than drown in apathy.

JANUARY 26

PRACTICING AND PREACHING

Oh, that my actions would consistently reflect your decrees!
PSALM 119:5 NLT

We have an enormous resource for living righteously. God's Word is filled to the brim with his decrees, and humans have spent millennia interpreting it, studying it, and trying to grow closer in their understanding of the heart of God. No amount of head knowledge about God, however, translates into action. This is the plight of the psalmist as he cries out, "Oh, that my actions would consistently reflect your decrees!"

The psalmist is a man with a heart for being righteous. The 119th psalm is the longest, and its theme is one of devout obedience. This writer understands that his actions often fail to live up to what he professes and what God has decreed. Much of faith is a process of God weeding out hypocrisy in our lives that has snuck in through the years. God is a holy God, and he will not be satisfied with a man whose words contradict his actions.

Dear Jesus, search me and know me. As I learn to know you, may you also know every part of me and make my actions consistently reflect your decrees.

JANUARY 27

LIVING FOR SELF

He died for everyone so that those who receive his new life will no longer live for themselves. Instead, they will live for Christ, who died and was raised for them.
2 CORINTHIANS 5:15 NLT

What wakes us up in the morning? What is the inspiration behind our rising, working, and choosing to rest? When we live for ourselves, we might be generous and kind, but ultimately, we use those things to improve ourselves. We will be these things because we know it is good for us. Even when we do all the right things, the heart can have a selfish outlook.

Christ "died for everyone so that those who receive his new life will no longer live for themselves." Even without a reward, we aim for virtue for the love of Christ. We should have deep within us the desire to live for Christ. Any Christian man who lives for himself, even while trying to be virtuous, will find himself burned out and unsatisfied. His virtue has to be built on a foundation of selfless love, otherwise it will not persevere.

Oh Jesus, I am all for you. In my virtue and my life, I live for you. I dedicate this day to your glory and the grace you have shown me.

JANUARY 28

CHILD OF GOD

See what great love the Father has lavished on us, that we should be called children of God! And that is what we are! The reason the world does not know us is that it did not know him.
I JOHN 3:1 NIV

The pains of this life bear testimony to our great inner comfort. No matter the magnitude of mockery, hatred, and persecution, the great love lavished on us by our heavenly Father is even greater. Without him, we are worms in the dust unable to even breathe apart from his blessed providence. For us, he went beyond giving us a life of highs and lows on earth. He stepped down from heaven to bring us up with him.

We are children of God, and that means we are familiar with the blessing of heaven. Earth is a blessing too, and it's the only blessing the world knows; God has chosen us to know his blessing beyond this place. We have been granted to be like him in spirit, rise above this earth's limits, and be enraptured with our Savior in eternity. What a blessing it is to know him and be known by him.

Oh Lord, thank you for raising me above this world. Thank you for making me one with you in spirit and giving me the title "Child of God."

JANUARY 29

WATCHING OVER US

The LORD himself watches over you!
The LORD stands beside you as your protective shade.
PSALM 121:5 NLT

People like to speak of guardian angels watching over them, but God doesn't delegate his work. No, he thinks we need special attention, so "the LORD himself" watches over us. He keeps an eye on us and makes sure we are exactly where he wants us to be in his plans. He is both our heavenly Father and our "protective shade" who shields us from the evil that wants to consume us.

As men, we are often put in roles of protection. Whether it's for a friend, family, a coworker, or even a stranger, God might call us to stand between someone and danger. In that moment, we are acting as the protective shade someone needs. It might be emotional help, taking care of someone, or physical protection. In all situations, we act as men protected by their Lord and Savior Jesus Christ.

Oh Lord, you yourself are watching over me. You protect me when Satan would cause me harm. Give me the courage to do the same for those around me.

JANUARY 30

THANKFUL IN LOVE

> Give thanks to the LORD, for he is good his love endures forever.
> 1 CHRONICLES 16:34 NIV

We are to be thankful in the love the Lord has for us. This is not a thankfulness of compulsion forced on us by a petty God. It is thankfulness born out of sincere appreciation for the radical work of God in redeeming us from our sins and brokenness. Yes, a God who shows pity to undeserving, rebellious individuals who want nothing to do with him truly is good.

We rejoice over such love especially because it "endures forever." It is not temporary or conditional; it continues. Can this be said of our love for other people? Do we continue to love people when they hurt us or are inconvenient to us? Do we love the annoying or the rude, or is our love for someone based on how much they love us? We are to set an example of love for those around us and especially for our Christian brothers and sisters. We are to show the unconditional love of God for which we rejoice.

Oh God, thank you for your love. Help me show it to those who do not deserve it just as I do not deserve it.

JANUARY 31

FEAR AND SERVE

"Only fear the LORD and serve him faithfully with all your heart. For consider what great things he has done for you."
1 SAMUEL 12:24 ESV

These words, said by Samuel to the wayward people of Israel, ring true for every generation. He is trying to pierce through their hypocrisy and hardened hearts with his words. He wants to convince this people to forfeit their eyeservice to the Lord in exchange for total surrender of their hearts. God will be happy with nothing less. There is good reason for this surrender in "what great things he has done for you." God may not have led us through the desert for forty years, but we have personal deserts we have endured with God.

The fear which Samuel beseeches the people to have is not typical fear. It's not terror or the thought that something bad might happen. It is a holy, reverential fear born out of adoration and respect. When we consider all the great things God has done for us, from the smallest favors to the greatest deliverances, this awe will take over us.

Oh God, may I render fear to you and you alone. No other is deserving of my faith and service.

FEBRUARY

Early the next morning, while it was still dark, Jesus woke and left the house. He went to a lonely place, where he prayed.
MARK 1:35 NCV

FEBRUARY 1

FALSE HOPE

This is no empty hope, for God himself is the one who has prepared us for this wonderful destiny. And to confirm this promise, he has given us the Holy Spirit, like an engagement ring, as a guarantee.
2 CORINTHIANS 5:5 TPT

Paul says, "God himself is the one who has prepared us." Too often, we think of our spiritual journeys in terms of ourselves and our work, like reading devotions, but our sanctification is first and foremost the work of God. He is making us for a "wonderful destiny" with him. He is preparing us for a future far better than anything we could achieve. Since this is God's work, not ours, God gives us hope in him that he will carry out this plan.

This hope is the Holy Spirit. When we feel the presence of something other than ourselves, we are assured of God's hand in our lives. We remember we are not alone; we are beneath the rod of a shepherd directing our steps. The Holy Spirit, as he renews us in supernatural ways, acts as our guarantee and as a taste of heaven.

God, please give me hope for the day. Remind me of my forever home and let that be my comfort in times of trial. Increase the work of your Holy Spirit in me.

FEBRUARY 2

ROOTING DOWN

Let your roots grow down into him, and let your lives be built on him. Then your faith will grow strong in the truth you were taught, and you will overflow with thankfulness.
COLOSSIANS 2:7 NLT

It's natural to push upward while looking for comfort and support from beneath. We pursue our work, goals, and success, and we look to family, coworkers, health, and more as our support beneath us. If the support beneath us wavers, we waver, and our attention is stolen from our goals as we turn it toward our support base. We need emotional, physical, and spiritual support to flourish. If we aren't rooted in these things, we have nothing to push off from.

Paul says, "Let your roots grow down into him, and let your lives be built on him." God is the one soil our roots can always cling to. Our physical support might fail, and those who often lend us emotional support might fail, but the spiritual support of the Lord will stand. From this support, "your faith will grow strong in the truth ... and you will overflow with thankfulness." By rooting ourselves in Christ, we grow stronger and develop a better thankfulness for the support we do have.

Lord, teach me today to root myself in you. Teach me to be dependent on you in faith.

FEBRUARY 3

KNOWLEDGE'S EXCELLENCE

The excellence of knowledge is that wisdom gives life to those who have it.
ECCLESIASTES 7:12 NKJV

Solomon calls the life of the wise "the excellence of knowledge." The greatest part about knowledge is that those who cultivate it into wisdom are filled with life. This is clearly the case observed in every person who avoids the pitfalls and sins of life. Knowledge and wisdom, according to Solomon, are more than head knowledge. They are precepts, commandments, and understanding that is internalized by "those who have it." The wise live and breathe wisdom.

The Bible says wisdom comes from hearing the Word of God. Unfortunately, when we slip away from regular scriptural devotion, we are more likely to have trouble in our lives. This trouble then distracts us further from reading the Word which would give us life and comfort us in trouble if we only made time for it. If we would only break the cycle.

Lord, make me a man of wisdom. Give to me life by filling me with knowledge and wisdom from your Word.

FEBRUARY 4

STONY HEARTS

"I will give them singleness of heart and put a new spirit within them. I will take away their stony, stubborn heart and give them a tender, responsive heart."
EZEKIEL 11:19 NLT

Without Christ, our hearts aren't just broken; they need replacing. We are so thoroughly corrupted, so far from the image of God in us, that our hearts are wholly against the grace of God until he rejuvenates us with a heart transplant. The Lord says, "I will take away their stony, stubborn heart." Our hearts are born stony and thus impervious to requests and unwilling to respond to others. Our hearts are stubbornly stuck in wayward ways out of habit and pride.

God has appointed for us tender, responsive hearts. They break with heartache, rise with elation, hurt with the hurt of others, and feel deeply. What might seem to be weakness is the absence of false strength. Those with stone hearts might seem resilient, but they have killed a part of themselves to do so. The heart is a muscle, and the stonehearted have lost use of it. Strength lies in weakness.

Lord, please renew in me a heart of flesh. Give me tenderness that responds to the hurt and triumph of others.

FEBRUARY 5

TEMPTED EVERY WAY

He understands humanity, for as a Man, our magnificent King-Priest was tempted in every way just as we are, and conquered sin.
HEBREWS 4:15 TPT

Our problems are unique to us. Every man has moments, if not years, of feeling burdened and alone in his pain. The temptations and struggles we go through are often overlooked or made light of by our friends or lovers. The magnitude of a man's fear of vulnerability comes from his personal past and from cultural standards. Many do not understand that, but Jesus understands. As today's verse says, "Our magnificent King-Priest was tempted in every way just as we are, and conquered sin."

He knows the struggles, he knows the power of immorality, yet he also knows how to conquer them all. He will never make light of our weakness. Christ is so great in humility that despite our weakness, he is honored to be let into our hearts during our darkest moments. He is honored to be our Lord and eternal friend. Who else do we have, so perfect in understanding, to hold on to?

Oh Jesus, thank you for experiencing my pain. Thank you for taking upon yourself the flesh of humanity so I would not be alone in my experiences and temptation.

FEBRUARY 6

EXALT AND PRAISE

LORD, you are my God;
I will exalt you and praise your name, for in perfect faithfulness you have done wonderful things, things planned long ago.
ISAIAH 25:1 NIV

If we let it, life can become a sea of difficulty and pain trying to drown us. It can be beyond suffocating. Isaiah lived in an Israel torn apart by sin and idolatry, and he was no stranger to heartache himself. Yet out of this pain and strife, he sings a song of exaltation and praise. He turns his eyes to God's glory and favor rather than the negative parts of his life, and this brings him joy and peace.

Isaiah declares, "I will exalt you and praise your name, for in perfect faithfulness you have done wonderful things." No matter the circumstances, we will never have a burden which God does not warn us about. He will never lie about his promises or deny his own faithfulness. We can expect a life of hardship, but it will not be a life of unpredictable hardship or neglect on God's behalf. When we call, he answers.

Oh Jesus, please make me a man of praise this day. Make me a man who loves you and honors you with his voice.

FEBRUARY 7

UNKILLABLE

Love never gives up, never loses faith, is always hopeful, and endures through every circumstance.
I CORINTHIANS 13:7 NLT

This passage from the apostle Paul is used at weddings as a romantic picture of love, but it has a darker, more sober side. Love "endures through every circumstance." After being betrayed, after being forgotten, after being purposefully crushed, love bounces back. In spite of being a beautiful emotion, love can feel like a cancer that won't leave us. Even after the object of our love is found completely unworthy and doesn't want our love, our love lives on.

Sometimes love is unkillable, and God made it this way to give us a taste of the divine. We will never be more like men of God than when we love someone who has pushed us away and given us hurt and pain; that is the love God has for us every time we sin against him. Will we turn to the God who loves us or push him away like the people in our lives push us away?

Oh God, your love is perfect and holy. It is an unkillable force we have a taste of in

this life. Give me the strength to love as you do even when it hurts.

FEBRUARY 8

TRANSCENDENT

"My thoughts are nothing like your thoughts,"
says the LORD.
"And my ways are far beyond anything you could imagine."
ISAIAH 55:8 NLT

The Bible is full of symbolism. The ark of the covenant, the angels of Ezekiel, even the last supper all act as symbols of the higher truths Jesus is trying to teach us. If we were like God, he never would have displayed his heavenly truths through physical counterparts. When we, as creatures of God's making, set ourselves on the same level as him, it displays an incredible level of arrogance. As beings created by God, we can't in any way be his equals.

This is reason for great awe but also great humility. Men often like to have the upper hand in an argument or speak with assurance, yet God only knows how petty we are to consider ourselves wise. In light of God's mighty thoughts and ways, no amount of understanding in our minds or hearts can come close to the understanding we have left to learn.

Oh God in heaven, how deep and vast is your understanding! I can't begin to fathom the enormity of who you are. All I can do is stand in awe and praise you.

FEBRUARY 9

GREATEST CONFIDENCE

"This is the confidence we have in approaching God: that if we ask anything according to his will, he hears us."
JOHN 5:14 NIV

A man without confidence is not necessarily humble. We can be proud and have doubt, fear, and hatred lurking in the corners of our lives. It's equally dangerous to have our confidence in the wrong places, and this includes in ourselves. We become bullish brutes with more action than intelligence.

Jesus wants us to have confidence in the right things, and he is our greatest confidence. Our confidence in Jesus includes our interactions with Jesus himself. According to the verse, "If we ask anything according to his will, he hears us." God is not fickle or subject to unwarranted anger. The more we lay aside our selfish ambitions, and the more we take on the Lord's will, the greater our confidence will be in approaching the throne of grace.

Dear Lord, please be my confidence today as I enter the world. Make me a man marked by confidence in my heavenly Father rather than my own prowess.

FEBRUARY 10

YOUR TREASURE

"Where your treasure is,
there your heart will be also."
LUKE 12:34 NIV

Who sits on the throne of your heart? Imagine you are in a room with everyone you know watching through a window. In an instant, the thing you desire most is given to you in that room, and everyone can see. The crowd is the catch. Many of us don't want everyone to see what we want. For many of us, we would be stuck in that room with a sexual idol, infinite wealth, or our dream career. What would be in your room?

God wants us to treasure him the way he treasures us. He wants this for our sake because nothing else will satisfy the aching desire in our hearts. Jesus is the ultimate source of satisfaction, but he will only satisfy us if we put him first. If we have anything else on the throne, Jesus will be the biggest thorn in our side.

Almighty King, be the treasure of my heart. Be my Lord, be my love, be my everything! I am nothing without you, and I desire your presence.

FEBRUARY 11

GOD OF REST

Jesus said, "Come to me, all of you who are weary and carry heavy burdens, and I will give you rest."
MATTHEW 11:28 NLT

In our striving and toiling, our effort and slow sanctification, do we remember we worship a God of rest? We worship a God who recharges us when we are spent and doesn't expect us to live in continual anguish. He is full of mercy for our shortcomings, and he has never turned us away from necessary relief.

Jesus addresses "all of you who are weary and carry heavy burdens" in this verse, and his offer is especially relevant today. The world is fast-paced and demands unnecessary amounts of busyness. Ever since the invention of the lightbulb, we have had the easy option to outdo the sun itself in productivity, but this isn't always a good thing. A man willing to live a quiet life and be content with what he has will find great contentment. He will find the world's race is vain and has no reward in and of itself.

Dear Jesus, I pray over myself and the other men around me. Please give us rest in a restless world. We need you.

FEBRUARY 12

HEART WISDOM

*Wisdom will enter your heart,
and knowledge will fill you with joy.*
PROVERBS 2:10 NLT

Wisdom and knowledge are usually associated with our minds while emotions, like joy, go with our hearts. To see these traits combined, as they are in this verse, is a revelation. Wisdom is actually of the heart, and it acts there. Wisdom of the heart tells us when to love, when to be patient, when to act, and when to wait. Heart wisdom makes a boy into a man, and when wisdom enters the heart, it does bring joy.

Everyone desperately needs heart wisdom. Head knowledge can't fill us with joy if our hearts are rotten. Rotten hearts take that knowledge, turn it against people, and use it to feed an inner spiral of negativity. Knowledge of the head is useless without wisdom of the heart, and it can make a man into a great force of evil.

Dear God, thank you for the true wisdom that feeds my heart. May it enter into me today. I welcome your wisdom with open arms; use me, Lord.

FEBRUARY 13

WRAPPED IN GOD

What a God you are! Your path for me has been perfect! All your promises have proven true.
What a secure shelter for all those who turn to hide themselves in you!
You are the wrap-around God giving grace to me.
PSALM 18:30 TPT

What does it mean to be a man? As a man, how do you live a life of righteousness? It might feel like you have to pour efforts into a thousand things, and God does require complete devotion, but in the end, a life of righteous manliness is awestruck worship. If we keep our eyes on our problems, we will have a front row seat to our destruction. The man who conquers his problems is the one who raises his eyes to God and keeps them there.

The psalmist wraps himself in God, for being fully enveloped by our Savior is the perfect path toward happiness. God is a "secure shelter" because he doesn't just insulate us from our problems; he solves them. His promises prove true when we trust him with our lives rather than selfishly holding on to them.

Jesus, how great and wonderful you are! I pray today for a life of awe and worship to focus my heart on you as my only object of exaltation.

FEBRUARY 14

HELPLESS

The Spirit helps us with our weakness. We do not know how to pray as we should. But the Spirit himself speaks to God for us, even begs God for us with deep feelings that words cannot explain.
ROMANS 8:26 NCV

We don't have the ability to do anything of consequence on our own. All the beauty and goodness produced by the secular world is God's gift to them and not vice versa. Without God, we are mumbling fools unable to even desire his light, grace, and goodness. We are brought to a place of repentance only by the grace of God. After being born again, as this verse says, our prayers continue to depend on the Holy Spirit to gain expression.

Paul says, "The Spirit himself speaks to God for us." How can the Spirit speak for us if we aren't in the Spirit? If we live with the world and don't set our minds on the Lord, what will the Spirit tell God on our behalf? Even if it is wordless, we can live in communication with the Lord. The Spirit waits upon us with patience for this reason.

Dear Lord, please teach me to lean on you in prayer and in life. Teach me to express myself through the Spirit's voice when my voice fails.

FEBRUARY 15

NEEDLESS ANGER

A gentle answer deflects anger, but harsh words make tempers flare.
PROVERBS 15:1 NLT

Everyone is responsible for their actions, but that doesn't mean we are free to incite people's rage. If we raise harsh words against someone, tempting them to anger, woe to us for tempting them. If they resist, they have been made stronger, but we are still at fault for our recklessness. A good man keeps the peace whenever it is reasonable. He does not cause needless anger because through Jesus, he has risen above the world's emotional tumult.

The writer says, "A gentle answer deflects anger." As men, we have the power to not use strength. Rather than win an argument, we have the power to subvert its genesis. We can end it before it begins. To achieve this, we must sacrifice our prideful desire to win. We must put on the calm face of manhood and set aside the petty dealings of this world.

Oh God, I pray over my words. Please use them for righteousness. May my words subvert anger rather than cause it.

FEBRUARY 16

CELEBRATION

The LORD your God is with you;
The mighty One will save you.
He will rejoice over you.
You will rest in his love;
He will sing and be joyful about you.
ZEPHANIAH 3:17 NCV

This verse from the prophet Zephaniah is a unique picture of God rejoicing over and celebrating his children. The verse says God "will sing and be joyful about you." When was the last time we pictured God, our heavenly Father, celebrating us? As men, the disapproval of our fathers is one of the easiest things for us to internalize. A stray comment from a father can affect us decades into the future. God wants to rewrite that.

God wants us to know he approves of us and loves us. He knows when we are trying our hardest, and he knows we are limited by being human, but he is proud of us nonetheless. Think about that: God is proud of you. He is with you; he will save you and rejoice over you so you can rest in his love. What a blessed, perfect father to have!

Lord, thank you for your fatherly nature. Thank you for loving and caring for me in ways I deeply need.

FEBRUARY 17

DELIGHTED IN RIGHTEOUSNESS

Give me your heart.
May your eyes take delight in following my ways.
PROVERBS 23:26 NLT

What grabs our attention? Is doing the right thing enough for us, or has it lost its luster? Righteousness can't go out of season or fade. It is eternally good, pleasurable, and delightful to the right heart. The writer says, "May your eyes take delight in following my ways." He does not want his son, whom he is addressing, to take the right path begrudgingly. He wants him to pursue righteousness heartily without looking to temptations on the side of the path.

Our eyes teach us. We learn when we fix our sight on something and choose to study it to understand its intricacies. If the eyes of our hearts are on something unworthy of its affection, like sexual idolatry or money, then we won't be able to stay on God's path. We are only on his path when we are looking at him. Once our gaze wanders, our hearts follow.

Oh Lord, make me delighted in righteousness. Make my heart alive by your love; do not let my heart grow cold in seeking you.

FEBRUARY 18

BETTER ONE DAY

*A single day in your courts is better than a thousand anywhere else!
I would rather be a gatekeeper in the house of my God than live the good life in the homes of the wicked.*
PSALM 84:10 NLT

What do we value, and where do we long to be? There is more danger in a comfortable life than in a tumultuous one, for we begin to consider this world our home when it is not. We were made for heaven. Just as the psalmist cries, it is better to live a single day in the house of God, resting in his presence, than to live an eternity elsewhere. The psalmist declares he would rather be a gatekeeper, the lowest of the servants, in God's house than be exalted in the house of the wicked.

As men, we are given many opportunities to be exalted at the cost of our faith. We will be offered job opportunities that compromise our morals; relationships, ones that don't deepen our faith and bring us down, can develop. In these times, it's important to remember where we stand: heaven is our home, faith is our compass, and this world is a fading dream.

Dear Lord, I praise you for the eternity you have promised me. Please give me tenacious faith to search after you in the midst of earthly comforts.

FEBRUARY 19

GOD'S ULTIMATE PLAN

"You cannot add any time to your life by worrying about it."
MATTHEW 6:27 NCV

Jesus warns us we can't alter his plan. It is set in the strongest stone. Worry won't help us; neither will all the begging or the pleading in the world. If it is against God's ultimate will, it won't happen. We have only to surrender our lives to his plan and seek to understand it in every small decision we are given. In giving our decisions to him, we will find ourselves following his plan rather than worrying about losing our own.

Jesus says, "You cannot add any time to your life by worrying about it." What unchangeable thing are you worrying about? What do you know you can't change God's mind about, yet you try anyway? Jesus wants men who struggle with him and seek him passionately, but he also wants men who will surrender themselves to their ultimate leader.

Dear God, I know your plan is unshakeable. I know no one can change what you have decided. Why should I try to alter your perfect will? Help me trust your plan

FEBRUARY 20

WORRY ENTERS

"I repeat it: Don't let worry enter your life. Live above the anxious cares about your personal needs."
LUKE 12:29 TPT

Is there anything we don't worry about? We worry about money, our health, our character, what people think about us, and anything else imaginable. Life can devolve into nothing but worry and leave us sleepless and stretched thin. We fool ourselves into thinking that worry is fine as long as it doesn't cripple us. It's okay as long as it makes us stronger, right? These are not the words of Jesus. His yoke and burden are light and free of the weight of worry.

Jesus found this command so important he repeated it. He says, "Live above the anxious cares about your personal needs." These are the holes in our faith through which worry enters in. The personal needs for food, comfort, sleep, and security all prone to becoming weak spots. They are the areas we especially need to surrender to God in humble trust.

Oh Lord, please step into my worries today. Let me see that the anxious cares I have over my personal needs are in vain. You will provide for me through the coldest nights. Be my reason not to worry, Jesus, and calm my heart.

FEBRUARY 21

UNTROUBLED AND UNAFRAID

"Peace I leave with you. My peace I give to you. I do not give to you as the world gives. Don't let your heart be troubled or fearful."
JOHN 14:27 CSB

God does not call us into a mindset of fear and trouble but of fearlessness and compassion. He wants men who love dangerously, live selflessly, and give themselves up for his will. As he says in John, "Peace I leave with you; my peace I give to you." Jesus will not give us pleasant circumstances; he doesn't promise us people who will love us. He promises peace to weather every circumstance, mount every defense, and conquer every worry. No situation is stronger than the Lord's peace.

"I do not give to you as the world gives." When the world gives, it gives with caveats, conditions, and ulterior motives. This is not the giving of Jesus. He gives us his peace unconditionally because we are his brethren and children in the faith. We are to do the same and act as men of unconditional love and mercy. He wants us to love as he has loved us.

Dear Lord, I will enter today in your peace. I will cast my anxieties on you, and I will entrust my situations to you.

FEBRUARY 22

DRAWN BY KINDNESS

"I have loved you with an everlasting love;
I have drawn you with unfailing kindness."
JEREMIAH 31:3 NIV

In the world of flesh, we find empty versions of love. We find deep love ultimately rooted in selfishness and kindness that turns sour with a moment's notice. The goodness and love we do receive in the world are gifts from God to a wayward people; it is not characteristic of the world. We yearn for a better way, a way of sacrificial love and kindness, and God draws us in with this kindness.

He is not like the world, for it is not in harmony with his spirit. He is full of love for us and ready to give of himself in every way. He has loved us with an everlasting love and draws us to himself with unfailing kindness. He calls us to be of the same heart and to bring in the weak and brokenhearted rather than let them suffer in loneliness. He wants to make us into men of inclusion who love radically and whose kindness never fails.

Jesus, only you have loved me perfectly. Please perfect this same love in me. Teach me to let go of myself in holy surrender.

FEBRUARY 23

UNTOLD BLESSINGS

If your faith remains strong, even while surrounded by life's difficulties, you will continue to experience the untold blessings of God! True happiness comes as you pass the test with faith, and receive the victorious crown of life promised to every lover of God!
JAMES 1:12 TPT

Happiness. What a concept to consider in our bustling world of goals, dreams, and needs! Some men give up seeking happiness and look for something else instead; others so hard for happiness they never find it. Truthfully, every man's innermost heart aches for happiness, and the majority of us have simply numbed ourselves to this ache.

"True happiness comes as you pass the test of faith." That is our encouragement in times of temptation, hopelessness, and difficulty. The desire for God's own happiness emboldens us to have faith, to be kind when we are terse, and to be strong when we feel weak. Happiness can be ours by surrendering our lives to God.

Dear Lord, please strengthen my faith when I am surrounded by life's difficulties. Be the light in my eyes that makes me continue when I would rather quit. I believe in your untold blessings, Jesus.

FEBRUARY 24

GENTLE AND LOWLY

He takes care of his people like a shepherd.
He gathers them like lambs in his arms and carries them close to him.
He gently leads the mothers of the lambs.
ISAIAH 40:11 NCV

Jesus Christ is perfect in humility, and we can't replicate the level of selflessness in his heart. Despite our lowly position, he is still lower in his humility. Even with our delicate dispositions and human fragility, we are still not as gentle as him. He excels beyond us in every virtue. As Isaiah describes, "He takes care of his people like a shepherd." He is a caregiver of sheep who knows their weak frames and aimless minds yet leads them with a sense of dignity and worth.

As men, we look to Christ as our example of leadership and virtue. Where he would be gentle in his moral perfection, we have more reason to be gentle considering our sinfulness. We can be strong like a lion and gentle like a lamb because he proved to us it could be done. We are created to gather the weak and the broken in this world and carry them in our arms.

Dear God, please make me into a man excelling in gentleness and strength. May I be as you are: a kind and loving shepherd perfect in humility.

FEBRUARY 25

SLOWED DOWN

Since we are surrounded by such a huge crowd of witnesses to the life of faith, let us strip off every weight that slows us down, especially the sin that so easily trips us up. And let us run with endurance the race God has set before us.
HEBREWS 12:1 NLT

What is slowing us down? What drags us back when we want to push forward? God wants to free our faith of all burden that might weigh us down. The sins of the past, the worries of the future, and every grievance in between no longer have a hold on us. We are free. We are forever free. The grave has been conquered, and death has been swallowed up; we can live in freedom and run life's race with endurance.

Men were made to be passionate and live with unfettered drive that pushes them deep into the heart of God. They were made to run as example of integrity, faith, and endurance. Are we willing to take this on? Are we willing to set our eyes on Jesus and let go of all other goals and infatuations?

Dear God, give me the passion to run the race set before me. I can't do it on my own.

Please give me passion and make me the man you want me to be.

FEBRUARY 26

ACHIEVING STABILITY

Teach those who are rich in this world not to be proud and not to trust in their money, which is so unreliable. Their trust should be in God, who richly gives us all we need for our enjoyment.
I TIMOTHY 6:17 NLT

Wealth brings a sense of stability. When we have money, we have pre-bought possibility. None of us wants money as just pieces of paper. We want money so we can use it, or at least know that if we need something, we can get it. But money is fickle, and what seems valuable today can disappear in the blink of an eye. Paul instructs Timothy to remind his church of money's unreliability and why it's a bad basis for pride.

Almost everything is a bad basis of pride. Nothing we achieve can bring stability because we are finite creatures. Our pride should rest in God because we can trust him and his secure hold on us. We are proud not because we have him but because he has us, and nothing can snatch us from his almighty hand. He is a generous God too, and he "richly gives us all we need for our enjoyment." Wealth does not lie with money but with God.

Mighty God, open my eyes to where my trust is and where it should be. Keep it with you, Lord; keep it with you.

FEBRUARY 27

BROTHERLY CARE

By helping each other with your troubles,
you truly obey the law of Christ.
GALATIANS 6:2 NCV

Jesus loves to see his children unified. He loves to see them bound together through the compassion and grace he first displayed to them. In this way, they become more like him than they could otherwise. Christianity is both a religion of the individual and the congregation. We are only redeemed if change occurs on a heart level, in our innermost soul, yet our faith only develops to its truest self while in community. We are "helping each other with your troubles," as Paul says.

The law of Christ is built on love. It's built on perfecting the believer's soul through heart changes rather than sacrifices, offerings, and ceremonies. For us, God's law is carried out through brotherly care, being there for others emotionally, and serving them when they need a helping hand. This is the law Christ wants us to obey.

Loving Christ, please show me how to follow your law as you intended it: through love and compassion. Give me humility and a servant's heart.

FEBRUARY 28

DWELLING IN FAITH

Christ will make his home in your hearts as you trust in him. Your roots wil grow down into God's love and keep you strong.
EPHESIANS 3:17 NLT

According to Paul, "Christ may dwell in your hearts through faith." It is a great and wonderful thing to have Christ always with us. When we have our hearts "rooted and grounded in love" and want Christ to dwell in our hearts through faith, we are in a great place indeed. However, it is important to note that Paul says it is "through faith" that Christ dwells in our hearts.

If Christ is not dwelling in our hearts, then what is? Something else might be taking the place of Christ in our worship and admiration. Perhaps it is money, sex, or any idol imaginary. Christ won't share the throne of a man's heart with any other god; he is jealous for us. He wants to dwell in us through faith, but he won't give us that faith so long as we hold on to this world.

Dear Jesus, please dwell in my soul through faith today. Root my spirit in love and cast out all false idols from my heart.

MARCH

"I myself will go with you, and I will give you victory."
EXODUS 33:14 NCV

MARCH 1

BEFORE ALL

*He is before all things,
and in Him all things consist.*
COLOSSIANS 1:17 NKJV

Men are finite creatures. We are wrapped up in our struggles and cast down by the cares of our circumstances. We exist in a world that has lasted for thousands of years before us and will last after we disintegrate in our graves. When it comes down to it, we can't rely on ourselves as responsible witnesses. We are not all-powerful or all-wise, and we aren't meant to be. God designed us with the capacity for glory so we can glorify him as the one in whom "all things consist."

Reality holds together because God upholds every detail as the Creator. He has given us the ability to comprehend this but not to achieve it ourselves. We are made to be worshippers and to stand in awe at the God who is eternal and perfectly providential. In every way, we are the reflections of his nature, bound to a finite world.

All-Knowing God, you are so great. You are perfect in eternity before and after all

things. You hold all together in perfect balance; you deserve my every praise.

MARCH 2

GIFT OF VIRTUE

It is more blessed to give than to receive.
ACTS 20:35 NIV

It is good for men to be givers. When men are in families, they have the blessing of providing for their families. When men are single, they have the blessing of being there for their friends and serving their communities. When we receive, we are given material goods that perish. Jesus' words in this passage, as quoted by the Apostle Paul in Acts, ring true. Jesus knows what is best for us, and he knows it is better to receive spiritual rather than earthly blessings.

When we give, we receive the gift of virtue. We are allowed to forget ourselves for a moment and be free of our anxiety and self-focus. Other times, the giving takes on an extreme nature, and we are made to give beyond our capacity. This too is a work of the Lord, and it's ultimately a greater blessing than we can comprehend in the moment.

Lord, thank you for every chance you give me to give of myself. Thank you for the opportunity to grow rather than shrink no matter the cost.

MARCH 3

CREATOR AND REVEALER

The LORD is the one who shaped the mountains, stirs up the winds, and reveals his thoughts to mankind.
AMOS 4:13 NLT

The prophets were heralds of God's plan and his glory. They lifted up the image of God for the nation of Israel to see so everyone would realize they were not gods. God is too mighty to compare with our puny level of agency. In this verse, the prophet Amos says, "The LORD is the one." Lest there be any mistake, he is saying, we need to remember it is God, the Lord, who created the world of wonders around us.

According to the prophet, the Lord is also the one who reveals the world to us. Our thoughts are faint reflections of an omniscient God, and he, the source of all wisdom, reveals his thoughts to us. He reveals to us the thought of repentance, charity, wonder, and perspective. The Lord Jesus is the source of all creation and revelation.

Dear Lord, I praise you, for you have created this world and revealed to me the meaning of it in great glory.

MARCH 4

EMPOWERED THROUGH WISDOM

Every Scripture has been written by the Holy Spirit, the breath of God. It will empower you by its instruction and correction, giving you the strength to take the right direction and lead you deeper into the path of godliness.
2 TIMOTHY 3:16 TPT

This passage from Paul to Timothy was given at a time when Scripture was not in great supply and not collected in one text. To have a complete Bible would have been an unheard-of luxury, and we have it at our fingertips each day. Think about the power of the living Word, "written by the Holy Spirit, the breath of God." These words in our hands are not like any other words we read, and they have the power to transform us into the image of our heavenly Father.

According to Paul, these words of God have the ability to "empower you by its instruction and correction, giving you the strength to take the right direction." All of us need to plunge headfirst in the direction of godliness, and there is no other way to do this apart from the Word of God. It is there to give us instruction and correction in ways we can't see ourselves.

Holy Spirit, please be at work in me through the power of your holy Word. Let it instruct, correct, and empower me to be a different kind of man.

MARCH 5

NEW LIFE

Celebrate with praises the God and Father of our Lord Jesus Christ, who has shown us his extravagant mercy. For his fountain of mercy has given us a new life—we are reborn to experience a living, energetic hope through the resurrection of Jesus Christ from the dead.
1 PETER 1:3 TPT

Peter is bold when describing our relationship to God. We do not just have, but we experience "a living, energetic hope." Before Christ, our lives were dull and lacked the depth of meaning and life we were made to experience. By redeeming us, Jesus didn't just change our status from "destined for hell" to "destined for eternity." He wholly and completely gave us a new life both now and for eternity. Yes, this is something to "celebrate with praises!"

God's love for us is extravagant. Every spiritual gift, holy comfort, and truth is given freely and abundantly. We need only sit at the Savior's feet and learn from him. He has given us a new life, and it's a life of humble joys and new identity. Like Christ, the old self has died, and we are alive with him.

Oh Lord Jesus, thank you for your grace in giving me a new life I don't deserve. Today, enliven and energize me through your hope.

MARCH 6

IN HIS PRESENCE

Seek the LORD and his strength;
seek his presence continually!
1 CHRONICLES 16:11 ESV

Men are created to be seekers. We are created to be filled with purpose and to push through in times of difficulty and trial. Not all things are worthy of our pursuit or seeking. There are relationships best left in God's hands or jobs not worthy of our time and energy. Above these things, though, are many possible gods unworthy of our adoration and praise.

"Seek the Lord and his strength," the verse says. Seeking the wrong path and the wrong gods fills our lives with death and weakness. These pursuits degrade us and corrupt our hearts from the inside. The only deity who can fill us with strength through our worship is the God of the Bible. He is the only one whose presence we should continually bask in. He is the only master who will fill us with strength by our adoration and devotion. Lives of happiness and purpose are lives where we "seek the Lord and his strength."

Dear Lord, raise my eyes to heaven. Remind me of my purpose and your glory. Give me a heart for your presence.

MARCH 7

CRAVING

This world is fading away, along with everything that people crave. But anyone who does what pleases God will live forever.
I JOHN 2:17 NLT

Our lives are defined by desire. Life tears us between our desires, other people's desires for us, and God's desires. The apostle John says, "Anyone who does what pleases God will live forever." He is telling us not to live for our desires and satiation but to seek to please the Lord through our hearts and ensuing actions. By living for God's desires instead of our own, we transcend the world's limitations.

We must transcend this world if we don't want to fade away with it. Those who live for today are doomed to die with it while those who live for a holy tomorrow can be comforted in hope. We are made for a greater reality we can only dream of. The comforts and satisfactions of this life echo heaven, but they aren't the real thing. God's desire is for us to reach his heavenly reality and enjoy it with him.

Lord, give me the strength to not be controlled by "everything that people crave."

Make my life pleasing to you so I may live forever in your presence.

MARCH 8

PUREST FAITHFULNESS

These troubles come to prove that your faith is pure. This purity of faith is worth more than gold, which can be proved to be pure by fire but will ruin. But the purity of your faith will bring you praise and glory and honor when Jesus Christ is shown to you.
I PETER 1:7 NCV

All these aspects—praise, glory, honor—are loftier than the thoughts we face on an average day. Few of us are thinking about what might bring us praise and glory while we are at work. Yet when troubles come our way, we search for the meaning behind our pain and trials if we are faithful. The worst thing we can do with hard times is not learn from them. God gives us hard times to deepen our faith, to prove it is pure, and to grow our understanding.

Peter says, "The purity of your faith will bring you praise and glory and honor when Jesus Christ is shown to you." What a consolation to hold close! The situation might not feel worth it now, but when Jesus comes, our many troubles will prove to be our medals of honor. The bravest, most glorious men are the ones who don't shy away from difficulty but welcome it as a blessing to their faith.

Dear Jesus, give me endurance in hardship so my faith would show pure. Give me faith to endure when I would quit.

MARCH 9

MINDSET

Be thankful in all circumstances, for this is God's will for you who belong to Christ Jesus.
1 THESSALONIANS 5:18 NLT

Thankfulness is not the product of kind circumstances but of a kind mindset. A man of gratitude is not made through comfort and ease; he is made in the unbeatable hope born through appreciation of the cross. Christ Jesus died for us and felt every pain imaginable when taking on our punishment. There is no eternal hell waiting for us anymore, no separation from God, and nothing that happens on earth can change that.

Happiness and goodness are found through a mindset of gratitude. When we start appreciating the good God has given us rather than being consumed by the woes in life, we will see how good Jesus has been to us. This isn't possible to see through pessimism. Pessimism will discolor our vision and obscure the glory of God from our sight. We were made to lift our fellow man's eyes up through the appreciation of the divine and the immovable gift God has given us.

Dear Lord, thank you for this day. Thank you for your love and your sacrifice for me.

I pray you would give me an untiring hope willing to weather every storm.

MARCH 10

STRENGTHENED

We also pray that you will be strengthened with all his glorious power so you will have all the endurance and patience you need. May you be filled with joy, always thanking the Father. He has enabled you to share in the inheritance that belongs to his people, who live in the light.
COLOSSIANS 1:11-12 NLT

In our culture, strength and a short temper are often linked. We might think of a bull stomping his feet when we think of power. A bull, however, is raised and owned by a person because the bull has no strength of mind or temperament to control himself. True strength is manifested in self-control, patience, and endurance. A man who isn't ruled by his desire to escape adversity is a real man indeed. He will be put in charge of impatient, brash men who don't exercise control over their spirits.

According to Paul in today's verse, the power to be patient and endure is found in Jesus Christ. He strengthens us with his "glorious power." Beyond this, he fills us with joy and shines his light on us. What a glorious blessing it is to be favored by God and to belong to his inheritance. In light of this blessing and his offered strength, we can be clothed in boldness and confidence.

Dear Jesus, I know I am a weak, fallible man. Through your strength, make me mighty for your glory.

MARCH 11

BROKEN WALLS

He himself is our peace, who has made us both one and has broken down in his flesh the dividing wall of hostility.
EPHESIANS 2:14 ESV

Reconciliation has been given to us, but we can turn from it. When Jesus Christ died for our sins, he forgave us more than we will ever have to forgive another person. He was wronged in every possible way and totally and completely forgave it. He was in the right, we were in the wrong, and he turned the other cheek. With this forgiveness held out to us, we have the power to forgive all the things people have done to us. We have the power to walk in peace knowing that if God can forgive us our sins, we can forgive too. Will we?

In today's verse, Jesus Christ's body broke down the walls between us and God. Christ's flesh, the body he lived and died in, is our source of reconciliation. For a world torn apart through wrongdoing and falsehood, the Christ who did no wrong can bring it back together. He took every bias, stereotype, and hurtful word on his back when he hung on that cross and said, "It is finished."

Dear God, thank you for your peace. Thank you for forgiving me; help me forgive others.

MARCH 12

SLAVES AND HEIRS

You are no longer a slave, but God's child; and since you are his child, God has made you also an heir.
GALATIANS 4:7 NIV

In today's verse, Paul was correcting the Galatians in their lack of spiritual autonomy. He was ashamed of them for submitting their minds and hearts to a yoke of rules and regulations. We often do the same. We take on the disciplines and man-made constructs that accompany Christianity and forget the heart of our faith. The words "you are no longer a slave" are both freeing and convicting. They remind us of our foolishness in forgetting true Christianity, and they free us from our earthly burdens.

Faith is frightening. Good men often fear their ability to sin. They fear their impurity, their rage, even their lethargy. Fighting these demons through faith and grace is not as easy as putting up rules and barriers for ourselves. To address our sin righteously means a change of character, not a change of circumstances, and taking on the uncertainty of being an heir of righteousness rather than bound to the laws of the flesh.

Dear Lord, please give me faith where I would prefer certainty and rules. Give me trust in you where I can't seem to find it.

MARCH 13

NEVER PASSED OVER

God is not unjust; he will not forget your work and the love you demonstrated for his name by serving the saints—and by continuing to serve them.
HEBREWS 6:10 CSB

Sometimes our work feels insignificant. It seems we slog away at the Lord's work only to be passed over for every promotion and honor. We wonder why we try to apply ourselves and if it matters. This is the struggle faced by fathers caring for children in the middle of the night or men at work weighed down by the negativity of their coworkers. It's a real struggle, and it has been a crushing blow for many Christian men.

But what does the writer of Hebrews say? "God is not unjust; he will not overlook your work." The love we show when no one cares, the way we go above and beyond for no admiration, are still admired by our Lord. He appreciates our work and will one day tell us himself. We will receive an unfading crown of glory for the eternal work of today.

Dear God, please give me comfort and resilience to not give up. Remind me that the

love I show today has a purpose and will bring you glory.

MARCH 14

JOYFUL HEART

> With joy you will draw water from the wells of salvation.
> ISAIAH 12:3 NIV

Where is our source of joy? What determines our happiness and sets the pace for the day? It's easy to let our temperament be ruled by morning coffee, work culture, or familial happiness. It's tough to rise above these things and make the focus on salvation determine our joy.

What does Isaiah mean by today's verse? Salvation is more than just a baptism that washes over us once; it's a deep well to be replenished by day in and day out. It continues to support us well past our conversion, and the joy of that salvation is a mighty mindset to live in. When we can find joy in our salvation, we will always have joy. We will also grow closer to Jesus in holy appreciation for how he saved us.

Joyful Jesus, I lift my highest thanks to you. I love you, Lord, for you saved me when I didn't deserve a thing from you. Let this be the well of my sustenance and the source of my deepest joy.

MARCH 15

MAN'S PURPOSE

The Sovereign LORD has given me his words of wisdom, so that I know how to comfort the weary.
Morning by morning he wakens me and opens my understanding to his will.
ISAIAH 50:4 NLT

Isaiah's words ring true for the life of every man. Isaiah was a man of compassion who waited on the Lord every morning for new understanding and to have his eyes opened for what God, not he, wanted to do. He was a man of faith through and through. Above himself, he put the needs of the weary and the weakened. He prioritized their comfort and gave them the Lord's own words of wisdom.

Isaiah was able to work with confidence because he knew his Lord was "sovereign" or the highest authority. Despite the weariness and brokenness around him, he knew the Lord was still sovereign. He was still in control and able to protect everyone who fled under his wings. Isaiah loved his Savior because his Savior was able to protect him and bring healing to the people he cared for.

Dear Lord, please give me words of wisdom the weary need to hear. Make me an encouraging man who puts the needs of others first in my life.

MARCH 16

BROTHERLY AFFECTION

Confess your sins to each other and pray for each other so that you may be healed. The prayer of a righteous person is powerful and effective.
JAMES 5:16 NIV

    Confessing sins, praying with each other, looking for healing: these intimate tasks are far from the average male relationship. The bond between two brothers in Christ is incredibly important but rarely seen. David and Saul's son Jonathan had an intimate, affectionate brotherhood, but their precedent has not been followed often. How many of us confess our sins to each other? How many of us speak words of healing?
    We can see the Lord work through our holy interactions with Christian brothers. When we lean on each other, carrying each other's burdens, we grow spiritually more than we could imagine. Letting down our barriers and embracing each other's vulnerabilities is a difficult task, but with difficulty comes great reward, and this is

no different. James wants us to have this special bond, become righteous through it, and bear effective prayers in righteousness. Our righteousness is often only achieved with the help of our brothers in Christ.

Dear Lord, please give me the courage and the environment to rely on my Christian brothers. May I be a blessing to them and not a weight.

MARCH 17

PASSING SHADOWS

He will once again fill your mouth with laughter and your lips with shouts of joy.
JOB 8:21 NLT

This conciliation given to Job seemed impossible. Job was destitute at this point. His riches had vanished. His family had died or left him and told him to do the same. Even his health had been taken away from him, and he had no comfort but the scratch of the dust to console him. Laughter? Joy? These things were far from the mouth and heart of Job.

Our path will walk through patches of darkness, but these are just shadows passing over us. The depression, anxiety, or any other difficulty we face is not eternal. God is eternal. His glory, peace, and joy are eternal things we look forward to. The seemingly endless darkness we are suffocating in will pass and be gone. It will end just as God promised Job, and we will once again be filled with laughter and shout shouts of joy as Job eventually did too.

Dear God, please give me faith that this too shall pass. May I trust you through the

thick blackness I am in; I know it has an end in you.

MARCH 18

BECAME HUMAN

> The Word became human and made his home among us. He was full of unfailing love and faithfulness. And we have seen his glory, the glory of the Father's one and only Son.
> JOHN 1:14 NLT

Jesus became flesh for our sake. He took on the weakness of a human body, felt human temptations, and went through the pains of human life for our sake. He did it for us and proved himself glorious in it. He was the very Word of God, the will of God, and a person of the Trinity in the flesh. He was perfect and without flaw, fully satisfied in and of himself, yet he chose to demonstrate his love for us by being made flesh.

What would it look like for us to take this level of vulnerability? For us, as men, to embrace the weakness of those around us and show love instead of disdain? Jesus was willing to stoop down all the way from heaven, but often we are unwilling to humble ourselves with the smallest act. It is good for us to seek the "unfailing love and faithfulness" Jesus showed us so we might be men who show it to others.

Dear Lord Jesus, thank you for your unfailing love. Thank you for your faithfulness and for coming from heaven to earth to show the way.

MARCH 19

FAVOR OF GOD

The LORD is good to those whose hope is in him, to the one who seeks him.
LAMENTATIONS 3:25 NIV

There are hundreds of religions seeking to find the favor of the gods or god they worship. In Baal worship, the Israelites would even sacrifice their children in fire to find the favor of the false god of the harvest. There is nothing that has not been sacrificed, burned, or torn apart for the sake of divine favor, yet we need only do as this verse from Lamentations says, and we will have the favor of God.

Hope in him; that's it. We just have to hope in him and seek him, and he will bless us. So many others have sought these same blessings from false gods and given up all parts of themselves in sacrifice, yet we have only to trust him, and he will do it. A man's heart is an idol factory, and we will gladly put another god before the one true God. Can these other gods deliver us? Can they be good to us the same way Jesus is?

Dear God, you are the one true God. Thank you for the blessings you have given

me. Thank you for your abundant favor which I in no way deserve. I will seek you and put my hope in you.

MARCH 20

IN RETURN

"Do not judge others, and you will not be judged. Do not condemn others, or it will all come back against you. Forgive others, and you will be forgiven."
LUKE 6:37 NLT

When we put our faith in Christ, the wrongs we should be punished for are forgiven, yet on this earth, a system of reciprocity still affects us. If we hurt others, they will likely try to hurt us. If we are cruel, we will be treated cruelly. As Jesus says in this verse, "It will all come back against you." It's important not to condemn others because we will surely mess something up ourselves and then realize how unworthy we were to condemn someone else. More than this, we will realize how much we were testing God's forgiveness by not offering forgiveness to others.

The blessings we receive through good actions are not to be shrugged off. In this life, it's helpful to be in the good graces of those around us. By storing up favors from others, we pave a smooth path for ourselves that can also help us share the gospel more easily.

Dear Jesus, I know I am not worthy of your forgiveness; please teach me to share it with others willingly. Teach me to be a blessing to those around me today.

MARCH 21

HIDING GOD'S PRESENCE

"Let your light shine before others, that they may see your good deeds and glorify your Father in heaven."
MATTHEW 5:16 NIV

Our virtues, along with our achievements, are not the light of the gospel Jesus is speaking about here. The light we shine is the light of God's presence. It is the goodness, safety, and love that comes from a godly environment. When we, as god-fearing men, allow others to taste the presence of the Lord, we are shining our light. The good deeds through which we glorify the Father are deeds of compassion, selflessness, and kindness. These deeds draw attention not to us but to our Father in heaven.

It is also a blessing to us to shine a light because it transforms our souls into places of peace and safety. Where can we be lights today? Is there an area at work, the gym, or home where a spirit of apathy or darkness reigns? Jesus is calling us to walk into that area as a light.

Dear Jesus, take my darkness and wash it in light. Make me a light of your presence to bring others into proximity with you and your good deeds.

MARCH 22

WHAT WE KNOW

"For those who listen with open hearts will receive more revelation. But those who don't listen with open hearts will lose what little they think they have!"
MARK 4:25 TPT

It's not enough to read God's Word and regularly delve into theology. For us to grow in wisdom, we have to acknowledge how little we know. Our minds are small and incapable of understanding vast loads of what God would like us to know. All we can do is learn faithfully and quietly as we try to better understand how we fit into the beautiful universe God created for us to steward. As Jesus warns, "those who don't listen with open hearts will lose what little they think they have!"

We can be sure our hearts are closing when we want to speak more instead of listen. If we always have an argument on the tip of our tongues that someone needs to understand, we are about to lose the little wisdom we have. The same is true when we read for the sake of reinforcing our arguments. God doesn't want us to use his words as ammunition in theological arguments. He wants us to learn in humility.

Dear Jesus, I am more arrogant than you ever were. You, the Son of God, are so far beyond me in both wisdom and humility. Make me your student.

MARCH 23

A SELFLESS LIFE

Don't be selfish; don't try to impress others. Be humble, thinking of others as better than yourselves.
PHILIPPIANS 2:3 NLT

Jesus' commandments are intended to glorify us but not always in the way we think. We might think our greatest glory would for others to admire our knowledge and look up to us for our achievements. What our glory actually is, though, is far different and rooted in a servant attitude. It involves letting go of ourselves and our pride to focus on others rather than ourselves.

Paul admonishes us: "Be humble, thinking of others as better than yourselves." Most of us are uncomfortable with the thought of being worse than others. We need a sense of success or superiority to feel secure. Christ calls us to the opposite, and this radical shift in mindset is difficult to reach. Christ wants other people, not us, to be our focus. He wants us to honor and admire them rather than ourselves.

Oh Lord, why is it so easy to focus on myself instead of others? Strip away my pride.

Make me a servant always looking to bless rather than be blessed.

MARCH 24

SWEET REST

When you lie down, you will not be afraid; when you lie down, your sleep will be sweet.
PROVERBS 3:24 NIV

Every man knows the feeling of anxious rest. We leave work and go to bed, but work follows us home and makes itself our companion. It demands our attention and makes us tense; responsibilities weigh on our minds all night. Perhaps we are afraid in our rest. It could be bad finances, poor health, or something else. No matter the reason, our rest is easily stolen by the world of worry.

This verse is especially welcome to people burdened by responsibilities and fears. The writer says, "your sleep will be sweet." This kind blessing washes away the care crushing us and restores our peace after a long drought. Yes, to lie down and not be afraid, to experience the sweet restfulness of sleep, is a blessing from God we can enjoy shamelessly and freely.

Dear Lord, you give me rest. Please restore my sleep tonight. Let me know you will carry my burdens through the night.

MARCH 25

UNDERSTAND AND EXPRESS

May the Lord lead your hearts into a full understanding and expression of the love of God and the patient endurance that comes from Christ.
2 THESSALONIANS 3:5 NLT

We can only express something after we understand it. We can't express the love of God toward others if we don't understand his love for us. We might know in our minds that he loves us, but perhaps it has not sunk into our hearts. Perhaps we consider ourselves unlovable or think no one could ever forgive us for the terrible things we have done. There are a lot of reasons why we might not understand the love God has for us.

If Jesus had foregone the cross and instead just told us he loved us, we might have reason to doubt the depths of his love. But he did not do this. He, with patient endurance, walked the way of pain and bled for our sin on the cross. He took the nails to prove his love for us and to prove that yes, he knows everything wrong about us, but he loves us anyway. That is the love and endurance he wants us to express.

Dear Jesus, thank you for dying on the cross for me. Thank you for giving up your life so I might have it.

MARCH 26

RELIABLE DEFENDER

God is my shield, saving those whose hearts are true and right.
PSALM 7:10 NLT

When we rely on God through moments of temptation, our faith in him during moments of fear is stronger for it. We look at how he protected us from temptation, and we are assured of his ability to defend us against the evil one. The man who gives into temptation regularly will question God's ability or desire to protect him. That is why the psalmist specifies that God protects "those whose hearts are true and right."

It's easy to forget the value of righteousness when our lives are always comfortable. When we are faced by difficulties bigger than ourselves, however, we reap what we have sown. If we have sown faithfulness and righteousness, we reap assurance. If we have sown doubts and sin, we reap fear. This psalm is a warning to us during times of comfort and urges us to continue in righteousness and truth.

Dear God, keep me straight and true. Be my shield today and help me trust in you when life's difficulties loom large.

MARCH 27

PURSUING WHAT MATTERS

Whoever pursues righteousness and love finds life, prosperity and honor.
PROVERBS 21:21 NIV

Whatever we put our minds to achieving will shape who we are. If we put our minds to a career, that career will shape us in its image. The writer of Proverbs admonishes us to pursue what matters so we will be shaped into people who matter to others and find the life, prosperity, and honor we so deeply desire. The narrow path is the difficult one, but it is also the one which ultimately gives us what we want most.

What have you been pursuing? Are you slowly being eaten away by lust, greed, or ambition? Perhaps you have been pursuing something without even knowing. Whatever false god sits on the throne of your heart, it can't make you happy the way Jesus can. It can't heal you, or make you joyful, or give you the life you desperately need.

Dear Lord, please give me life and honor, but first, give me a desire for righteousness and love. Make me a man who pursues what matters rather than running headlong into a world of trouble.

MARCH 28

GOD OF LIGHT

> LORD, you give light to my lamp.
> My God brightens the darkness around me.
> PSALM 18:28 NCV

God does not provide for us alone but also for our surroundings. Rather than simply sustaining our souls, he also clears a path for us in the desert and gives us light to see the next step. The psalmist boldly declares, "My God brightens the darkness around me." The other gods of Canaan could not do that. They couldn't shed light in the pitch blackness or open the eyes of the blind. Yahweh alone can do that. We have a sustainer in Jesus Christ, the light for all nations.

Without God, we are clothed in utter darkness, and our eyes are shut. We are beyond lost with no ability to do anything but feel through the darkness and cry out for help. To have the Lord give light to our lamp, to have him brighten Satan's devastating darkness, is a blessing beyond all measure. We have only to glorify him and recognize the great splendor radiating from his presence around us.

Dear Jesus, please give light to the darkness around me today. Help me see; without you, I am utterly blind.

MARCH 29

AS WE ARE

We can all draw close to him with the veil removed from our faces. And with no veil we all become like mirrors who brightly reflect the glory of the Lord Jesus. We are being transfigured into his very image as we move from one brighter level of glory to another. And this glorious transfiguration comes from the Lord, who is the Spirit.
2 CORINTHIANS 3:18 TPT

Most people can relate to the feeling of hiding who they are for the sake of looking appropriate. Whether we are visiting our in-laws for the first time or sitting in a job interview, it's advantageous to put our best foot forward. Jesus, however, wants us unveiled. He wants the true, raw, us at our worst and our best. He wants no counterfeit version to prop up in front of the real us.

What is the result of this spiritual honesty? Paul says that by removing the veil from our face, we become mirrors who brightly reflect the glory of the Lord Jesus. By putting aside our fake selves, we can be transformed into the image of God. Men often feel the need to look strong at all times, but that is not the man God wants. God wants vulnerability.

Dear Jesus, help me open up to you. Take the real me, Jesus, and make me reflect your glorious splendor. I am nothing if I am fake.

MARCH 30

GLORIOUS SPLENDOR

You, O Lord, your mercy-seat love is limitless,
reaching higher than the highest heavens.
Your great faithfulness is so infinite, stretching
over the whole earth.
PSALM 36:5 TPT

God's every attribute stretches from everlasting to everlasting. To picture this, the psalmist uses images his fellow believers could see for themselves: "the highest heavens" and "the whole earth." In reality, nothing physical could compare with the infinity of God's love and faithfulness. We can sin against him time and time again, test his grace even after repenting, and he remains faithful to us and with nothing but mercy for our souls.

The psalmist says that God's faithfulness stretches over the whole earth. If God were not faithful to the world, he would have stopped sustaining it a long time ago. He could have given up on the world's cultures many times; instead, he chooses to reach out his hand in love and give them year after year to search for him and find him. His heart for the nations never fades or grows dull in its affection.

> **Dear Jesus, may I be a man with the love and faithfulness of my Savior. There are none to compare with you, Lord. In all things, you are infinite.**

MARCH 31

FINALLY HEALED

"He will wipe every tear from their eyes, and there will be no more death or sorrow or crying or pain. All these things are gone forever."
REVELATION 21:4 NLT

Every man carries a wound in his heart. It might be the disapproval of a father or hurts sustained from an old lover. Perhaps it's adverse experiences from a chaotic, violent environment. Whatever it is, healing can be brutal. Sometimes, we feel fully the holy comfort of the Lord as he takes away the wounds from our conscience; other times, they return without mercy. With these scars of our past on our minds, the prospect of heaven is all the sweeter.

John says, "All these things are gone forever." Imagine all our imperfections, pain, difficulty, and wounds washed away for all eternity. What a beautiful thing it is to be healed forever with no worries about change or discomfort. Yes, the Lord's mercy may feel heavy while on this earth, but his favor will one day turn our trials into medals of honor.

Dear Jesus, thank you for your final revelation. Thank you for its comfort in times

of hardship. Thank you, Lord, for the beauty of it all.

APRIL

"Don't be afraid. Just stand still and watch the LORD rescue you today."
EXODUS 14:13 NLT

APRIL 1

TENDER LEADER

Tell me in the morning about your love, because I trust you.
Show me what I should do, because my prayers go up to you.
PSALM 143:8 NCV

In today's verse, the psalmist lifts his eyes and his requests to God. To the psalmist, God has a twofold identity. He is a tenderhearted father but also a leader. The writer looks to God as a source of intimacy and affirmation but also a source of direction. He leans on the Lord, reminding him that "my prayers go up to you," and he requires the Lord's direction to know what to do. The writer is vigilant to listen and rises early in the morning to hear about the Lord's love and grow in his trust.

Dedication, dependency, and a deep love of the Lord don't come from the law. They don't come from our religious efforts or even our habits. The quality of the psalmist's heart comes from his focus on God's work and an ensuing appreciation for what Jesus has done. In our lives, the same is true; greater passion and virtue result from deeper appreciation of our Lord.

Lord, thank you for your love. In the words of the psalmist, please show me what I should do because my prayers go up to you.

APRIL 2

LOVE'S WORTH

*Many waters cannot quench love; rivers cannot sweep it away.
If one were to give all the wealth of one's house for love, it would be utterly scorned.*
SONG OF SOLOMON 8:7 NIV

As men, we were made to love. We were made to love each other, love God, and live passionate lives of love. God didn't put passion inside us so he could subjugate it. He wants to direct that passion, which "many waters cannot quench," and he wants to use it for his glory. No one except God fully understands the worth of true love; the author labels it better than "all the wealth of one's house."

The words of Solomon's bride in this verse are full of resilient imagery. Love stands up to harsh circumstances and survives. The love God desires for his children is like a rock anchored in a stream. It faces continual opposition and struggle, yet it holds on. The love of God is a force that binds us to him and gives us resilience beyond our measure. It truly is worth more than all possessions. It is the perfection of the soul.

Lord, give me love beyond the measure of my soul. Give me love to make me stand strong and fight for those I love.

APRIL 3

FALSE HOPES

It is better to take refuge in the LORD than to trust in people.
PSALM 118:8 NLT

The unnamed psalmist behind this passage is speaking candidly on the pain of being let down by people. He knows human beings are not trustworthy creatures; they are prone to change in disappointing ways. From experience, most of us would agree with him. Almost everyone has been betrayed or hurt by people who changed their word or character when we didn't expect it. Life has many of these unwanted surprises.

Christ is the perfection of human character, and that is a very real and lovely thing. It means he is all the things we expect from other people. He will not let us down, and he will love us the way we have yearned for. He will be there when we need him. Perhaps the ill experiences we have with people occur to show us just how excellent Christ's character is.

Oh Jesus, I do not deserve you. I don't deserve the love you have shown me or the kindness I have received from you. Thank you for always being there for me.

APRIL 4

IDLE LIVES

All hard work brings a profit, but mere talk leads only to poverty.
PROVERBS 14:23 NIV

A man should be a model of hard work as he seeks to honor his God. Through the way he does his job, he should seek to display the character of Christ and the dependability of a Christian man. The writer of Proverbs says, "All hard work brings a profit." Even those cheated out of their wages or receive only losses on their labor get the profit of a stronger character. They are still blessed with the honor of growing in resilience, fortitude, and strength. No matter the size of the job, whether it be a corporate office or a home kitchen, the lessons are there.

Finally, the writer also warns that "mere talk leads only to poverty." Work is a place of building relationships and sharing the kingdom, but if nothing is accomplished, it is no longer a place of work. The best spirit we can have at work is productivity combined with patience. We must have an eye for the eternal value of whatever we do.

***Oh Lord, please make me a good worker.
Bless the work of my hands this day.***

APRIL 5

LIVING WITH FAITH

"Don't worry about tomorrow, because tomorrow will have its own worries. Each day has enough trouble of its own."
MATTHEW 6:34 NCV

It's not easy to hand our cares to God. He is not visible and rarely speaks in words like a person. Often, the way we give our cares to him is by simply letting the thought of them go. Jesus himself tells us in this passage, "Don't worry about tomorrow, because tomorrow will have its own worries."

In our desire for control, we want to worry about every day ahead of us to gain a semblance of control over the bad things that might happen. A responsible man is especially susceptible to worry. God never promised us a long-term understanding of what would happen in our lives; he only said that he would lead us day by day. We have to live with faith if we want to rest at night and not let our cares consume us. We do enough by living life well; we don't need to control it.

Oh Lord, I give you my cares for tomorrow. Today's energy is for today's problems. Please remind me of that. I can do nothing outside of your plan.

APRIL 6

EVENTUAL REST

"There are many rooms in my Father's house; I would not tell you this if it were not true. I am going there to prepare a place for you."
JOHN 14:2 NCV

Life's difficulties are outweighed by eternity's glory. There is no end to peace in heaven. Every positive thing we have ever experienced will be consummated in heaven. The beauty of every sunrise, the feeling of holding a loved one's hand, the glory of a new song, and every conceivable joy we know have their home in eternity with God. Those who scorn heaven and give no care for their eternal resting place don't know what they are missing; if they did, their attitude would be far different.

It's beautiful that Jesus is preparing a place for us. He loves us tenderly, and despite our sins and our mistakes, he wants to give us a good home with him and the Father. What a blessing it is to have a Savior who loves us so unconditionally no matter our sins and evil past. Nothing compares with this blessing.

Oh Lord Jesus, I am not a pure man. I am a sinner, it's true, but I will lean on your

grace and forgiveness today and for all eternity.

APRIL 7

ADMITTED WEAKNESS

If any of you needs wisdom, you should ask God for it. He is generous to everyone and will give you wisdom without criticizing you.
JAMES 1:5 NCV

An admitted weakness is a weakness on the way to becoming a strength. When we are blind to a weakness, it is as its strongest. Being blind to our need for wisdom is one of the greatest threats to our faith as our arrogance can convince others we are wiser than we are. It's vain of us to consider ourselves wise in light of the infinite depth and breadth of God's thoughts. There will never be a moment when we can understand even a percentage of Jesus' wisdom.

What James is likely addressing in this passage is moments where we lack specific wisdom over a situation. Perhaps it's a move, or a job choice, or a relationship, but we often lack knowledge over a specific situation. In these times when we need wisdom, we should simply ask for it. Jesus will assuredly bless us with the wisdom we need.

Dear Jesus, please help me find the wisdom I am lacking in the situation on my mind. I want to avoid unintended consequences to others or myself.

APRIL 8

BROTHERLY FRIENDSHIP

Let us not neglect our meeting together, as some people do, but encourage one another, especially now that the day of his return is drawing near.
HEBREWS 10:25 NLT

Friendships between men are increasingly rare. Outside of college and the military, there are few opportunities for men to create lasting friendships. The friends we make at work or church are often friends of circumstance whom we let slip by. The friendship the writer of Hebrews is speaking of, however, is built purposefully with Jesus at the center of it.

There is likely a friendship we could deepen. It might be someone we hadn't considered, like a neighbor or another man at church. Every candidate, as long as they are likeminded in their faith, have the opportunity to become a brotherly friend to keep us accountable and encouraged. King David called these male friendships better than the love of women. They are incredibly powerful in the development of our faith, and a key strategy of the devil is to disrupt them.

Oh Lord, please strengthen my male friendships and nurture new ones. Let them be for encouragement and Christian accountability. May they strengthen my faith, and may I strengthen theirs in return.

APRIL 9

THANKFUL FOR EVERYTHING

Give thanks for everything to God the Father in the name of our Lord Jesus Christ.
EPHESIANS 5:20 NLT

Americans have a holiday for giving thanks, and it's one of the few ways society has incorporated thankfulness into its culture. God doesn't need us to be thankful so he can feel good about himself, but we need to give thanks to grow in gratitude and humility. Thankfulness is one of the easiest ways to become humbler without having to experience pain or failure. It's also a healthy expression of our reverence for what God has done for us.

Paul admonishes us to "give thanks for everything to God." This is a high order if we consider number of things we can be grateful for. As long as there is air in our lungs and thoughts in our heads, we have reason for thankfulness. If there was most-neglected commandment, it is probably the commandment to be thankful. Starting today, we can change that.

Dear Jesus, please work in my heart to renew me. Give me a mindset of gratitude that honors you, Lord, for all the ways I have been blessed.

APRIL 10

SOFTENED THROUGH WISDOM

How wonderful to be wise, to analyze and interpret things. Wisdom lights up a person's face, softening its harshness.
ECCLESIASTES 8:1 NLT

The wise are often portrayed as cynical. If the world's darkness is its prevailing feature, as many believe, the more we understand, the more we are dismayed. This is only half the truth. The wise see and understand more evil than the foolish, but they can also see the goodness in the world with new appreciation. The things they "analyze and interpret" are not all bad; God's promises and holiness are also deserving of our analysis and interpretation.

If we want our hearts lightened and the weight of our consciences lifted, we should pursue wisdom. Wisdom is the perfecting virtue that leads to new character and outlook. It takes an old, tired man and gives him hope and optimism for the day. Only a cruel God would create wisdom to cause dismay, and we can be thankful this is not the case.

Dear Jesus, remind me of the goodness of wisdom. It is right and enlivening to understand things better than I currently do. I have so much to learn.

APRIL 11

WALKING ALONGSIDE

Make allowance for each other's faults, and forgive anyone who offends you. Remember, the Lord forgave you, so you must forgive others.
COLOSSIANS 3:13 NLT

Christians often find themselves in the mindset of correcting others. They see a problem, and all they can think of is solving it. The issue with this is that we know, from personal experience, this is not how we deal with our personal faults. None of us became perfect overnight. We had to learn we would always be flawed and have faults, and the best we can do is walk with Christ as he slowly works them out of us.

Making allowance for others' faults takes practice and conscientiousness. We need to see the tendency in ourselves to hold things against others, and we need to recognize when we are trying to solve people's problems for them. All too often, they just need someone to be with them or listen the way Jesus listens to our prayers.

Dear Jesus, teach me to make allowance for the faults in others. I am not perfect, yet

I live with myself and my flaws. May I have the same attitude toward others.

APRIL 12

SUFFERING PATIENTLY

So then, those who suffer according to God's will should commit themselves to their faithful Creator and continue to do good.
1 PETER 4:19 NIV

This verse from Peter gives us a high standard for suffering. Suffering, according to the will of God, is a difficult concept. We know in our heads that it's possible, but in our hearts, we struggle to see how a God who loves us would make us go through the things we endure and witness. Why would a faithful, loving creator do us harm?

Christ lets us suffer for the perfection of our souls. He does not afflict us himself; he simply allows the suffering to take place, and he would never make us suffer in a way he does not understand himself. He lived and died to relate to every level of suffering. There is no depth of pain our Savior Jesus Christ has not felt. No level of betrayal exists which Christ has not felt to the fullest degree. We can suffer patiently because he suffered patiently, and he knows how long we can last.

Dear Jesus, please give me a patient spirit who suffers according to your will. Teach me to commit myself to your hand in these times.

APRIL 13

WEIGHT OF GLORY

Our momentary light affliction is producing for us an absolutely incomparable eternal weight of glory.
2 CORINTHIANS 4:17 CSB

What if you were stuck for all eternity as the man you are today? If all chance of improvement were gone, would you be happy with who you are? Perhaps we should not scorn "the momentary affliction" that shapes us into better versions of ourselves. Jesus uses the time we are given on earth to shape us from selfish, conceited creatures into noble, holy children of God. He prepares us for heaven by acclimating us to the "weight of glory" that awaits us.

Paul describes this weight of glory as "beyond all measure." When we say heaven is greater than we could imagine, even that is an understatement. There is no telling the glory of God that awaits us, and we only glimpse it through occasional experiences. This promise of future glory is our greatest blessing that lights our path and gives us hope in darkness.

Dear Jesus, please prepare me for the weight of glory that awaits me. Remind me

of the magnificence ahead; may it dampen my light affliction.

APRIL 14

HUMILITY HIDING

Humble yourselves under the mighty power of God, and at the right time he will lift you up in honor.
1 PETER 5:6 NLT

Humility does not show itself. It is at its fullest when it grows inside of us without others knowing or taking notice. Humility doesn't bring praise and attention because it makes us realize we are not the main character of the story. It shows us who we truly are: small beings overshadowed by a magnificent god of mighty power. Despite this, God takes the humble and exalts them. God loves humility as one of the greatest virtues, and he wants it to be seen and role modeled.

We do not grow humbler in times of peace and satisfaction. According to Peter, we grow in humility "under the mighty power of God." After we have given up fighting and struggling, we realize we are weak and that the main character is Jesus. We realize it is worthless to fight Jesus, and we surrender by offering up our bodies and souls wholly to him in glory and praise.

Oh Lord, remind me of your worth. You are worthy of love and adoration; please take the throne of my heart for yourself. I give myself to you, God, so I may worship you in humility.

APRIL 15

FEARING THE SITUATION

*When I am afraid,
I will put my trust in you.*
PSALM 56:3 NLT

Life is full of fearful situations: losing a job, losing a lover, moving, facing health problems, and temptation are just a few. In these situations, we usually fear uncertainty. What if we don't find work? What if we don't recover? We also fear the pain of loss. It's okay to be afraid as long as we can turn that fear into trust. Jesus does not put fearful situations in our lives to cripple us but to remind us of our fragility so we can grow in faith.

The psalmist says, "I will put my trust in you." This is easier said than done. Putting our trust in Christ means not making comfort or certainty our goal but only Christ and his kingdom. We must come to a place where we can look at pain and uncertainty as part of an unpredictable life. We can trust in Christ for constancy.

Lord, give me faith today to put away fear. Take the fearful situation I am in and use it to grow my trust in you.

APRIL 16

NEWNESS

If anyone is in Christ, he is a new creation. The old has passed away; behold, the new has come.
I CORINTHIANS 5:17 ESV

Baptism is the traditional ceremony celebrating repentance and salvation. It would be a misunderstanding, though, to consider it a mere symbol of washing away our sins. Baptism is a powerful sacrament in which God adopts us into his family. Baptism is death and resurrection. It symbolizes how we are not just redeemed but recreated by the blood of Jesus. He takes the old self and replaces it with the new self.

How do we deny this truth? When we accepted Christ in our hearts, we died to sexual immorality and every kind of insidious sin, yet these sins often make their way back into our lives and, worst of all, we let them. We let our old, dead habits come to life again, and we subsequently die to Christ. This is both wrong and foolish. The pleasures of our old ways are incomparable to the glory of being a child of God.

Dear Jesus, please forgive me when I forget about my newness of life in you. My old self has passed away and you, Lord, are making me new.

APRIL 17

FOUNTAIN OF GOOD

*Splendor and majesty are before him;
strength and joy are in his dwelling place.*
I CHRONICLES 16:27 NIV

No one can give to anything to God; he is the giver of all things. If we offer up everything we have to the poor, he gave us the idea and the humility to do so. No matter the act, no matter its virtue, it is ultimately God who completes it. Even someone who is not saved owes their kind demeanor to God who blesses them with virtue even when they rebel against him in their heart.

"Splendor and majesty are before him," the verse declares. "Strength and joy are in his dwelling place." God is seated in the perfection of everything good we have ever known. He is the fountain of all good, and from him flows the beauty and the richness of everything we know. We have only to live in praise of him and his glory. We give him our hearts and service in humble gratitude for the grace and love he focuses on us.

Oh Jesus, how magnificent you are seated on your throne! You are beyond comparison and deserving of my every honor.

APRIL 18

COVERED BY LOVE

Above all, love each other deeply, because love covers over a multitude of sins.
I PETER 4:8 NIV

It's not common for men to show love. Love has often been portrayed by our society as feminine, and this makes it lack the holistic meaning the Bible ascribes to it. Few of us know what it looks like for men to "love each other deeply" or to show that love at work or in society. How would we know when the world discourages it so thoroughly? The best way the world can multiply sin is by shaming it because where love abounds, it "covers over a multitude of sins."

How can we appropriately and sincerely demonstrate love toward others? Love is not gushy or obscene. It does not draw attention to itself or its actions, but in humility, it seeks the betterment of others. To love is to bless others however we can. It's a powerful act and greatly humbling. It turns our attention away from ourselves and toward others for the sake of God's glory.

Oh Lord, please make me a man of love. May the sins of my past be covered by the love I show today, God. Only through you can this be done.

APRIL 19

NOTHING REJECTED

Everything God created is good, and nothing is to be rejected if it is received with thanksgiving.
1 TIMOTHY 4:4 NIV

Our lives are inherently corrupt. Cynicism and apathy sneak into every perception we have of the world. We tell ourselves things are going to break down, people are never as good as we think, and we listen to pessimists before optimists every time. It's easier not to be disappointed if we lower our expectations, and no one can argue with that. But this does not lead to any improvement, and pessimism enables us to look on apathetically as the world burns.

God is fiercely optimistic. He loved his people, met their scorn, suffered their crucifixion, and chose to be the king of hope anyway. He is beyond the pettiness of pessimism, and he wants to see the world transformed with hope and acceptance of truth and beauty. As Paul says, "Everything God created is good." Do we honestly live in this truth? Do we receive his world with thanksgiving or sit back and mock it with the other commentators? It's time to get our hands dirty and plant hope in place of brokenness.

Oh God, make me as fiercely hopeful as you. Make me strong as you are. I am willing to put aside my cynicism for you, Jesus.

APRIL 20

PERFECT PROVIDER

"Your Father knows exactly what you need even before you ask him!"
MATTHEW 6:8 NLT

This verse holds a priceless gift. We don't have to bargain with God. Despite our infirmity and weakness demanding his attention every day, we still receive the utmost level of blessing. No matter our need, his ability to provide for that need is greater. He does not use his transcendence as a reason to look down on us and degrade us; instead, he stoops to our level, so we feel cared for and loved.

God is our perfect provider, and nowhere else can we find such a combination of ability and willingness to serve our needs. There are many things we might think we need, and which seem to be neglected by God, but often God is showing us how to make do without them. Man does not live by bread alone, and God provides for our spiritual needs more regularly than what our flesh wants.

Dear Lord, please give me faith in your provision today. Thank you for giving to me while I did not deserve it. May I show the same love to those around me.

APRIL 21

TRUE COMPETENCE

We don't see ourselves as capable enough to do anything in our own strength, for our true competence flows from God's empowering presence.
2 CORINTHIANS 3:5 TPT

According to Paul, "our true competence flows from God's empowering presence." Every skill, job qualification, or other asset we bring to the table is brought to us through the empowering presence of God. Just by being near us, God brings opportunities and the willingness to make us strong. On our own strength, as Paul says, we are incapable of anything. It's insufficient for any meaningful task.

The heart of humility is realism. It's the willingness to see things how they are, and it shows us we are weak. Realism sees that our true competence comes from God and alone, we are worthless. This is not self-degradation but rather the beautiful truth of our existence. Despite the world's pressures on us to be men of responsibility, integrity, compassion, and fairness, we can rest in the truth that we are none of those things, but we can be through our true competence in Christ.

Oh Jesus, all my strength is in you. I have nothing without you, and I praise you for all you have blessed me with this day. Thank you for your empowering presence.

APRIL 22

FAITHFULLY STRENGTHENED

The Lord Yahweh is always faithful to place you on a firm foundation and guard you from the Evil One.
2 THESSALONIANS 3:3 TPT

It's easy to forget that God is faithful not just in providing for our physical needs but also in providing for our spiritual needs. We are not expected to resist temptation alone. Depression and anxiety are too strong for us to face on our own too. Only by God's providence are we able to face struggle of any sort in our lives. When we put Jesus first, between us and the difficulties we face, our trials don't stand a chance.

Paul says, "The Lord Yahweh is always faithful to place you on a firm foundation." How well does this describe us? Do we rather feel more tossed around than firmly placed? We often mistake our circumstances for our foundation. Our jobs, health, and even our communities are not always faithful. They are not our foundation; our foundation is our relationship with Jesus. He is the firm foundation we can always count on.

No matter the chaos of life, Jesus remains faithful.

Oh Yahweh, you are faithful. You are true. Today, be my spiritual foundation. Please keep me from slipping and hold me firmly in place through every tribulation.

APRIL 23

CAPTURED BY IGNORANCE

See to it that no one takes you captive through hollow and deceptive philosophy, which depends on human tradition and the elemental spiritual forces of this world rather than on Christ.
COLOSSIANS 2:8 NIV

A man's mind is a fortress. When Christ takes over, it's protected by his strength and power, and the chinks in the walls are repaired one by one. The enemy, constantly assailing the walls, knows this, and he sometimes opts for the front door. If we are not guarded by knowledge, we will let down our guard for the wrong people and their ideas. These hollow philosophies are appealing to the simpleminded, and only through sharpening our minds with the Word of God can we see through them.

According to this passage, the only philosophies worth believing are founded on Christ. A philosophy which depends on Christ takes to mind the needs of his children and dealing with them kindly and respectfully. It is absolute in its truth and does not reduce the truth to win an argument. Hollow philosophies lack all these things.

Oh Jesus, fill me with your truth. Let your strong, compassionate philosophies guard me against the hollow words of the enemy. Only you can defend me, God.

APRIL 24

STEADFAST ROCK

"He is the Rock, his works are perfect, and all his ways are just. A faithful God who does no wrong, upright and just is he."
DEUTERONOMY 32:4 NIV

Jesus is perfect both in record and in heart. He has no mistakes or dark past, and in his heart, he has righteous pride coupled with perfect humility. He can relate to the filthiest of sinners yet remain pure. It Not only is Jesus perfect, but everything he has done is too. The verse says, "His works are perfect, and all his ways are just," and we see this all around us. If not for the fall, the goodness we see in everybody and everything around us would be fully mature and perfectly beautiful.

As men, we are called to be solid rocks for our community. We are called to be a source of safety and steadfastness and hold still when situations go chaotic. With Christ's example in mind, we look for peace when there is rage and patience when there is anxiety. Each opportunity is a chance to be an example of Christ's character for others.

Oh Lord, you are perfect in steadfastness and justice. Remind me today that you remain with me when everything else abandons me. I know I can always trust in you.

APRIL 25

THE HUMAN PROBLEM

God has made everything beautiful for its own time. He has planted eternity in the human heart, but even so, people cannot see the whole scope of God's work from beginning to end.
ECCLESIASTES 3:11 NLT

Each and every human being faces the same problem. God created man as both a physical and spiritual creature, and this leaves him torn between two realities. As Solomon points out here, we are limited by time, and our experiences of beauty don't last. Yet we also have eternity planted in our hearts, and somehow, unlike any animal, we know deep down it would be right to live forever. The moments of deep meaning we experience tell us there is more to life, but we don't quite know what.

Only God can fill the hole in our hearts. We can numb the pain with pleasure and secondary pains, but in their right mind, every man and woman knows they are missing something. There are thousands of religions all over the world searching for the answer to this human problem, but only Christ can answer it.

He recognizes that "people cannot see the whole scope of God's work," but one day, if they put their trust in him, they will.

Oh Lord, why am I so desperate for answers? Please, God, give me faith in your answers.

APRIL 26

FREE OF BONDAGE

> This is the message we have heard from him and declare to you: God is light; in him there is no darkness at all.
> 1 JOHN 1:5 NIV

Darkness is a world of bondage. Satan's greatest desire is for our slavery. Whether it is through prudish pride or greedy lust, he would gladly take us for himself. Many a man has considered the light a place of rules and expectations. This made the darkness appear like a freedom from legality. The reality is that legality and carnality are both forms of slavery. Living in the light means becoming a slave to righteousness not through laws but through desiring God.

We can praise God as the only master we will ever have with a wholly good spirit. John says, "God is light; in him there is no darkness at all." If there were specks of darkness in our Lord, we would have no way of trusting his character. He would be unpredictable and at war with his own character. As it is, he is completely righteous, shedding light wherever he goes. How can we be of the same spirit and cast out all remnants of darkness from our souls?

Dear Jesus, please free me from all bondage. Make me like you in character so I can be one in the light.

APRIL 27

MAGNIFICENT DESTINY

> We have become his poetry, a re-created people that will fulfill the destiny he has given each of us, for we are joined to Jesus, the Anointed One. Even before we were born, God planned in advance our destiny and the good works we would do to fulfill it!
> EPHESIANS 2:10 TPT

Every man has a magnificent destiny God has planned for his life. He is not reserved for a meaningless life or a dull one; his life is a unique tool God plans to use to bring himself glory and honor. Paul says, "We have become his poetry." We are beautiful expressions of God's Word. Of all the words to describe the life of God's children, "dull" is not one of them.

According to Paul, we are "a re-created people that will fulfill the destiny he has given each of us." What destiny have we been scared to embrace? What have we been too scared to fail at to try? God is with us to face every adventure. He wants us to be men of passion, action, and feeling and not men who sit on their couches and let life happen to them.

Dear Jesus, before I was born, you had planned the great things I would do through you. Please work wonderfully in my mind and heart today.

APRIL 28

FRUITLESS PAIN

Unless the LORD builds the house, the builders labor in vain.
Unless the LORD watches over the city, the guards stand watch in vain.
PSALM 127:1 NIV

If we are to put ourselves through tribulation or trials, it had better be for a reason. To go through pain without reaping a reward of faith is the worst of both worlds, yet this is the predicament we land ourselves in all too often. We build our frail houses and watch over our insecure cities as though our efforts could accomplish anything. We can't accomplish a thing except by God's power, and the pain of doing things alone is not a pain he intended for us to experience.

The psalmist says, "Unless the LORD watches over the city, the guards stand watch in vain." This is true of heart, mind, and soul too. If we don't trust the Lord in faith, then our attempts resist temptation, seek honor, and gain wisdom will be fruitless. These are only accomplished by faith and not our efforts or vigilance. Jesus only wants our efforts as long as they are offered to him and no further.

Oh Jesus, why do I keep trying to do on my own what only you can do? Teach me to give my work as an offering to you. Please bless and keep it.

APRIL 29

CRUSHED BY SIN

It is for freedom that Christ has set us free. Stand firm, then, and do not let yourselves be burdened again by a yoke of slavery.
GALATIANS 5:1 NIV

Sin is not freedom. Letting go of God's plans for us and giving in to temptation is not freedom. It's the heaviest yoke of slavery we can bear, and we are too weak to bear it without being crushed. When a man surrenders to temptation, the devil makes him feel like he is embracing his greatest destiny. What that man is actually doing is surrendering to his enemy so he can be torn apart and destroyed.

Paul admonishes us to "stand firm." We have to stand firm against slavery today. It might mean resisting sexual temptation or an old coping mechanism, but it could also be something else. Perhaps we are tempted to give in to legalism and lean away from faith. Perhaps we are tempted toward pride and the yoke of slavery we want is one of higher status or respect. Turn your eyes back to Jesus; he is the only light and good yoke.

Oh Lord Jesus, please give me strength to stand firm against the works of the devil. He is preying on my life, and I don't want to listen to his lies.

APRIL 30

ALIVE AND ACTIVE

The word of God is alive and active. Sharper than any double-edged sword, it penetrates even to dividing soul and spirit, joints and marrow; it judges the thoughts and attitudes of the heart.
HEBREWS 4:12 NIV

The writer of Hebrews describes God's Word as a slicing, sharp weapon. He says it "penetrates even to dividing soul and spirit, joints and marrow." This is an incredible power beyond what most people would attribute to Scripture. It takes us a moment to truly appreciate the meaning of the words here and the monumental change that can be wrought with the Word of God. What does it mean for the Word of God to be "alive and active"?

When we interact with the Word of God, we do more than read a book. We are reading something alive and active that can communicate with us beyond the context of its original audience. We can choose to read Scripture out of obligation, checking off a chapter here and a chapter there, or we can dig in to the richness of what God has to say to us. He would love to equip us with his piercing, incisive knowledge, if we would just listen to him.

Dear Jesus, please work in me through your holy Word. Take the chapters and books of the Bible and make them my dearest companions.

MAY

"The LORD himself will fight for you. Just stay calm."
EXODUS 14:14 NLT

MAY I

CALLED TO PEACE

Let the peace that Christ gives control your thinking, because you were all called together in one body to have peace. Always be thankful.
COLOSSIANS 3:15 NCV

Without God, our world is a peaceless world. It's divided and fractured. Before God came into our hearts, we lived in hurt and trouble. We were not at peace. Miraculously, he called us into his peace even though we did not deserve it and had no right to demand it. The peace Christ gives is a healing balm for every wound. It is to be appreciated beyond every pleasure of this earth.

This admonition from Paul is coupled with a commandment: "Always be thankful." The key to letting peace control our thinking is found in thankfulness. If we are thankful for what we have, we won't be ill-tempered over what we don't have. If we are thankful, we won't find it necessary to complain or lose our temper. A peaceful man is a man with his thankful heart and eyes focused on what he has instead of what he lacks.

Dear Jesus, thank you for the air I breathe and the life you have given me. Make me a peaceful man for the sake of those around me.

MAY 2

PEACE AND RIGHT-LIVING

People who work for peace in a peaceful way
plant a good crop of right-living.
JAMES 3:18 NCV

We don't know how valuable peace and "right-living" are until we experience them. When we are no longer surrounded by conflict or battle chaos in our interactions, life is healthier. This is not just for our sake but for the sake of those around us. Peace and right-living gives people space to grow. Within the family of Christ, there should be an atmosphere of support and healthy relationships.

Outside of the church, we can expect a lack of peace and righteousness because the truth of the gospel is not being lived out. By working for this atmosphere of peace outside of the church, we further the gospel. By being men of peace, we make ourselves promoters of the gospel of peace. This in turn leads to the harvest of right-living that James speaks about.

Dear Jesus, please make me a promoter of peace in the world. Help me demonstrate this peace to others in my personal life as well.

MAY 3

DIVIDED HEART

"You will seek me and find me when you seek me with all your heart."
JEREMIAH 29:13 NIV

If you divide your heart among competing goals, Jesus will not compete. He will not share the throne of your heart with other gods, and he will not let you find him while simultaneously searching for something else. Jesus is not in the market for a divided heart but for a wholehearted heart that wants one thing: the Savior. To the person with this heart, Jesus promises himself. He promises to give all he is without cost or sacrifice on our part.

What a blessing to receive what we seek! We are not like those who give birth to wind or chase after ghosts. We are among a priesthood that searches and finds what it's looking for. Our goal is not questionable in character or subject to change; it's perfectly available and desires our wholehearted pursuit. Today, thank God for the joy of living with purpose rather than confusion.

Dear Jesus, please accept my total heart. Take it from me and use it for your glory.

All I want, Lord, is to honor and worship you in every way I can.

MAY 4

HOLY CAREGIVER

You gave me life and showed me kindness, and in your care you watched over my life.
JOB 10:12 NCV

Wounded soldiers are assigned medics to attend to them. They aren't expected to mend and heal their own bodies but are instead entrusted to the care of an expert. Jesus is our expert medic. As Christian men, we are battered and tossed by temptation and hardship, and our strength is miniscule in comparison to the fight. We need a holy caregiver who is kind and powerful enough to heal our wounds and watch over our lives.

Every man has wounds. For some, it is unattainable expectations from loved ones; for others, it is the self-hatred they feel over their mistakes and sins. These wounds can be sanctified, and they don't need to be repressed and forgotten. Jesus can use these wounds and help us understand them rather than fear them. He can heal us in a way we have barely dared to hope for.

Lord, I have needed someone to feel my pain and heal me for so long. Be that person, my Lord and holy caregiver.

MAY 5

PROOF

"I will give you hidden treasures,
riches stored in secret places,
so that you may know that I am the LORD,
the God of Israel, who summons you by name."
ISAIAH 45:3 NIV

God takes it upon himself to lend us confidence in our faith. He gives us experiences and testimonies that can't be explained without acknowledging his almighty hand at work. Isaiah declares, "I will give you hidden treasures, riches stored in secret places." What are these hidden treasures and riches? What makes them so valuable to us, and why would God bestow them on us?

These treasures and riches of old are the blessings we receive through walking faithfully with God. God spoke this verse to Cyrus, his anointed conqueror. God promised him success in his endeavors, and he was willing to prove Cyrus's faith worthwhile through tokens of success. In our lives, we find God blesses us with his treasures and riches as assurance of our faith, but it might not always be in ways we expect.

They may be small moments of peace or simple provisions we desperately need.

Dear Lord, please give me faith in your way for my life. Thank you especially for the tokens of assurance I find along the way. May my eyes be open to see them.

MAY 6

DIRTY SECRETS

"Nothing is hidden that will not be made manifest, nor is anything secret that will not be known and come to light."
LUKE 8:17 ESV

It is a common danger for Christian men to put up a façade. Yes, we have been saved by faith and grace from all our sins, but this is a lot easier to talk about in principle without the trouble of bringing up the sins we have committed in private. That would be too messy, we tell ourselves, so we shove sin into the closet so we can deal with it alone rather than letting it bother the people around us.

Our sin, however, is going to bother them anyway. If our hearts have sin, then those who love us will be able to tell and will be troubled by it. If the past has sin in it, those who love us would likely want to know and not reject us for it. Jesus warns us that "nothing is hidden that will not be made manifest," yet how difficult is it to live in light of this truth? How many of us are willing to expose our dirty secrets for the sake of healing and change?

Dear Jesus, give me the courage to not live in private. Give me the strength to recognize my sins and mistakes among those who love me. May I conquer them out in the open.

MAY 7

CONSTANT FAITH

By day the LORD directs his love,
at night his song is with me—a prayer to the
God of my life.
PSALM 42:8 NIV

As he gets tired and watches the night draw on, a man's inhibition naturally weakens. This is the reason behind many of the regrettable things we do in the evenings and at night. Things we know not to do in the daylight start to feel morally neutral after alcohol or plain drowsiness set in. This doesn't mean we are bound to sin, though, if our inhibition slackens for some reason. It just means we need to act as this psalm advises us to act.

This psalm from the sons of Korah declares, "By day the LORD directs his love, at night his song is with me." The psalmist is saying that God's love is directed through actions and plans, and at night, while at rest, the psalmist is still with the Lord in spirit. The psalmist's songs and prayers keep his mind centered on God rather than wandering to dark topics that don't deserve his attention.

Oh Lord, please be at work in my waking and sleeping. Teach me to be faithful at all times especially when should it be different depending on the time of day.

MAY 8

IDENTITY

"If you try to hang on to your life, you will lose it. But if you give up your life for my sake, you will save it."
MATTHEW 16:25 NLT

The men with the firmest sense of who they are in Christ usually let go of their ego long ago. They didn't become spineless or timid, but they gave up themselves for Christ's sake. Christ wants us to find our identity in him, but this isn't possible when we are holding on to an inflexible image of who we think we are. If we find ourselves getting defensive when someone questions our identity or insults it, then we have not truly let go of our lives for Christ's sake.

Identity is not an issue to be ignored. It takes active prayer and faith to trust in God's identity for us rather than our own. No one can live without a sense of who they are, and putting on a new identity in Christ is often a long and arduous process filled with doubts and revelations. It's okay to be uncomfortable and to take our time reaching Christ.

Oh Lord, my identity is in you. Show me what this means and guide me as I let go of my own version of myself.

MAY 9

WAITING AND READY

I can do everything through Christ, who gives me strength.
PHILIPPIANS 4:13 NLT

Most Christian men recognize they can do everything through Christ, but few of them are willing. If doing everything through Christ means taking on new pains and sacrifices, are we still willing to do it? Is the verse still inspirational when we consider the sacrifices we need to make to realize its full truth? Yes, we can do everything through Christ, but the path is steep and narrow.

God wants a man who is not controlled by comfort but instead masters his own sense of pain and suffering. This is only possible by trusting Christ's plan and knowing it will work out even when things get rough. He doesn't need us to be superhumans waiting and ready to act on his call. He only requires our trust, and then he will give us the strength we need to complete the tasks ahead of us.

Dear Jesus, the way ahead is rough, and I am not sure I can find the resolve to move forward. Give me the resolve, Lord, and give me the strength I require.

MAY 10

WISDOM AND WORK

Wise words bring many benefits, and hard work brings rewards.
PROVERBS 12:14 NLT

A good man supports his mind and body through wisdom and work. He leans on wisdom in many ways. By wisdom, he keeps his mind from falling into slavery. Wisdom helps him see the path the Lord has set and keeps his eyes toward his Savior. Through wisdom a man understands his surrounding and the people in those surroundings. As the verse says, "Wise words bring many benefits," and any man who accepts this will find it true.

The benefits of hard work are reserved for the indominable. If we are willing to die to ourselves and rise each morning to meet the day, we will gain mental resiliency beyond physical strength. Rather than being soft and easily influenced, our minds will grow sharp like swords, ready for every adversary and earthly challenge. Hard work is often more of a gift to us than anyone else we support through it.

Oh great and sovereign Lord, thank you for the gifts of wisdom and work. I praise you this day for the challenges created to strengthen me.

MAY 11

FILLED WITH JOY

Let all who take refuge in you rejoice;
let them sing joyful praises forever.
Spread your protection over them, that all who
love your name may be filled with joy.
PSALM 5:11 NLT

We can live lives of peace and joy. We don't need to live in guilt and shame over the past but can bask fully in the redemption of our Savior. All the wrongs we did to others and to ourselves are forgiven. Our past is wiped clean. We are no longer defined by the worst things we have done but are made new in Christ. In our new identity, we can glorify him and worship him with joy. Yes, the blessings the psalmist shouts in this verse are true of each and every one of us.

The psalmist asks the Lord, "Spread your protection over them." He is asking for security because he can't rejoice or sing for joy if he is unsure whether or not he is secure. But he knows he is at the mercy of God, and any number of things could crush him if God let it. We should be of the same mindset, knowing that our security is not our doing, but the Lord's.

Oh Lord, please make me filled with joy. Remind me of the glory of being a child of God, and I will glorify you for it.

MAY 12

NO EXCUSES

Ever since the world was created, people have seen the earth and sky. Through everything God made, they can clearly see his invisible qualities—his eternal power and divine nature. So they have no excuse for not knowing God.
ROMANS 1:20 NLT

There is no excuse for those who deny God's offer of salvation. Even when human testimony fails and Christians slander the name of God, "the earth and sky" are there to bear testimony to God's love. The world's continued existence is a testimony to the God's eternal power and divine nature. God is indeed visible in the created realm in a way often clearer than the words of men.

After accepting Christ into our hearts, we still make excuses for failing. When we ask for repentance, we often just ask God to pardon us because we didn't know better. But more than excuses, God wants change. He wants men who don't settle with their faulty state but push toward perfection. Are we ready to be men with no excuses? It's a high standard to put on ourselves, but it makes the grace of God all the more precious to us.

Dear Jesus, please forgive me for times I have offered excuses in place of repentance. I refuse to live with my sin.

MAY 13

DANGEROUS LOVE

Place me like a seal over your heart, like a seal on your arm; for love is as strong as death, its jealousy unyielding as the grave. It burns like blazing fire, like a mighty flame.
SONG OF SOLOMON 8:6 NIV

Love can cause extreme levels of elation and destruction. It can take the most dejected and turn them into kings, but it can also break apart families and destroy peace. Love is the all-engrossing decision to put someone else's needs above our own, and it is accompanied by powerful emotional levels that burn "like blazing fire, like a mighty flame." There is no telling what those emotions can lead to when we don't let God into our love.

Solomon's bride is singing to him a song of devotion and tenderhearted intimacy. She wants to be bound to her groom in a promise that lasts. Her words are full of passion, yes, but also loyalty unlike most of the pictures of romantic love we see today. What would it look like to pursue our romantic relationships this way? What would it look like to have a such a passion for our spouses or even life itself?

Dear Jesus, make me a man of love. Make me a man who lives with passion and unyielding jealousy for your plan so I can know your heart.

MAY 14

REST IN ADVERSITY

God is your confidence in times of crisis, keeping your heart at rest in every situation.
PROVERBS 3:26 TPT

Most of us avoid adversity. Where we lack comfort, we seek it. Becoming accustomed to comfort can lead to a fear of adversity, though, or make us severely uncomfortable with any kind of discomfort. Maybe we think we are okay with difficulty, but those around us might say our short tempers and complaints say otherwise. Being "at rest in every situation" involves a spirit of contentment and acts as a testimony to the hope within us.

What kinds of difficulty or adversity are we discontent in? It could be any number of things, but most likely it is something that frustrates us or ruins our day. In these situations, we need to pray for God to be our confidence and for him to make us at rest in every situation. We need God to make us into men who rule their temper rather than being ruled by it.

Dear Jesus, please be at work in my heart to make me content in every situation. Be my peace and my confidence.

MAY 15

PROMISE

The LORD's promises are pure,
like silver refined in a furnace,
purified seven times over.
PSALM 12:6 NLT

Unlike human promises, God's promises are as perfect as his faithful provision over the earth. Every day the sun rises on the earth is a renewal of God's faithfulness, so each promise in Scripture is indestructible. This is the same level of resilient truth found in the Lord who in eternity has felt the continual pain of man's unfaithfulness.

The psalmist says, "like silver refined in a furnace, purified seven times over." There is not a speck of error in the promises of the Lord. Down to the microscopic level, there is no minute dishonesty. His promises are pure, reliable beyond measure, and we have only to trust in them. To believe in them, though, we must know them, and to know them we must read his Word. What is stopping us from dwelling daily in the promises of the Lord?

Dear God, how strong and pure you are! Thank you for the salvation, security, and love you have promised me.

MAY 16

ACTIONS SPEAK VOLUMES

"Just as you can identify a tree by its fruit, so you can identify people by their actions."
MATTHEW 7:20 NLT

If we had only our actions to demonstrate our love, how would we act? Without affirmative words or compliments to offer, we would have to get creative. As it is, actions are our primary way of demonstrating our character. In today's verse, Jesus says we "can identify people by their actions," and his words are as true today as they were back then. It's vain to craft a persona through our words and demeanor if our actions and hearts are in the wrong place.

Today, ask those closest to you what your actions tell them. Often, we don't know ourselves half as well as we think, and external opinions have great value for this reason. Our words, actions, and opinions of ourselves should all agree. Only then can we be role models of righteousness for those around us.

Dear Jesus, I know I can never live up to your perfect image of righteousness, but I want to produce the fruits of righteousness that result from faithful repentance and living. Make me more like you in thought, word, and deed.

MAY 17

LOVABLE

"I love each of you with the same love that the Father loves me. You must continually let my love nourish your hearts."
JOHN 15:9 TPT

Men aren't shown enough tenderhearted love in our society. Some might think our society is too soft, but the opposite is true. We are either demeaned by people for our faults or shown a counterfeit love that is okay with our sin and leaves us feeling lost and unable to grow. The love Jesus has for us bleeds with compassion and acceptance of who we truly are and pushes away all the sin encrusted on our souls.

One of the main obstacles to our Christian growth is considering ourselves unlovable. Yes, we have heard Jesus loves us, but in light of our shame and the repulsive images of our past in our minds, who could actually love us? We say Jesus loves us, but secretly we doubt it. The greatest way we can improve ourselves and be the men our world needs is to know we are lovable and loved by Jesus.

Dear Jesus, strip away the leathery crust of sin suffocating my heart. Make me know, deep down, that I am loved in my brokenness.

MAY 18

BE LIFTED UP

Humble yourselves before the Lord,
and he will lift you up.
JAMES 4:10 NIV

By humbling ourselves, we lift up Christ. By putting aside our fame, we shout his. He deserves the praise and glory, and when we learn this, we learn contentment. Our greatest joy is not found in being lifted up by God but in being humbled by him so we can enjoy his exaltation. If he lifted us up without humbling us, our enjoyment would be tainted with pride and broken ideas.

What does it look like to humble ourselves? What actions can we take in humility today? It might mean going next door to help a neighbor or responding kindly to a rude email. For some men, it involves learning to listen more than speak. Whatever it is, the ways we can humble ourselves is our path to exaltation and joy.

Oh God, only you can lift me up. Please do not lift me up before you teach me to be a man of humility and servitude. Teach me how to live in humility before you.

MAY 19

RIVER FROM GOD

"Look at the new thing I am going to do.
It is already happening. Don't you see it?
I will make a road in the desert and rivers in
the dry land."
ISAIAH 43:19 NCV

Rivers don't flow through dry lands for many reasons. The water the river brings may be lost to evaporation or sink into the sand leaving no water for the end of the river's path. In order for a river to run through a dry desert, the source of the river must overflow with an abundance of water. Isaiah is declaring that God is going to make one of these rivers, and he is going to bring an abundance of this "new thing" to where there are only old things and desolation.

When God blesses us, he often does so where we need it most; he blesses our deserts with water. To the most broken parts of our hearts, he brings healing. To the most starved, he brings food. For a man feeling alone and misunderstood, he brings his own companionship and understanding. God is a god of new things who is ready to act in ways we do not expect.

Oh God in heaven, give me faith for the coming rivers. Give me trust in your way and your actions. You will surely do what you have promised; I have only to wait.

MAY 20

PASSIONATE LOVE

*I will show my love to those who passionately love me.
For they will search and search continually until they find me.*
PROVERBS 8:17 TPT

The love of God is revealed to "those who passionately love" their God. There are few things Christ despises more than the lukewarm. If we are to do anything, he wants the full measure of our manhood poured into the task. He wants his children to "search and search continually until they find me." When have we ever lived up to such life, passion, or purpose?

If we desire to see and comprehend the love of God, all we have to do is search for it. It is a straight path but is a difficult one. It takes grit, determination, and endless drive based on a deep appreciation of the Lord. To be a Christian man is to be a full-hearted believer whom others can count on. To be a man is to search continually.

Oh God of life, fill me up this day to meet the battle. I am nothing without you, and I need your blood in my veins.

MAY 21

BY OUR SIDE

Because you are close to me and always available, my confidence will never be shaken, for I experience your wrap-around presence every moment.
PSALM 16:8 TPT

The Psalms are a wealth of intimate prayers between man and God, and today's verse is no exception. The psalmist praises God for his nearness or "wrap-around presence." God is perfectly close to us, and he is also perfectly available and never a moment away. As the psalmist testifies, this is our source of confidence. No matter who seeks to harm us or how great their strength is, nothing can separate us from the love of God or diminish his power.

There is also a flipside to God's presence. Sometimes, we find it inconvenient for him to always be nearby. The things we do in the dark or in our minds, where we think we are safe to think and do what we want, are still subject to the searching eye of God. Acts of sexual impurity, cheating, and our prideful thoughts never escape the eye of our omnipotent Lord.

Oh God, thank you for your nearness and faithfulness. Thank you for always wrapping around me in protection and provision. Please clear the darkness from my mind today.

MAY 22

PURPOSEFUL PEACE

Work at living in peace with everyone, and work at living a holy life, for those who are not holy will not see the Lord.
HEBREWS 12:14 NLT

Peace and holiness never come to those who don't want them. Peace can exist both in our minds and our relationships, and holiness can only be seen in our relationships when it is seen in our hearts. The Hebrews author tells us to "work at living in peace" because peacemaking is important to God. He is unwilling to abide with sin, yet he can confront it peacefully and still overpower it.

To not live in holiness is to live apart from God. We can't be near him if we are not holy; his very being rejects anything unholy. The moment we turn to our addictions and idols for fulfillment is the moment we lose God's presence in our hearts. He will not live in a heart that has something else on its throne, for he is holy in his jealousy for us.

Oh God, I commit my heart and mind to you. Make me holy and use my words to bring peace to every situation.

MAY 23

EVIDENCE

The Holy Spirit produces this kind of fruit in our lives: love, joy, peace, patience, kindness, goodness, faithfulness.
GALATIANS 5:22 NLT

We can fake our faith for the world, but God, and those closest to us, will see the lie because they will not see love, joy, peace, patience, kindness, goodness, or faithfulness. Only genuine faith can produce these pieces of evidence. Without faith, we lust in place of love, pleasure instead of joy, apathy where there should be peace, and a host of other counterfeits for the virtues God would give us if we asked him.

When we look at our lives, what fruit of the Spirit do we find lacking? Every man is his truest self when the entirety of the fruit of the Spirit is within him. When he is the man God desires him to be, the Holy Spirit will produce the missing fruit in his life so others will know God is working in him.

Oh Jesus, please give me a sincere faith that produces the fruit of the Spirit I can't find elsewhere. I can't pretend to have these virtues, so please grow them in me.

MAY 24

DIFFERENT WEALTH

He is so rich in kindness and grace that he purchased our freedom with the blood of his Son and forgave our sins.
EPHESIANS 1:7 NLT

Men are expected, by the world and by the church, to accumulate wealth. We are seen as being our best selves when we are providing for a family, watching over their future, and giving them financial security. This pressure can be a heavy weight that pulls a man down to his knees and breaks his resolve to live. Jesus himself felt pressure to provide for his global family, but he chose to provide them with a different kind of wealth. He chose to be rich in kindness and grace and to bless his children with the wealth of virtue even when he withholds material wealth.

What would it look like to pursue a different kind of riches? What if others knew us as men rich in virtue even if we were poor materially? God never promised us riches, but he did tell us we could always count on him for the riches of the Spirit. Perhaps our anxiety will lessen when we stop searching for the wrong riches.

Oh God, why have I been looking for the wrong wealth? Remind me of true riches and your life of material poverty.

MAY 25

WHOLE BEING

I wait for the LORD,
my whole being waits,
and in his word I put my hope.
PSALM 130:5 NIV

When you wait for the Lord, does your whole being wait with anticipation? Do you fill your mind with his Word or with your own words? Waiting on the Lord is an active, vigilant mindset. It's not time passed easily; it involves the fixation of our will on God's future plan and seeing it come about. The psalmist waited for the Lord with his heart, mind, and soul. Are our lives this prayerful and patient, or are they filled with anxiety and impatience?

Everyone has something that they need to wait for. It could be anything from a job promotion to a child on the way. The world does not expect men to be patient or faithfully wait on the Lord for his will to pass. They expect men to be products of their circumstances, but the glory of God raises a man above this. God wants men who wait on him and fully trust his power.

Oh Lord, I will wait on you. I will take the things I worry about and lay them at your feet as I wait for your will to pass.

MAY 26

ONE ANSWER

There is salvation in no one else! God has given no other name under heaven by which we must be saved.
ACTS 4:12 NLT

As long as their soul is not completely darkened, everyone is searching for the same thing. Everyone wants to find meaning in the madness, to understand why we are here, and to find reasons for pain and beauty. The world is full of answers people have made for this question; see every religion apart from Christ. We are all on a sinking ship and praying desperately for a lifeboat to appear, but sometimes the lifeboat is difficult to accept.

Are we willing to deny everything we are for the sake of salvation? We can seek salvation in other places that don't mean the death of our selves. We can seek salvation in work, lust, alcohol or stimulants, even in psychological health, but only God can satisfy our thirst. Every other coping mechanism delivers less and less the more we ask. To be saved is to die to who we are and all we take pride in. Once everything is stripped away and only God remains, we will see there was no other way.

Oh God, thank you for your thirst-quenching salvation. Strip away all that I am in pride and worldliness and make me your child.

MAY 27

STRONG IN WEAKNESS

I'm not defeated by my weakness, but delighted! For when I feel my weakness and endure mistreatment—when I'm surrounded with troubles on every side and face persecution because of my love for Christ—I am made yet stronger. For my weakness becomes a portal to God's power.
2 CORINTHIANS 12:10 TPT

Our weakness is where God is ready to work his strength in us. Where our self-centered pride ends is where Christ begins. As Paul says, "I'm not defeated by my weakness, but delighted!" It's an uncommon mindset. Men are not taught to delight in weakness or told to "endure mistreatment" to be made stronger. Paul knows the vital truth: endurance is a result of repeated failures and not repeated successes.

Where do we feel defeated by our weakness? Where has the love of Christ caused us to be hated, beaten down, and persecuted in every way? This is the area we must surrender to God so his power would manifest in us. Then, we can grow resilient in that power and not be disappointed.

Dear Jesus, I rejoice in the areas where I have no reason to be proud so I might be proud of how you act through weakness.

MAY 28

WEALTH IN WAITING

True godliness with contentment is itself great wealth.
I TIMOTHY 6:6 NLT

Nothing good comes easily. There is always a cost, and for human beings, the cost is often patience. God has made life this way on purpose to produce "godliness with contentment" in his children. A man without self-control is like a city with all its walls torn down (Prov. 25:28), and how can a man gain control over his emotions and plans if not through waiting? Contentment is the most difficult feeling while waiting because we have no idea if or when the fruition of our waiting will come to pass. Once we learn to trust God with every outcome, we will find this contentment and be the godly men he wants us to be.

If God only wanted to give us material prosperity, he wouldn't need to make us wait. He would give us everything we want immediately. God instead chooses to give us wealth of the spirit, and he blesses us with this through our waiting. There is wealth in the waiting; we need only find it.

Oh God, please give me contentment where I have frustration. Give me the godliness only found through you.

MAY 29

BACK TO LIFE

Why am I discouraged? Why is my heart so sad?
I will put my hope in God! I will praise him
again—my Savior and my God!
PSALM 42:11 NLT

The mind of a man is prone to brokenness. Life's circumstances affect our mental wellbeing. As the psalmist was brought down through sadness and discouragement, he had to forcefully pull himself back into a mindset of life. He had drifted into death and stagnation, and with God in mind, he reminded himself of the promises he needed to think about.

Our situation is no different. When we fall into a mire of hopelessness, we will not be able to pull ourselves out until we do so with great force and desire. God gives men times of despair to perfect their spirit and will. He wants us to be strong and to push toward him in faith even when we can't see him. This is impossible apart from his power, so we must rely on his power even when we can't see it.

Oh God, life's dark struggles overshadow me. Give me hope in the unending grace

flowing from your throne and give me the strength to run toward it.

MAY 30

IMMOVABLE AND GENTLE

My dear brothers and sisters, stand strong. Do not let anything move you. Always give yourselves fully to the work of the Lord, because you know that your work in the Lord is never wasted.
I CORINTHIANS 15:58 NCV

How many men can be described as immovable yet gentle? Men who don't let anything move them are often stubborn and ignorant and negate the virtue of steadfastness. Jesus is steadfast in his holiness and perfection, but he is also the most merciful individual ever to exist. He proves this dichotomy is not just possible but glorious in its balance of strength and understanding.

This verse from Paul is a call to strength, work, and steadfastness. He doesn't make room for the halfhearted or those willing to give up the fight. He demands, "Always give yourselves fully to the work of the Lord." What does this look like in our lives? Where do we see the Lord working, and where have we stood back while other Christian brothers reap the harvest?

Perhaps it is time we join in the bounty awaiting those who pursue the Lord with all their heart.

Merciful God, this day is precious to me as an opportunity to live fully for you. Please work in my mind and produce the steadfastness I need to hold on to you.

MAY 31

MARKED BY JESUS

Dear friends, let us love one another, for love comes from God. Everyone who loves has been born of God and knows God.
1 JOHN 4:7 NIV

When we love as Jesus loved, selflessly and utterly, we show the world we are marked by Jesus. We demonstrate we have been touched by a higher power and have the virtues of our Lord and Savior. We are no longer bound by the selfishness of this age or the burdened heart of our society; we have gone beyond these things in holy redemption. As John says, "Everyone who loves has been born of God and knows God."

John says this to his "dear friends." He was full of love for his audience no matter the conditions. John had been loved unconditionally by his Savior, so he loved his brothers and sisters unconditionally in return. Are we willing to be men who love the unlovable? Are we willing to put aside our grievances and love the broken and hurtful people around us? Jesus did this for us, and we have no part with him if we don't do the same.

Oh God, how you have loved me! You have made me a new man, and I want to show this through the love now overflowing in me. I pray your love would shine from me and give you glory.

JUNE

Listen to my voice in the morning, LORD.
Each morning I bring my requests to you and
wait expectantly.
PSALM 5:3 NLT

JUNE 1

SPIRIT AND BODY

> We do not lose heart. Though outwardly we are wasting away, yet inwardly we are being renewed day by day.
> 2 CORINTHIANS 4:16 NIV

We are both spirit and body, and these two sides are often at war. For Paul, his flesh was "wasting away," but the spirit inside of him was "being renewed day by day." This level of perseverance is easier to read than practice. According to Matthew 26:41, "The spirit is willing, but the flesh is weak." We are often ready and willing in spirit, but once our flesh begins to tire, we lose heart. The spirit can rule over the flesh and bring it through difficulty only through the Holy Spirit's power.

What would it look like to not lose heart in our lives? Where are we discouraged and brought low, and where are our bodies and minds too tired to fight back? Men were made to be broken for the Lord but never broken by the world. We were made to be beacons of hope and endurance for those around us, but this is only possible if we walk in faith through our tribulation.

Eternal Lord, please give me the faith to not lose heart. Give me the strength to stay strong in you while my body wastes away.

JUNE 2

POWER BEYOND MEASURE

"You will receive power when the Holy Spirit comes on you."
ACTS 1:8 NIV

This promise was the consolation Jesus gave his disciples before ascending to heaven. His disciples were powerless without the hand of God, and they had seen this at Jesus' crucifixion. All but one of the disciples fled Christ, like scattered sheep, because suddenly he was not there to support them. They needed a friend even more intimate than Christ to support them and keep them on the right path, and this friend was the Holy Spirit.

The power of the Holy Spirit empowers us to live out the gospel mission fruitfully. He empowers us to go beyond regret and shame and into new hope and glory. He shows us that our lives are no longer defined by our mistakes but by living a holy and loving life for Jesus. What old vestiges of our former lives are waiting to be cast off in exchange for the Holy Spirit's power? What is dragging us away from the glorious life God intended for us?

Oh Jesus, please give me power beyond my measure to leave behind my old life and cling to you. Help me live with hope and passion for you.

JUNE 3

LETTING GO

There is a time to cry and a time to laugh.
There is a time to be sad and a time to dance.
ECCLESIASTES 3:4 NCV

Holding on to Jesus, pushing endlessly toward him and putting first, doesn't mean always feeling passionate or happy. Christ didn't design one-dimensional people, and he expects us to cry and laugh throughout our lives. Burnout awaits the man who is only comfortable when he feels like he is achieving or fighting for something and never allows himself to rest.

The man of greatest value to those around him is the one appreciates emotion. God designed our hearts for a wide spectrum of emotion, and the man who denies himself this will also deny others the same thing. It is good to be merciful to oneself because it's the best way to learn how to be merciful to others. What area of life or memory do we refuse to process? Perhaps we have been hiding from something we need to cry over.

Oh Lord, please be near me through the diverse experiences you put in my path. I

have no way to live without you, so please give me strength for the day.

JUNE 4

FAMILIES

God decided in advance to adopt us into his own family by bringing us to himself through Jesus Christ. This is what he wanted to do, and it gave him great pleasure.
EPHESIANS 1:5 NLT

Every Christian is brought into God's family and bound together through the fatherly and brotherly love of Christ. This family isn't made out of desperation or circumstance; it's a planned community of believers that gives Jesus "great pleasure." The glory of having a family of renewed and redeemed individuals was so appealing to Jesus, he was willing to die to obtain it. Everything about this plan, this thing that "God decided in advance," took great sacrifice. The measure of this sacrifice is the measure of God's desire to have us in his family.

Not all men are called to get married and start a family. For some men, the family they create is not linked through genetics but through love and care. The communities we make around us are reflections of the family community God created. There is great reason to rejoice over the unofficial families around us because that is ultimately how God brought all gentiles into his family.

Lord, thank you for families bound through blood or bound through choice. Show me who needs a family and how I can answer that need.

JUNE 5

HOLY REST

"My presence will go with you, and I will give you rest."
EXODUS 33:14 ESV

Any man who perpetually refuses to rest is not functioning as the best version of himself. God created a holy rest for his saints, and it rejuvenates them so they can continue their faithful work with new energy. Without rest, there is no end to the wear and tear that breaks us down. Rest is not laziness, and there is no glory in denying rest for the sake of working a little longer. Rest is itself a kind of work; it takes dedication and practice. In today's verse from Exodus, God promises, "My presence will go with you." His presence is the source of our rest.

It gives security and protection so we can let our guard down. Without God's holy presence, we are at the mercy of temptations and trials that try to pull us off the narrow path. God's presence does surround us, however, and this allows us to rest at any time Jesus finds fit.

Jesus, please continue to provide for me through your holy rest. Lend your presence to me always so I can rest in both peace and danger.

JUNE 6

LAW OF LOVE

Love completes the laws of God. All of the law can be summarized in one grand statement: "Demonstrate love to your neighbor, even as you care for and love yourself."
GALATIANS 5:14 TPT

Just like that, Paul takes the entirety of the Pentateuch (the first five books of the Bible) and condenses it into a single word: love. God is love. He is the perfect image of giving up oneself for the sake of others. God's heart burns with love for his beloved, and so we could have this same love, he wrote the entirety of the law. By showing us our impurity, he revealed to us what it means to love him and be like him. To be like God is to love him and our neighbors just as he loved us.

As Christians, we often make things more complicated than they are. We make our Christian walk into a set of dos and don'ts, and we are frustrated by those who do things differently. This is the trap the Galatians fell into and why Paul labeled them fools. The most dangerous thing we can do to sanctification is add or subtract from what God made it to be: love shown to our Savior and our neighbor.

Dear God, please teach me to show love. Teach me to fulfill your law in the simplest way.

JUNE 7

GETTING STUCK

> Now is the time for us to progress beyond the basic message of Christ and advance into perfection. The foundation has already been laid for us to build upon: turning away from our dead works to embrace faith in God.
> **HEBREWS 6:1 TPT**

In Matthew 5:48, Jesus told us to be perfect. He knew we would never reach this goal, but that doesn't mean he wanted us to give up or settle for less. The phrase the writer of Hebrews uses is "advance into perfection." It's an aggressive, effort-filled sentence. With the Word of God as our foundation, we build our lives into ever-better temples for Jesus. We don't stop with the additions and renovations, but in holy reliance, we become temples of reverence and holiness.

"Now is the time," the verse says. It is not time to get stuck, be men of weak character, or be men that settle. Now is the time to progress and push deep into the character of God. There is no better time than now. What are we waiting for? Do we need any reason beyond pleasing our Lord and Savior?

Perfect Jesus, make me into the man you want me to be. I will not settle with my flaws. I will give them to you to be ironed out and made righteous.

JUNE 8

ONLY THE PATIENT

The LORD must wait for you to come to him, so he can show you his love and compassion. For the LORD is a faithful God. Blessed are those who wait for his help.
ISAIAH 30:18 NLT

Patience is a valuable virtue to God. It must be; he perfects it in us through an incredible amount of waiting. He also waits for us as today's verse says. Once we walk away from our pride and wait on him, he is ready to shower us with his blessings. His love and compassion are waiting for us, but we must let go of our desire for instant gratification. His love and compassion will not stop waiting either. The Lord is faithful, and no matter who we are, he will wait for us to turn to him.

We are rich beyond measure with a God abounding in faithful patience. No one on earth had us in mind for millennia or foresaw our existence for ages. No one else has watched us sin and cheat on him and continued to love us anyway. What a God rich in love and patience! He has stored up his blessings but only for the patient of heart.

Dear Lord Jesus, how great you are in patience! Please make me a man slow to anger and abounding in love and faithfulness.

JUNE 9

DRAW NEAR

Draw near to God, and he will draw near to you.
JAMES 4:8 ESV

God can't approach a heart hostile to him. He won't make peace with a man who is unpeaceful. Before we can be redeemed, we are often broken and humbled until our pride is stripped away and we are willing to draw near to God. The comfortable, satisfied man is not one who draws near to God. James also says that God never rejects a penitent sinner. "He will draw near to you," the verse says. Unconditionally, God will do it.

What are we drawing near to? What idols sit in place of God's holy presence? It might be a coping mechanism, like alcohol, or something darker like depression. Whatever we draw near to, we will grow into its image. We will find ourselves consumed by the thing we are near, so it's important we draw near to the right thing.

Dear Lord, teach me to draw near to you every day. Make me a man consumed by your passion and will instead of my own.

JUNE 10

CONFIDENCE

Blessed is the one who trusts in the LORD, whose confidence is in him.
JEREMIAH 17:7 NIV

For a man, life is a confidence game. We are pressured by our male peers into being confident, yet we are also shamed for it by others. Our confidence is the key to our success at times but ruins things in other situations. What is the Lord's plan for confidence, and how do we honor him in the way we act toward others?

The confidence the prophet Jeremiah speaks of is a confidence of trust. He is confident in the Lord the same way a son is confident because of his trust in his father's greatness. Jeremiah is bold and ready for every situation because he knows he is in the hands of the Lord, and he trusts him. To honor those around us, our confidence must not depend on our achievements or level of strength. It must be as constant as the Lord's providence and faithfulness toward us.

Oh Lord, you know how much I need you. Please work in me this day and give me the confidence that comes from you alone.

JUNE 11

LEFT WANTING

*Oh that I might have my request,
and that God would fulfill my hope.*
JOB 6:8 ESV

God has given every man a host of wants and desires that he leaves unsatisfied. It might be for short or long periods of time, but other times, it's forever. There are some men who will never move a rung up the corporate ladder or others who will never be in a romantic relationship. God has not messed up by placing these desires in a heart left wanting. Job was in this place of wanting as he cried out to God, and he received a complete response.

After all his pains, Job did not receive a hearty congratulations from the Lord. God met him with rebuke over his impatience and pride he had even as he writhed in the dust with open sores and diseases. It is not our lot to be frustrated or angry over God's decisions. He gives us desires to perfect us in patience, and no matter the timetable he decides on, we have only to rely on him and pray to him in holy dependence.

Oh God, the waiting can feel like it's killing me at times. Please perfect me through my requests and my hopes as I am left wanting.

JUNE 12

THE LORD IS ALWAYS

The Lord is always good and ready to receive you. He's so loving that it will amaze you—so kind that it will astound you!
And he is famous for his faithfulness toward all. Everyone knows our God can be trusted, for he keeps his promises to every generation.
PSALM 100:5 TPT

It's easy to question the Lord's reliable nature. We are surrounded by people who are unreliable, act out with no warning, and change their predictable behavior. Just when we think we know what to expect, we learn we're wrong. This conditions us into thinking that no one is constant or reliable, and we can never be sure of what anyone will do. But this is not the case.

Christ is the perfection of all human emotion. "He's so loving that it will amaze you—so kind that it will astound you!" the psalmist writes. More specifically, he says, "The Lord is always good." Always. No matter what. We can rely on the Lord and his constant, outstretched arm, and we are to mimic his reliability. How many of us aim to be predictable, good, reliable men?

Oh God, if only I could be like you in faithfulness and constancy. Keep me always by your side so I might grow to be like you.

JUNE 13

ENDLESS GRACE

*From his fullness we have all received,
grace upon grace.*
JOHN 1:16 ESV

What man has fully considered the depth and the breadth of God's grace for him? Can we appreciate how much he changed us, down to the core of who we are, or how many sins he covers for us every day? Men are born as rebels against God, and the evil in them is deep in their hearts. There is nothing good in us apart from what God has granted in his mercy, and then through his atoning death, he renews all that we are.

Even after redemption, we sin constantly. Think about every lust-infected thought, every moment of pride, every speck of selfishness, and remember that any of it is enough to separate us from the love of God. What a blessing to receive God's grace! We receive his grace in redeeming us and then his grace in upholding us. We have nothing to gain from this world if we do not have this.

Lord, thank you for the grace you have given me in your death and resurrection.

Thank you for the love and grace you pour out on me every day.

JUNE 14

HIGHEST STANDARD

"Love your enemies, do good to them, and lend to them without expecting to get anything back. Then your reward will be great, and you will be children of the Most High, because he is kind to the ungrateful and wicked."
LUKE 6:35 NIV

To be a child of something is to resemble it. The walk of faith is a process of becoming more fully a child of God each and every day. We can't continue to grow if we forfeit God's standard for our own. Once we decide his perfection is too high to attain or his demands on us are too great, we will cease to grow in his image. Luke 6 is Jesus' dismissal of the human standard of excellence. Whatever we think is good enough is not enough, Jesus says, and only perfection will do.

As men, we are called to hold ourselves to a standard we know we will never achieve in this life. We are called to not just be good fathers, brothers, leaders, and followers but to be perfect ones. Once we stop improving, we regress. With God, there is only one direction we can travel healthily, and it's toward him.

Oh God, make me in your image. Make me righteous where I am lacking and fill me with your passion to run this race.

JUNE 15

TEACHABLE NATURE

"Listen to the truth I speak: Whoever does not open their arms to receive God's kingdom like a teachable child will never enter it."
MARK 10:15 TPT

It is not common to aim at being teachable. It's an uncommon brag. How many of us have the humility to always want to learn from others rather than teach them? When it comes to the kingdom of God, Jesus says a teachable nature is non-negotiable. He says we must have the humility of children and open arms to receive.

As men, Jesus calls us to excel as both leaders and followers through the path of humility and self-forgetfulness. If we want to be like Jesus, we have to do away with our pride. Humility does not mean we have to be doormats, but it does mean we have to dispense with everything we hold to be ours. This allows us to step into every situation Jesus gives us, from leadership to servanthood, without any sense of entitlement. This is the same path Jesus took.

Oh Lord, remind me of the truth you spoke to your disciples. Remind me how little my pride matters and make me teachable.

JUNE 16

ALWAYS FILLED

> May you always be filled with the fruit of your salvation—the righteous character produced in your life by Jesus Christ—for this will bring much glory and praise to God.
> PHILIPPIANS 1:11 NLT

Many would describe life as a series of valleys and mountains. Between the shadows of death and the mountains of the Lord, there doesn't seem to be any continuity. Yet continuity is exactly what the apostle Paul wishes for his readers in Philippi. "May you always be filled with the fruit of your salvation," he declares. This does not necessarily mean feelings of joy and elation. Fruit is the result of a relationship that puts Jesus first in the believer's life.

The things which Paul wishes for his readers to have continuously are not emotions but "the righteous character produced in your life by Jesus Christ." We can't always count on satisfaction, and often our character feels like it is tested far more than it is displayed. Still, this brings glory and praise to God, and he is most honored when we are filled with character no matter the situation.

Lord, fill me continuously. Make me righteous no matter the circumstances and reliable to others through you. By your name I pray this.

JUNE 17

FIX YOUR GAZE

*Let your eyes look straight ahead;
fix your gaze directly before you.*
PROVERBS 4:25 NIV

Many men let their minds wander wherever they like. They have no actual control over their thoughts and ultimately their actions. Their eyes are allowed to look side to side at every distraction whether it is good or evil. This is not uncommon; it's true for all of us at times. Only through active faith can we learn to control ourselves through Christ.

The writer says, "Fix your gaze directly before you." This only works if Jesus is directly before us. If we are headed in the wrong direction, the path straight ahead is poisonous to us. Fixing our gaze directly before us is disaster. The freedom of self-control and focus are only achieved while traveling in the right direction. Only Jesus can complete this work in us, and he will only do it when we put him first in our lives.

Oh Lord, please do a great work in me today. Put me on the path that leads to you and restore my control over my mind,

thoughts, and gaze. Give me the self-control I lack without you.

JUNE 18

REFUGE

Keep me safe, my God, for in you I take refuge.
PSALM 16:1 NIV

This psalmist is a man wholly given to his Lord and Savior. He has put Jesus first and has forsaken all other sources of refuge and safety. The world is against him, and God is for him. He cries out, "Keep me safe, my God." Yes, it is his God, for he has put aside the pleasure of idols and the idol of pleasure for the sake of knowing Jehovah as his sole deity.

Do we find ourselves taking refuge in God? If we were fired today, what would we do first? Probably yell, call someone, or look through help wanted ads. Few of us would have the immediate reaction to pray. The problem that often assails us is we don't take refuge in God, but we expect his help. The Lord will not sustain those who don't lean on him. Whatever we lean on in times of difficulty will be what we can expect help from.

Oh Lord, there is no deity like you. Please hold me. I have no other to lean on, and I need you in this moment.

JUNE 19

WELL PLANNED

Commit your actions to the LORD,
and your plans will succeed.
PROVERBS 16:3 NLT

What makes a good plan? Thousands of books claim to have the key to successful planning and the execution of those plans. There is a wealth of strategies, tactics, and everything in between to ensure our feeble man-made plans deliver what we want from them. But the Bible says, "Unless the Lord builds the house, those who build it labor in vain" (Ps. 127:1 ESV). There is no assurance that our plan will be successful without God. He wants our plans to be following his will which will never fail.

The writer says, "Commit your actions to the LORD." The root of our success is found in our smallest steps and actions. We find harmony with God's plan when we yield to him even the smallest portions of our lives. Our thoughts, actions, and sentiments must all be rendered to the Lord of lords if he is to use us in his will.

Dear God, thank you for your care and love. Today, I give you my actions; please sanctify them and my earthly plans for your will.

JUNE 20

OUR PRIDE

"Blessed is the one who isn't offended by me."
MATTHEW 11:6 CSB

It is natural to take offense. Deep down, men know they are weak and subject to injury, so they defend themselves by being insulted. This defensiveness is born out of a fear of being destroyed by our enemies. God, however, does not want to be our enemy. Repenting of our sins means looking at what we thought were the offenses of an enemy and realizing they are the remarks of a lover.

Jesus says, "Blessed is anyone who takes no offense at me." Of the many things Jesus has said, we can dismiss none of them. We must take every remark he has made as gospel truth, and even when it conflicts with our deepest opinion, our opinion must give way. Only then will we be blessed as Jesus promises. Only then will he cease to be our offending enemy and begin to be our closest friend.

Dear Lord, please work inside my heart. Give me the faith to let go of my offenses and accept your words. They are true.

JUNE 21

CONSTANT IN PRAYER

LORD, every morning you hear my voice.
Every morning, I tell you what I need,
and I wait for your answer.
PSALM 5:3 NCV

Putting Jesus first means making him our first thought and our first breath in the morning. It means giving our anxieties to the Lord instead of fixating on them. Putting Jesus first is a commitment of the mind born out of holy dependency and being constant in prayer. David put forth his requests "every morning," and he would wait on the Lord for an answer. His prayer was an active conversation and not just a podium for his fears and anxieties.

Putting Jesus first is the calling of every Christian, and for men, this involves dying to ourselves in a unique way. We must learn to give God control of the things we have been given control of and learn to recognize we are only stewards of his world. The responsibilities he gives us are a blessing made to shape us, and he still expects us to go to him for everything we need.

Oh God, I need you desperately. Hear my call in the morning and give me an answer. What am I without you, Jesus?

JUNE 22

PURPOSE

We are convinced that every detail of our lives is continually woven together to fit into God's perfect plan of bringing good into our lives, for we are his lovers who have been called to fulfill his designed purpose.
ROMANS 8:28 TPT

We usually can't see how God's plan is working, and that can make life difficult. It's difficult because the pieces start to look like they fit together as a different plan that ends in our destruction, and we begin to doubt God's hand at work behind the scenes. However, it does not matter if we can see how God is working in our lives as long as we are convinced he is working. What would it look like to put aside our worry in light of this truth?

The verse calls us lovers who have been called with a purpose. God already has a purpose for everything happening in our lives, and we have only to wait until we can see how. He has a purpose for us, too, and he will accomplish this purpose through uncertain circumstances more often than not.

Dear Lord, please convince me today that you have a purpose for everything happening right now. One day, it will make sense. Amid the uncertainty, convince me that your purpose and plan remain.

JUNE 23

DIFFICULT PROGRESS

I am certain that God, who began the good work within you, will continue his work until it is finally finished on the day when Christ Jesus returns.
PHILIPPIANS 1:6 NLT

This admonition from Paul is a comfort for anyone facing setbacks. God made man with the capacity for failure, even on the road to success, and often failures teach us more resiliency than success. The thing we need to remember is that no number of failures can change the power of repentance and turning away from our sin does not guarantee perfect fidelity even for the finest saint.

For some, it is controlling their anger; for others, it's conquering a sexual or substance addiction. It could be anything, but whatever the "good work within you" that God is working at, it will be brought to completion. As long as we die to ourselves every day, we have the assurance of sanctification and of God working in us slowly but surely. We will not see the ending in this life, but on the day that Christ

Jesus returns, the work will be complete, and we will rest in the peace of our righteousness.

Dear Jesus, I know I will not win every fight, but please give me the strength to never stop trying. Give me the faith to continue despite all failure.

JUNE 24

FEEBLE EXISTENCE

"Look at all the birds—do you think they worry about their existence? They don't plant or reap or store up food, yet your heavenly Father provides them each with food. Aren't you much more valuable to your Father than they?"
MATTHEW 6:26 TPT

We worry about existence because it's fragile, but perhaps that is the reason we shouldn't worry about it. Perhaps life is so precarious, it's on the brink of ending at any moment, and only by God's grace do we continue to live. Perhaps he has a plan for us and if it were not for his will, we would have died long ago. Unlike the birds, we know life is uncertain.

We are not on the same level as the birds of the air or any other animal. We are made in the image of God with a capacity for the full range of emotion. We mean more to him than any animal because they do not have the same harmony with his spirit. Why would he care less for us? We are his chosen stewards, and it's pointless for us to discount our worth.

Dear Lord, please work in my heart to end my anxiety and fears. Show me I have no reason to be afraid for my existence because you will take care of it.

JUNE 25

HIS BLESSED PRESENCE

Surely you have granted him unending blessings and made him glad with the joy of your presence.
PSALM 21:6 NIV

David was happy because he had been given his heart's desires. The greatest requests he had, which he laid at the feet of the Lord, had been granted to him, and the king's heart was overcome with joy. Most importantly, he was given what he desperately wanted because he had wanted the right things. He had not desired fame and fortune but the still and mighty presence of the Lord. Fame and fortune were still given to him, along with "unending blessings," but these were second to the joy he received from being near to God.

What does your heart want? A man's heart was designed to desire. We are not sinful to want. God wants us to pursue our desires wholeheartedly, but he also wants us to have the fullest desires. He wants us to put aside our lesser wants and lusts for the sake of his noble, pure, and wholehearted love.

Dear Lord Jesus, may your blessed presence be my greatest desire. May it be the thing I long for and seek out. Thank you for the blessings you have granted me this day.

JUNE 26

GOD'S PASSIONATE LOVE

Christ proved God's passionate love for us by dying in our place while we were still lost and ungodly!
ROMANS 5:8 TPT

God's love for us is like a fire that can't be quenched or deep waters that can't be withheld. His love for us is passionate and unstoppable by any force of man or hell. What he wills, he accomplishes. What he desires, he obtains. We did not choose God but were chosen by him out of love. Perfect love is more than an emotion; it's a selfless choice. Love is present when someone puts the needs of someone else above their own no matter what they feel at the time.

What kind of love do we display? Would the world describe us as men of love? When our coworkers or friends are lost and ungodly, we must have the courage to love them passionately and selflessly. We must have the courage to love as Jesus loved us. Otherwise, we will have no idea what the love he has for us is like.

Dear God, thank you for loving me while I was unlovable. Thank you for finding worth in me as a worthless sinner and bringing me into your family. You are beyond comparison.

JUNE 27

LABOR IN VAIN

It is in vain that you rise up early and go late to rest, eating the bread of anxious toil; for he gives to his beloved sleep.
PSALM 127:2 ESV

It's easy to correlate our success with our level of effort. How much are we willing to sacrifice? How much are we willing to give? In our functionally atheistic minds, we factor God out of our plans. We forget that if God does not build the house, the laborer works in vain. What God requires of us is not a quota of work but a spirit of humility.

At the heart of overworking is two things: pride and mistaken mindset. In pride, we think our efforts amount to something. We think we can attain glory by our miniscule strength. But that is not all; we are also mistaken and confuse righteous devotion with single-mindedness. God wants us to be wholeheartedly devoted to him but not to the work he has given us. According to the verse, God "gives to his beloved sleep" because he knows our human limits and does not need our physical work to prove our devotion.

Lord, remind me of the limits of my capabilities. Give me a full measure of godly devotion and not just a devotion to work.

JUNE 28

WHAT'S WITHIN

Above all else, guard your heart,
for everything you do flows from it.
PROVERBS 4:23 NIV

The world and even those closest to us only see the outside of us: what we say and do. They build a picture of who we are based on what they know, but they often can't say why we are the way we are. They don't know exactly what's inside and the struggles we face every day on a moment's scale. In the case of all men, only God knows the heart.

The writer starts with "above all else." The matter at hand is supremely important, and all else is to be put to the side. The actions and words people see spring from our hearts like a garden, and just like a garden, we need to keep the weeds out and protect the good things that grow there. Good men do not come to be good passively; they are the result of active heart-guarding and cultivation. If we want to be better versions of ourselves and grow close to God, we must guard our hearts above all else.

Lord, be the fence around my heart that keeps its garden for you and your purposes.

Use my heart for everything you have planned for it.

JUNE 29

OVERCOMING DEMONS

"I have told you all this so that you may have peace in me. Here on earth you will have many trials and sorrows. But take heart, because I have overcome the world."
JOHN 16:33 NLT

Jesus warns us, "Here on earth, you will have many trials and sorrows." He warns us because he knows these trials and sorrows are a certainty. He will not remove the obstacles in our path, but he will equip us to move past them and not let them overcome us. That's why he says, "Take heart, because I have overcome the world." The truth is not that we can conquer all things through Jesus; Jesus himself has already conquered all by dying on the cross.

Where are we looking for peace in our lives? It might be at work, with family, or with friends, but wherever it is, Jesus wants to offer us his peace. He wants us to take his light burden rather than the weight of anxiety we carry. He wants us to have peace in him because in the world, we will not.

Dear Lord, I want to take heart. Help me not be afraid as I put my hope in you instead of this world. Please give me the peace I can't find anywhere else.

JUNE 30

JUST CALL HIM

"Call to me and I will answer you, and will tell you great and hidden things that you have not known."
JEREMIAH 33:3 ESV

There is so much for a man to learn. Whether it's how to do a job or care for those closest to us, we are at a loss on our own. The arrogant will think they understand, but those around them will disagree. Yet as the Lord says through his prophet Jeremiah, all we need to do is call to him. We can accept our lack of knowledge and choose to ask him for what we need.

Most people learn to pray as a way of speaking to God, but it is vain to pray without waiting for an answer. God says, "Call to me and I will answer you." He wants us to pray to him so he can answer. He wants us to humbly listen. Listening is far more difficult than speaking, but the man who listens to God will also learn to listen to others, and he will have the right words for them when they need it. God will share the "great and hidden things that you have not known."

Lord, I will listen to you today.

JULY

This is the day the LORD has made; let's rejoice and be glad in it.
PSALM 118:24 CSB

JULY 1

OUR POWER

*Anxiety weighs down the heart,
but a kind word cheers it up.*
PROVERBS 12:25 NIV

They say there is strength in numbers, but there is power in words no matter their number. Our words have the power to kill, give life, and do everything in between. Do we appreciate this? Anxiety afflicts nearly everyone we see on a day-to-day basis and especially those under the most strain. This demon, anxiety, can be conquered through a single kind word. What power is this?

The issue most of us have is we don't realize how much people take what we say seriously. We say whatever we think. We get frustrated with our friends and family and tell them why, but we don't realize how much we are crippling them. Is someone being defensive? They feel they have to be because someone is criticizing them. If they do not fight back, they will be crushed by the weight of their words. Imagine what a kind word could do instead.

Heavenly Father, remind me of the power you have given me. Make me in your image

of strength and meekness. Meekness is choosing not to hurt others, and strength uplifts them.

JULY 2

IMMORTAL INHERITANCE

*My flesh and my heart may fail,
but God is the strength of my heart and my portion forever.*
PSALM 73:26 NIV

This psalm of Asaph is the expression of a man whose soul rests in his Savior and nothing less. He has let go of everything of this world including his own body and heart. Nothing will drag him away from his holy pursuit of the Lord or make him cast lots for possession of anything earthly. He can say, "God is the strength of my heart." His strength, his ability to act and endure, is not based on circumstances but on Christ alone.

If heart and flesh failed, where would we find ourselves? Would we be crushed and leave behind a world that meant everything to us? Hopefully, we would leave our loved ones with the greatest difficulty and not health, riches, or pleasantries. God desires a man whose strength is in the Lord and whose portion is in eternity.

Dear God, thank you for giving to me a portion in heaven rather than here on earth. Thank you for your strength which supports my every step.

JULY 3

ETERNAL COMFORT

I am convinced that nothing can ever separate us from God's love. Neither death nor life, neither angels nor demons, neither our fears for today nor our worries about tomorrow--not even the powers of hell can separate us from God's love.
ROMANS 8:38 NLT

Fear is often the imagining of a possible undesirable situation. When fear is not addressed at a current enemy or source of pain, it's telling us to pay attention to something that reason has not brought to our attention. Therefore Paul, at the conclusion of chapter eight, gives us indefatigable proof that every fear over losing the love of God is ill-founded and should be dismissed. There is no situation or power that can change our relationship to God once it has been established.

Paul points to every good and bad power and says none of them can cause the situation we fear. Not even demons, life, nor fear itself can change God's love for us. That is the beauty of it. Even if we are consumed by the fear of being separated from God's love, it remains with us and is ready to be received.

Dear Jesus, give me the assurance of your love today. When no one else is there for me, I always have you.

JULY 4

FAITH IN THE GOOD

Surely your goodness and love will follow me all the days of my life, and I will dwell in the house of the LORD forever.
PSALM 23:6 NIV

A strong man can be brought to his knees by cynicism. Any man can be destroyed by ceasing to see the good. This verse, the last in Psalm 23, declares with hefty optimism that David will indeed be surrounded by salvation both in life and in death. He fears no Sheol and no earthly pain, and he declares that despite them all, "goodness and love will follow me all the days of my life." This is the promise David holds before his eyes through every valley and storm.

David had a rough life as documented in the Bible. He faced betrayal, child-loss, and his own apostasy. His life proves there is no level of evil acting on our lives over which we cannot declare God's goodness. As long as we are saved, with that single comfort of redemption, we have a goodness that outweighs all hardships.

Dear Lord Jesus, I declare that my life is good. Please make me a man who fills others with the hope and optimism of the gospel.

JULY 5

MEN WHO FALL

Your words have comforted those who fell, and you have strengthened those who could not stand.
JOB 4:4 NCV

All men will morally fail God. Creation is broken, and so are we. We are not destined for lives of moral perfection. We are destined for imperfection that can lead to shame, bitterness, and feelings of futility if we are not careful. Job fell from both moral and circumstantial security, yet he praised God, saying, "You have strengthened those who could not stand." God leaned down to help people even when they did not deserve it.

Job says, "Your words have comforted those who fell." When we fall or are damaged and need comfort, the first place we should go is God's Word. He is our greatest comfort through difficulty and tribulation. When we can't walk, or stand, or go on, he is there to uphold us. He is there to guide us in his way and give our legs the strength to make the journey.

Oh Lord, please give comfort to me and those around me who have fallen under the

weight of this world's difficulties. Be near to us through our trials.

JULY 6

EVERYTHING

"If you can?" said Jesus.
"Everything is possible for one who believes."
MARK 9:23 NIV

It's so easy to fall into disbelief. We love the Lord, and we think we believe in him, but it never feels like we can count on him to come through. It feels like what we do doesn't matter because the plan Jesus has make no sense. Jesus saw this in his disciples as he responded, "If you can?" There are no ifs with God. God either wills it or does not, and our task is to search out his plan.

When something falls within God's plan for us, "everything is possible." Think about that: every difficult relationship, disease, or struggle in life conquered through belief. If we believe and rest in the Lord, we will either see our trials fall or see God take us through them.

Oh Jesus, remind me to put you first. When you are first in my life, everything falls into place.

JULY 7

VERY GOOD

God looked over all he had made,
and he saw that it was very good!
GENESIS 1:31 NLT

Have you considered what God was implying with "all he had made?" All of it—yes, all of it—was good. Over every speck of nature, every part of humanity, God declared it "very good!" Take a moment to look at your job, family, and heart. How much of it do you consider very good? Much of the human heart is eaten away by bitterness and resentment. Former wounds and pain make us question the inherent goodness in the world God created.

When we look in our hearts, do we consider ourselves very good? For many of us with an understanding of sin and repentance, we are stuck with a negative view of ourselves. All we see is sin, regret, and the wrongdoing we have done, but that is not the gospel. God has made us good, and he has redeemed us as good creatures. Intrinsically, we are now good, not evil, and the evil is only transient.

Oh Lord, you have made me good! You have looked on me and declared me good. Thank you.

JULY 8

APPROACH BOLDLY

Let us then approach God's throne of grace with confidence, so that we may receive mercy and find grace to help us in our time of need.
HEBREWS 4:16 NIV

In the heart of God lies a deep desire for men of boldness and confidence. He wants men who believe so heartily in Jesus' atonement and prioritize him so much, they find no trial or comfort compares to the overwhelming love and power of the Lord.

"Let us then approach God's throne of grace with confidence," the writer says. This is the throne of the one eternal God who has struck men down because they approached his earthly altar with pride in their hearts. What kind of sanctifying work was worked in us, and what kind of appeasement for the wrath of God must have been accomplished, to merit such confidence? Yet this is the only path. We are to be confident so "we may receive mercy and find grace to help us in our time of need."

All-Powerful God, remind me today of what Jesus did for me. He felt every pain so I could have access to your throne of grace.

Remind me again of his sacrifice and of its worth.

JULY 9

RUN WITHOUT BREAKS

Those who hope in the LORD will renew their strength.
They will soar on wings like eagles; they will run and not grow weary, they will walk and not be faint.
ISAIAH 40:31 NIV

God created man as a finite creature. Our fleshly bodies can't live forever, run forever, or work without sleep. Our small minds can't hold all knowledge or learn without breaks. We are weak, and we grow weary. For us to be children of God, however, we have to pursue the Lord without end. We must run without breaks, and for this task, Jesus offers us his own strength. He knows our limits and gives us the strength of the Lord so we can complete the grand mission of being children of God.

God wants us to be men who soar on wings like eagles and run and do not grow weary. He wants us to have passion and to inspire those around us as we push deeper into the heart of God. He wants us to be filled with life and not be dragged down by the weight of this world. His plan for us is not one of failure and dismay but of passion and endurance.

Oh Jesus, please give me strength when I am at the end of myself. Inspire me with your own endurance so I can soar and run without tiring.

JULY 10

GOOD WISDOM

The wisdom that comes from God is first of all pure, then peaceful, gentle, and easy to please. This wisdom is always ready to help those who are troubled and to do good for others. It is always fair and honest.
JAMES 3:17 NCV

Here, James characterizes the wisdom of God. The wisdom of God is not neutral, able to be used for good or evil, but it is necessarily right and will support the right course of action. According to James, "It is always fair and honest" and "ready to help those who are troubled." God's wisdom is above all pettiness and does not exist to be used as ammunition in arguments. To take God's words and use them for our purposes goes against their character.

How can we, as men of Christ, act in wisdom? First and foremost, we can display the character of wisdom. We can be "peaceful, gentle, and easy to please." We can be ready to help others with a kind word when they are troubled, and we can be fair and honest just as God's wisdom is. To be a man of God necessitates wisdom displayed through kindness and compassion.

Dear Jesus, please fill me with your kind, gentle wisdom. Make me a blessing of knowledge to others so I can breathe life into their troubles and woes.

JULY 11

UNOFFENDED

*A person's wisdom yields patience;
it is to one's glory to overlook an offense.*
PROVERBS 19:11 NIV

How easily are we offended? How quickly is our ego injured? This is the measure of our pride. The more we let go of ourselves and yield to the Lord's identity, the more we become unoffendable. We don't feel the need to defend ourselves to others or hold on to offenses. As we grow in godly wisdom, we grow in patience and confidence.

In 2 Chronicles, King Sennacherib of Assyria besieged Israel and began to taunt the God of Judah. King Hezekiah, a godly man, took deep offense at this. It was beyond disgraceful to him, and he brought his anger to the Lord who proceeded to destroy tens of thousands of Assyrian soldiers in the night. We must learn how to be insulted on behalf of others and especially God. It is to our glory to overlook our offenses, but when someone weaker than us is being offended, it merits our defense.

Dear Lord, please teach me to let go of my pride and overlook offenses. Teach me

also to stand up for your name and for the weak and poor.

JULY 12

MEN OF CONFIDENCE

Even when I walk through the darkest valley, I will not be afraid, for you are close beside me. Your rod and your staff protect and comfort me.
PSALM 23:4 NLT

David had seen many bloody wars. He was a man after God's own heart, and his faith had been tried and tested through many life-or-death experiences. For David, having faith meant more than living an easy life. It meant trusting Jesus in the face of enemy armies, trusting him in the wilderness as he was being chased by Saul, and trusting him as his own son sought to kill him. In these trying times, David found his confidence in the Lord's providence and wisdom.

In his mistakes and successes, David set one of the clearest examples of biblical manhood. He displayed the difficulties and trials of being a fallible man living before the face of a perfect God. That is the commission before us: to follow God with confidence, despite our flaws and sins, and show compassion and wisdom as we live in humility. We are like sheep guarded and guided by the hand of a divine shepherd.

Dear Lord, give me confidence in you this day. Teach me to follow you boldly wherever you might lead. I want to trust you through both my mistakes and successes.

JULY 13

IN ALL THINGS

Seek his will in all you do,
and he will show you which path to take.
PROVERBS 3:6 NLT

Here, the writer of Proverbs addresses people who don't know what to do with their lives. He addresses the conflicted soul who lacks direction or is wondering what path to take. His words also apply to those with paths and goals: "Seek his will in all you do." Christians are often criticized for seeking Christ in some areas of their lives while ignoring him in others. These charges of hypocrisy are often well-merited and shouldn't be scoffed at.

To be faithful in all things takes a lot of effort, and it's often not comfortable or convenient. To be a faithful man means more than settling into a regular routine of church and reading Scripture even though those are both tremendous help. Being faithful means taking time to analyze every part of our lives, submitting them to Christ, and offering him our thanksgiving. Yes, being faithful in all things is an all-consuming task.

Dear Jesus, please work in every inch of my life. Declare your lordship over my life. By seeking you in all I do, may I find your path.

JULY 14

PROTECTION AND COURAGE

> LORD, you are my shield,
> my wonderful God who gives me courage.
> PSALM 3:3 NCV

David wrote this psalm when he fled from his son, Absalom, who was seeking to kill him. Beyond the trauma of having his own son want him dead, David had to deal with the very present reality of dying if he wasn't careful with his next actions. Beyond a defense or attack plan, he needed bravery to process what was going on in his environment. He needed both protection and courage.

David praised his "wonderful God" for being both his shield and his source of courage. He was able to trust in the Lord because he was both a practical method of defense and a spiritual source of encouragement. David's God truly was wonderful to him and a great friend when those closest to him turned against him. We can take refuge in the same God. He is there to help us and save us when we need him. No matter the difficulty or pain, our God is present in every moment.

Dear Jesus, please be my protection and courage. Let my confidence be a testimony to those around me today.

JULY 15

LIVES OF STRENGTH

"Remain passionate and free from anxiety and the worries of this life. Then you will not be caught off guard by what happens."
LUKE 21:34 TPT

God is a god of great strength and passion. He designed man to be a vessel of that passion, living wholeheartedly and "free from anxiety and the worries of this life." Oh, to be free from anxiety! That would set us apart from our peers. God wants us to live above the cares and trials of this age, but it's difficult when we are so deeply immersed in it.

In this passage from Luke's gospel, Jesus warns his disciples about the day he returns. He wants them to be ready, so they are not "caught off guard by what happens." The only way to be ready, he says, is to "remain passionate." Jesus wanted his disciples and every man and woman to develop the right kind of cares and passions. He wants us to be full of passion for his gospel and for seeking his love and sharing it.

Dear Jesus, please make me a man of passion. Dispel my cares and worries so I am

not distracted from my goal of searching after you in all I do.

JULY 16

TRUE WITNESS

"When the Spirit of truth comes, he will guide you into all truth. He will not speak on his own but will tell you what he has heard."
JOHN 16:13 NLT

Everyone wants to be heard, but not everyone has something to say. The value of the Holy Spirit is that he is pure truth, and he wants to impart that truth to us. He is a true witness and will not lead us astray. Just as the verse says: "He will not speak on his own but will tell you what he has heard." Even the Holy Spirit, God himself, has a humble attitude. In this spirit of humility, he guides us, so we don't wander off the narrow path.

Prayers are a way for us to speak to God but also for him to speak to us. It is important to recognize this in our prayer lives and to spend time listening for the words of the Lord. We can trust him to lead us and guide us, but it will take much surrender and listening on our part.

Oh Lord, may I rely on your promise to guide me into all truth. Please lead me today. Don't let me wander off the path you have set for me.

JULY 17

STEADFAST

"For the mountains may depart and the hills be removed, but my steadfast love shall not depart from you, and my covenant of peace shall not be removed," says the LORD, who has compassion on you.
ISAIAH 54:10 ESV

God has filled his Word with promises, and most of them are promises of steadfastness and faithfulness. We can be sure of his love because he has proven it, time and time again, and recorded its testing throughout the Bible. God says, "My covenant of peace shall not be removed." When God makes a covenant, he does not break it. He can't because doing so would deny his character. His love is perfect and founded in eternity.

The first line of this verse from Isaiah uses imagery of physical destruction. It's important to note that mountains and hills are much more secure than most of the things we are afraid of moving. Our jobs or homes are more likely to be upset. Yet even if the mountains gave way, or the entire universe for that matter, God's love remains steadfast.

Oh God, please make me a man who loves as steadfastly as you do. Make me perfect in your love and faithfulness.

JULY 18

MAN OF MOTIVATION

Let us think of ways to motivate one another to acts of love and good works.
HEBREWS 10:24 NLT

Anyone can motivate their fellow Christians. As men, however, we are specially positioned to equip each other through brotherly affection. We can motivate one another by defeating negative peer pressure and instead spur one another on toward "acts of love and good works." This encouragement reminds our fellow men of the right way to act. When the world is pushing him toward hatred and selfishness, we can motivate him toward righteousness with a simple word or action.

Motivation often takes creative measures. The writer says, "Let us think of ways to motivate one another." We won't always know how to motivate someone right away, and we might spend time thinking about the best way to encourage our brothers in Christ. Everyone is different, so every man will need different words or actions to push them toward Christ. Thankfully, the Holy Spirit aids us in this creative work of motivation.

Dear Jesus, please give me the words or show me the right actions to encourage my brothers and sisters in Christ. Make me a good brother who motivates your children to good works.

JULY 19

FREE TO SUCCEED

You have been called to live in freedom, my brothers and sisters. But don't use your freedom to satisfy your sinful nature. Instead, use your freedom to serve one another in love.
GALATIANS 5:13 NLT

When Christ washes us free from our sins, he frees us from our sinful nature. He forgives us by washing us clean in his blood, and the sins of our past and future are likewise washed away. The sinful nature Paul is speaking of is not lust or gluttony but rather pride and legality. The desires of the flesh are not all animalistic. The desire to be under law, or to find salvation through ceremonies and sacrifices, is also of the flesh.

The Galatians were catering to their desire for legality. They were destroying each other's faith by spurring each other toward the old Jewish law rather than the grace and faith of the gospel. Are we choosing the easy path of rules rather than faith? It is one thing to set boundaries and another to give up the freedom of faith in exchange for chains.

Dear God, please teach me to live in freedom rather than bondage. May rules and laws be behind me, the cross before me, and a foundation of faith beneath me.

JULY 20

GIVEN A GIFT

By grace you have been saved through faith. And this is not your own doing; it is the gift of God.
EPHESIANS 2:8 ESV

A man who lives life satisfied is a man who knows his blessings. Many people with the riches and renown we wish for are actually cursed and only see what they do not have. When Jesus strips away everything we have, we are brought to the realization that we have a gift above all others: salvation. "And this is not your own doing," Paul writes. "It is the gift of God." In light of this gift, do we need anything else? Can broken relationships, disease, or loss take away from the glory of God's love for us? His grace extends the promise of eternal glory; our lives before that glory begins are short.

Paul says that "by grace you have been saved through faith." He has outlined for us the process of every single Christian's journey toward the cross. We have entered into relationship with God by the power of his grace, and our role in the process is one of trust and faith.

Generous God, you have loved me so much. If the world yields to me not a single blessing, I have this; you loved me and chose me when I did not deserve you.

JULY 21

CHANGE ALL AROUND

Let justice flow like a river,
and let goodness flow like a never-ending stream.
AMOS 5:24 NCV

The prophets were concerned for the individual salvation of every Jew, but most of all, they were concerned for the social state of their homeland. The sins of individuals had combined into a river flowing with sin and apostasy. They wanted change all around; they wanted this river of death they saw in Israel to be transformed into a river flowing with goodness and justice. They wanted society's atmosphere to change from toxicity to healing.

Do we ache with the same desire? Are we heartbroken by the issues of our society, and do we seek the wellbeing of our city or country? God wants men to be active in their communities and bring the gospel of change to all they know. He wants us to be agents of his renewal and seek for justice to flow like a river and goodness to flow "like a never-ending stream."

Oh God, please renew this world I am in. Bring your justice and goodness to those

who deserve none of your goodness, and that includes me.

JULY 22

BOASTING IN WEAKNESS

Each time he said, "My grace is all you need. My power works best in weakness." So now I am glad to boast about my weaknesses, so that the power of Christ can work through me.
2 CORINTHIANS 12:9 NLT

Our power is in our weakness. When we fail, we fall on Christ in reliance and brokenness. Life has no shortage of burdens ready to be strapped on our backs. Paul was no stranger to these pains, and he cried out to Christ in 2 Corinthians. He wanted the pain taken away and comfort to rejoin him, but that's not how God works. "My power works best in weakness," he told Paul. Imagine the disappointment of the apostle Paul when he realized his burdens were there to stay.

Can we be glad to boast about our weaknesses? Instead of praising what we are good at, do we tell people about all the ways we fail and how God makes up for it? Once we let go of our achievements and outer image of success, we will be able to bear the testimony of the Lord.

Oh God of wonders, you deserve all the praise. Help me rely on you as my testimony and let go of my own strengths.

JULY 23

BECOMING A MAN

> When I was a child, I spoke about childish matters, for I saw things like a child and reasoned like a child. But the day came when I matured, and I set aside my childish ways.
> 1 CORINTHIANS 13:11 TPT

There are behaviors and struggles appropriate to different seasons. When we are young boys, we endure being looked down on by our older peers, trying to control our temper, or discovering sexuality. When we mature, we progressively set aside our "childish ways." If we continue struggling with our childish ways, they will slowly but surely gain a stronger hold on us.

Paul says, "I saw things like a child and reasoned like a child." He knows it's unfair to judge children by the standards of adults because they have not been given the minds or bodies of adults yet. It's okay to struggle, grow, and develop so long as we don't get stuck somewhere along the way toward perfection. Jesus wants to walk alongside us as we become the men he envisions, and he doesn't plan to make us perfect overnight.

Dear Jesus, please work in me so I can mature and set aside my past ways. May my struggles not hold power over me; through you, may I conquer them all in due time.

JULY 24

GOD REPLIES

When I was in trouble, I called to the LORD,
and he answered me.
PSALM 120:1 NCV

When Baal and Asherah worshipers took over the religion of Israel, there were no responses. These false gods were made of wood and stone, and no matter how many times the pagan priests cut themselves, cried out, or sacrificed, they only received silence. Our God is unique because he answers us. There are times of trying silence when we feel he isn't there, but these are balanced by moments of beautiful communion we have with God as he speaks to us in the quiet of our souls.

We should pray as though God would answer. He is not a silent or passive deity. He does not intend for us to pray just so we can hear ourselves speak; he wants us to pray with minds ready to listen. Why should we call to someone who doesn't call back? He may respond in way we don't expect, but he will respond.

Almighty God, thank you for being a god who answers. Thank you for showing your care in the darkest moments. I give you all my glory and praise.

JULY 25

LOOKING BACK

It will happen in a moment, in the blink of an eye, when the last trumpet is blown. For when the trumpet sounds, those who have died will be raised to live forever. And we who are living will also be transformed.
1 CORINTHIANS 15:52 NLT

Work and pleasure are the primary motivations for the man of the world. He lives to wake up every morning and work and seek pleasures afterward in a myriad of ways. An eternity is awaiting us, though, in which we will deal with the consequences of our decisions. We will have to face how we lived our lives and whether we were truly living or just surviving. What will be our regrets, and what will we wish was different?

God willing, we will reach the resurrection with joy over how Jesus used us as agents of his change. God willing, we will look back on our lives as men who lived for the right things and sacrificed for those they loved. The doldrum of work, and the pleasures we enjoy without gratitude, will mean nothing to us then, and we will only have the work or pleasure we rendered to God.

Dear God, please take every hour of my day and sanctify it for your purpose. May I live for you in every moment and not just for pleasure and necessity.

JULY 26

EYES ON HEAVEN

In keeping with his promise we are looking forward to a new heaven and a new earth, where righteousness dwells.
2 PETER 3:13 NIV

Where is our focus, and what do we hope for? The apostle Peter tells his readers to keep "looking forward to a new heaven and a new earth." We all have pasts and memories that show the worse side of our character. No man is without regrets or mistakes, and some of them can be debilitating. But Peter does not want us to look back at our past and be dragged down; he wants us to look forward and be encouraged.

How beautiful our future is where "righteousness dwells" and there is no longer any weeping or suffering. The new heaven and earth will be a place of rest after our long journey, and we will be able to once and for all forget our pains and regrets. This is the future we eagerly await. Even better, it is the future Christ has promised to us, so it's a plan that cannot fail.

Dear God, thank you for the future I have to look forward to. Thank you for your new heaven and new earth and the promises they bring.

JULY 27

HEART OF WORSHIP

> Let everything that breathes
> praise the LORD.
> Praise the LORD!
> PSALM 150:6 NCV

Life is riddled with difficulty. Between the responsibilities of work, the trials of relationships, and bodily exhaustion, it's too much for any man to handle on his own. All too often, the only thing we manage to do is numb ourselves to the pain. The greatest thing we can do, however, is embrace this difficulty by praising the Lord in the midst of it. By giving our hearts in worship to our Creator and Redeemer, we are freed from much of the anxiety seeking to crush us.

Christ has felt every pain we can imagine. It has been said that the only way to heal our wounds is by looking into his. To worship Jesus is to turn our gaze to him in love, honor, and adoration. No one else is worthy of the throne in our hearts. He is perfect in humility and strength and stands as the greatest role model of manhood we have. Let us praise him on this day.

Dear Jesus, I long to worship you alone. No one else is worthy of my praise or highest adoration. Take the throne of my heart; it belongs to you.

JULY 28

INDEPENDENT IN VIRTUE

If we are not faithful, he will still be faithful, because he must be true to who he is.
2 TIMOTHY 2:13 NCV

God's virtues are independent of us. Paul testifies here that God's faithfulness doesn't depend on us also being faithful, but the same is true of every other aspect of God. He does not need the world to be happy, at peace, or be anything for his character to stay good. When Israel was at its most godless and child sacrifice had replaced right religion, God remained the same. Despite no one save a few remembering the name of Jehovah, Jehovah was still the same God he had always been.

God wants us to be of the same spirit. He wants men who don't need happy families, fulfilling jobs, or anything but Jesus. He wants us to remain faithful and good even if circumstances cause us distress or sorrow as the prophets experienced. For us to bear the clearest testimony, we must be independent in our virtue and free from the supporting structures of this world.

Dear Jesus, please make me a man with a clear testimony of godliness. Give me faith and righteousness in every circumstance.

JULY 29

SINGING TRUTH

Let the teaching of Christ live in you richly. Use all wisdom to teach and instruct each other by singing psalms, hymns, and spiritual songs with thankfulness in your hearts to God.
COLOSSIANS 3:16 NCV

Paul gives us practical ways for letting the teaching of Christ dwell within us. With all the distracting thoughts and experiences we process every day, it's easy to forget about the teachings of Christ until we are reminded of them again on Sunday. This is not a mindset of spiritual growth, and it will cripple us in the long run. Rather, through whatever way we find easiest, we are to let the teaching of Christ live inside of us in every small moment.

Paul encourages us to let wisdom proliferate through our singing. Few of us sing outside of church. The usual reason is we don't believe we are good enough, but God never required men to be talented vocalists. He wants our song to rise to him and be heard by those around us, not because our voices are angelic, but because singing is beautiful in and of itself as an expression of truth.

Dear Jesus, please work in my heart through the presence of your teaching in me. Let it be the life inside of me, and let it grow through my singing to you.

JULY 30

LIVING EMPOWERED

I pray that from his glorious, unlimited resources he will empower you with inner strength through his Spirit.
EPHESIANS 3:16 NLT

This blessing from the apostle Paul is of the greatest value for a man alive today. He reminds us first of God's "glorious, unlimited resources" and then he prays these resources would be used to empower us. He does not pray for us to be empowered in a physical, exterior way but in our spirits through an inner strength. What a blessing this is from Paul, and how marvelously it shows what we need to be men of God.

God does not need men with external strength alone. He would have promised us external strength if he needed it. He promised to provide internal strength. This strength is not always visible, but it makes us men whom others can look up to, rely on, and trust in. Inner strength is well beyond the value of external strength.

Dear God, thank you for your unlimited stores of kindness and how you lavish it on me. Please make me a man of inner strength this day.

JULY 31

FORGIVING ONE ANOTHER

Be kind to each other, tenderhearted, forgiving one another, just as God through Christ has forgiven you.
EPHESIANS 4:32 NLT

Forgiveness is not an easy task and definitely not one to be taken lightly. Jesus died for forgiveness; he did not just "get over" our sins against him or easily forget what we did. If we find it difficult to love someone who has wronged us, that's to be expected. That is why forgiveness is precious; it's difficult. It starts with what Paul says, namely being kind and tenderhearted, but it is often a long and slow process that takes time and dedication.

Whom do we resent in our lives? We are letting them have power over us by not forgiving them and not the other way around. We are letting the wounds they inflicted on us not heal, and that's painful. If we want to feel joy and Christ's forgiveness for us, we must forgive them and let their transgressions go.

Dear God, I am a man who has been wronged, but I have also wronged you. Please forgive me and teach me to forgive those who have wounded me.

AUGUST

His anger lasts only a moment, but his favor, a lifetime.
Weeping may stay overnight, but there is joy in the morning.
PSALM 30:5 CSB

AUGUST 1

ULTIMATE ACCOUNTABILITY

Nothing in all creation is hidden from God. Everything is naked and exposed before his eyes, and he is the one to whom we are accountable.
HEBREWS 4:13 NLT

Men in the church often have accountability partners to remind them of the grace God has instilled in their hearts. They meet often, discuss the important news in their lives, and care for one another. Before any other human being, God is our ultimate accountability partner. As the verse says, "Nothing in creation is hidden from God." We don't even have to tell him about something for him to know about it. We are accountable to him because of his perfect knowledge.

The words of Hebrews are graphic: "Everything is naked and exposed before his eyes." No matter our shame or the disgusting nature of what we have done, Jesus knows. He knows, and we have only to confess and trust in his forgiveness. Whether it happened in our heads or in our solitude, there is no point hiding it from God.

Omnipotent God, please forgive me for the sins I try to hide from you. Show me that you see me; there is no hiding from the eyes of God. May I learn to live with courage and faith before you.

AUGUST 2

WORK AND REST

He gives strength to those who are tired and more power to those who are weak.
ISAIAH 40:29 NCV

It is not a sin to be exhausted. God made man to work and fight for his goals, but he did not intend for him to do so without interruption. Life is full of rhythms, and one of these core rhythms is work and rest. As men, we acknowledge our limits and our dependency on God by stopping our work and resting in God's peace. By resting when we are tired, we are asking God for the strength to continue. When we are weak, we must call out to him for the power we need instead of searching for it by ourselves.

God will exalt the humble and, as the verse says, make strong those who are weak. As long as we believe ourselves to be strong, God will not exalt us. As long as we fill ourselves with pride over our power or ability, we will scorn God's blessing. We must put ourselves in a mindset of humility and recognize our power is only a fraction of what is possible.

Dear God, reveal my weakness. Humble me to call out to you for power. When my body and mind fail, may I fall on you.

AUGUST 3

HOLY CALLING

"Everyone my Father has given to me, they will come. And all who come to me, I will embrace and will never turn them away."
JOHN 6:37 TPT

Until Jesus gathers us into his new family, we are lost sheep. Beyond that, we are dead in our sins, and dead men can't make choices. We are completely dependent on the choice of the Father to give us to the Son so he could embrace us and bring us in from outside of his love. Thankfully, he promises to embrace us no matter what. No matter the sin in our past or the despicable state of our souls, Jesus has dealt with dirtier.

Every good man feels like a monster at some point in his life. Looking at the filthy state of his soul and mind, he wonders how anyone could love him, yet that is what gives God the most glory. Loving the unlovable, doing the impossible, and turning fools into wisemen is God's plan. He does not redeem all the people we would expect him to, and he delights in the unexpected.

Good Shepherd, what a blessing to find favor in your eyes. I pray today for all the people in my life who feel beyond your reach. Please embrace them, Jesus.

AUGUST 4

OPEN TESTIMONIES

"No one lights a lamp and hides it in a clay jar or puts it under a bed. Instead, they put it on a stand, so that those who come in can see the light."
LUKE 8:16 NIV

Sin is insidious and seeps into every area of life like a cancer. As men of Christ, we are fundamentally different from the men around us who do not have the Lord in their hearts. If we are God's, we think differently about humility, sexual integrity, honesty, and most other areas of life than our contemporaries do. They will want to know why.

The light illuminating our souls must be explained as the source of our differentness. When people ask about our conduct, speech, or decisions, Jesus must be at the center of it. He is our reason why, and we have to ascribe to him the glory he is due. His testimony is our joy, and we can share it without fear. A worthy goal for Christian men is to be a source of safety and fearlessness for others. How can this be seen in our testimony? How can we grow to share our story comfortably and without fear?

Oh Jesus, be first in my heart and in my conduct. Teach me to share your testimony with boldness.

AUGUST 5

SET FOR SUCCESS

The hope of the righteous is joy,
but the expectation of the wicked will perish.
PROVERBS 10:28 CSB

When our hearts are far from God, our plans are sure to disappoint. The writer of this verse is warning us about the absolute futility of ungodly plans. Righteousness comes from being near to Jesus, and being near to Jesus helps us understand his plans for us. Rather than laying out plans, we walk through hope. We place our hearts with God's plans which will always unfold, whereas our ambitions are like vessels tossed about by the waves and crashed on the rocks.

Are you setting yourself up for success? Whether you are a man who plans too much or a man who doesn't plan at all, you are setting yourself up for failure unless your plans are based on righteous hope. God does not want us to be apathetic or plan our whole lives out; he wants us to seek his perfect plans and live in light of them.

Dear Jesus, please bring me near to you. In being near to you, make me righteous, and in righteousness, give me hope.

AUGUST 6

DRINK DEEPLY

With joy you will drink deeply from the fountain of salvation.
PSALM 12:3 NLT

Most men live halfheartedly. They don't put their hearts into what they do, and they have no idea what true joy tastes like. The very idea of drinking deeply is foreign to them. That is not the life God calls Christian men to. We are to stand out for our wholehearted efforts in everything we do. We are to be different by living with passion.

As this verse says, our sustaining fountain is salvation. No matter the pain or suffering, no one can take our salvation from us. In every situation, a man can rejoice because he has the Lord, and that blessing will outweigh every sorrow. This is not just an encouragement to us; it's also for those around us if we tell them. We can be like support beams in times of difficulty by drinking deeply from the Lord's salvation when the world gives us nothing to rejoice over.

Oh God, make me a man who lives life wholeheartedly. May the source of my joy be your salvation which nothing in this world can take away.

AUGUST 7

DARK TIMES

> Smile on me, your servant.
> Let your undying love and glorious grace
> save me from all this gloom.
> PSALM 31:16 TPT

The world's darkness is felt keenly by those who know the light. David is acquainted with righteousness as a man after God's own heart. He asks for God's "undying love and glorious grace" because he has tasted it before. He knows how sweet it is to be comforted by the Lord. We are called to behave the same way and to let our pain and tribulation push us closer to God in holy dependency. A man can only stand independently if he is dependent on the Lord.

There will always come dark times in our lives, but that is okay. It's okay to feel loss, betrayal, anxiety, and bereavement if we feel them alongside our Savior. When we feel he is far away, we can cry out to him like David and continue to hope in him, so the darkness does not drown us. Man is perfected through difficulty, gloom, and remaining hopeful despite the circumstances.

God of light, you are my only hope in the darkness. I have no other plan, and I need your salvation. Please smile on me and save me, oh Lord.

AUGUST 8

BEYOND THE VISIBLE

Though you have not seen him, you love him; and even though you do not see him now, you believe in him and are filled with an inexpressible and glorious joy.
I PETER 1:8 NIV

Men are products of their environment. Their actions are determined by their past circumstances influencing them in current situations each day. They cannot rise above this. When life or the past is filled with adversity, they either crumble or go in search of meaning beyond the trials they face. Jesus is the meaning beyond our visible circumstances. Peter says, "Though you have not seen him, you love him." Men of Christ live by what they do not see.

Peter goes on to say, "You believe in him and are filled with an inexpressible and glorious joy." As men of Christ, we are to be fountains of that inexpressible and glorious joy. It's a tall order, but nothing short of it fulfills God's plan for us. We can acknowledge the trials of today and the pain of our past while living with joy anyway and praising the Lord for his glorious light.

Dear God, please make me a man not dictated by his circumstances. May my faith be in the invisible and my source of joy be in you.

AUGUST 9

RESPONDING LIKEWISE

All of God's promises have been fulfilled in Christ with a resounding "Yes!" And through Christ, our "Amen" ascends to God for his glory.
2 CORINTHIANS 1:20 NLT

In Christ, we have the answer to our every request. He has provided what we desired deep within our hearts. He is God's fulfilled promise as "a resounding 'Yes!'" In a world of rejections and discouragement, God holds back the tide of our doubts and criticisms with the action he has undeniably accomplished: sending his Son in the likeness of sinful flesh to take on our pride and shame and give us the power to live again.

How do we respond to the resounding "Yes!" from Christ? God created men to bring him glory and cry out, "Amen!" to his plans. We are made to turn others back onto paths of righteousness and bring them closer to our God and Savior. Just as Christ, full of passion and righteousness, declared "yes!" to our hopes, we respond likewise. With hope and strength, we shout back to Christ our honor and devotion.

Dear Jesus, remind me of the glorious promises fulfilled in you. Make me a man

who lives out your promises with great thankfulness and passion.

AUGUST 10

STUDY HIS THOUGHTS

His unforgettable works of surpassing wonder reveal his grace and tender mercy.
PSALM 111:4 TPT

In the works of God, we see his thoughts. Today's psalmist was a man rich in wisdom and wonder because he studied the works of his Creator. According to Proverbs 25:2, "It is the glory of God to conceal a matter; to search out a matter is the glory of kings" (ESV). Do we want to pursue glory? The best thing we can do is to study God's created world and Word in which he has concealed his wisdom. Admiring his "unforgettable works of surpassing wonder" will fill us up and sustain our hearts more than anything else.

Our lives often become task-oriented, and at the height of our productivity, we should stop to remember Jesus' unforgettable works. He wants to be the focal point of our attention, and we should look to him when we are most distracted. His grace and tender mercy will reorient our eyes to the cross and remind us of what truly matters.

Dear Jesus, fix my eyes on what you have done. In creation and in Scripture, may I see the glory of your handiwork revealing your character and wisdom.

AUGUST 11

CONFIDENT PATIENCE

If we look forward to something we don't yet have, we must wait patiently and confidently.
ROMANS 8:25 NLT

When others look at how we act, standing out from our peers in religious purity, we should be ready with a reason. We should be able to point to the cross of Jesus, saying he will return, and we desire to show him lives of fruitfulness. Yes, we "wait patiently and confidently" because there is so much reason for us to wait. If we squandered our days in pleasure and monotony, we would land in regret.

How do we fail to wait patiently? A man's life is a place of business and deadlines. It can be difficult to learn patience in our productivity-oriented culture. Opportunities to grow in patience can be found all around us whether it is taking the stairs instead of the elevator or learning to be calm when provoked. Jesus is a perfect example of patience; his life has many lessons in what it looks like to wait.

Oh Lord, help me wait confidently and patiently for your second coming. Teach me to spend my life on what matters to you.

AUGUST 12

GOD OF POWER

The LORD merely spoke, and the heavens were created.
He breathed the word, and all the stars were born.
PSALM 33:6 NLT

God exerts no effort in doing what everyone in this world could not do even if acting in unison. It is no struggle for him to put stars in place or to create a myriad of galaxies. The billions of dollars and man hours we spend on projects are nothing to him, and he smiles at our little plans that seem so grand to us. The psalm tells us that "the LORD merely spoke." Think for a moment about how little our voices can do in comparison.

A man is easily wrapped up in his own pride. He uses it to keep himself warm in this cold world, but it is not a worthy source of comfort. Our small achievements, our meager strength, are nothing to be proud of. God merely speaks and whole galaxies are born, and he wants us to be his blessed children; that is our source of pride. Our God is bigger than the noblest and highest aspirations any man has ever had about himself.

Mighty Jesus, you were the Word at the beginning. By you and through you, everything came into being. I praise you for this!

AUGUST 13

PRUDENT WORDS

Those who are careful about what they say keep themselves out of trouble.
PROVERBS 21:23 NCV

Any given man lands himself in trouble more often than he would like to admit. We live in a world of trouble with possible mishaps scattered around us like bear traps. The writer of Proverbs would like to help us avoid some of these less-than-desirable situations. Communication is a birthplace of trouble, especially bad communication, and this is done most often through our words. Being careful about what we say is the greatest way we can keep ourselves out of trouble.

Few men in this world are careful about what they say. Even within the church, most men work at being good but neglect to acknowledge how their words affect others. Being careful about what we say applies every time we communicate. Whether we feel spiritually strong or spiritually downcast, there is no grace for how our negative words will affect others. Careless words will cause harm no matter how many reasons we have for why our day was bad.

God, no matter the situation or my place spiritually, please give me care in what I say. Help me watch my tongue so I don't discourage my community.

AUGUST 14

HE HAS TOLD

He has told you what he wants from you: to do what is right to other people, love being kind to others, and live humbly, obeying your God.
MICAH 6:8 NCV

A man's purpose is to live in the love of God and learn each day to enjoy him. We find that when a man is at his best, other people can rely on him spiritually and otherwise. The verse says, "Love being kind to others, and live humbly, obeying God." There is no room for pride in serving others and living in obedience. Our ability to serve comes from our renewal in Christ, so it isn't our achievement.

There is no excuse for disobedience. It does occur in each of us, but that doesn't mean it's excusable. We have no good reason for our failures, because "he has told you what he wants from you." Every time we fail morally is another moment of God's grace covering us, and that must not be forgotten.

Oh Lord, thank you for writing your Word on my heart. Thank you for being present with me and giving me the privilege of being a blessing to others. Teach me to walk in humility.

AUGUST 15

TRACK RECORD

Those who know your name trust in you,
for you, LORD, have never forsaken those who seek you.
PSALM 9:10 NIV

Everyone has a reputation. Whether it is good or bad, people know us by our reputation. The longer we are in the faith, the better this reputation grows and the more it shows us to be children of the Lord. He has the perfect track record of faithfulness and has never once forsaken those who seek him. The psalmist celebrates this by declaring God's trustworthiness in an untrustworthy world.

Will we trust the only being who is perfect in trustworthiness? Are we willing to let go of ourselves for the sake of being held by the only solid rock? We are bound to waste every day spent seeking anything that is not the Lord. There is nothing to do but forsake all distractions that clamor for attention. We must instead lean on the Lord and seek his face.

Oh God, please be at the heart of my search. Be the one I need and the one I lean on. No one else is perfect in faithfulness, so teach me to put my faith in you.

AUGUST 16

MINDFUL OF GOD

I have always been mindful of your unfailing love and have lived in reliance on your faithfulness.
PSALM 26:3 NIV

How many men would describe themselves as mindful? The psalmist writing Psalm 26 is a mindful man who has "lived in reliance." To others, he might appear strong, independent, and focused on his situation, but he keeps his mind centered on God's love more than his situation. His outward independence is born out of reliance on the God of promise and faith. Every man of God in our lives who projects true confidence and intelligence has found it through being broken by the Lord in reliance and holy dependence.

Unfailing is the word the writer uses to describe God's love. More than just not betraying us, his love is constant. It is like a wooden beam that has been battered, stressed, and strained, yet continues to hold up the weight of a house. The human soul is that house. If we want to stand the test of time, God must be the beam supporting us.

Oh Lord, you alone are constant in love and faith. I yield my life to you, Lord. Only by relying on you will I find my strength.

AUGUST 17

ONE WAY

> "I am the way, the truth, and the life.
> No one can come to the Father except through me."
> JOHN 14:6 NLT

When Jesus said he was the only way, he was denouncing more than just other religions. Buddhism, Islam, and other religions will not get us to the Father, but neither will self-improvement, stoic endurance, or any inner philosophy we come to rely on. Jesus is the only way. If we want forgiveness, a clean conscience, or any semblance of healing from the Father, we must learn to let go of ourselves and cling to Jesus. He is the only path worth taking.

What other paths are we trying to take? What spiritual discipline or practice has replaced the presence of Jesus in our hearts? A relationship with Jesus is messy and humbles the proudest of men, and it's not easy. It involves apologizing to people we would like to never see again and seeking reconciliation in a lot of places that are not easy for us to handle. A man will never be who he is destined to be as long as he denies a relationship with Christ.

Dear Jesus, you are the only way to newness of life. No one else can heal my broken heart and make me new.

AUGUST 18

MERCY AND COMPASSION

"Show mercy and compassion for others, just as your heavenly Father overflows with mercy and compassion for all."
LUKE 6:36 TPT

Every man carries a power. When he is wronged, he must choose between mercy or judgment. A man of Christ knows he has been shown mercy and compassion by his Savior, so he readily extends the same mercy and compassion to others. This makes him different from his peers who have no easy way to deal with the wrongs inflicted on them.

It's not natural to be merciful and compassionate. When we are wronged, the natural thing to do is fight back and hurt whoever hurt us. This does not make us stronger, but it gives the illusion of strength. To be strong, we need to be like Christ and overflow with something the world is not expecting: mercy and compassion. It takes true strength to look at our wounds and afflictions and give their healing up to God in humility and understanding.

Merciful God, please work in my heart today. May I be a man of mercy who is not weighed down by his afflictions and wounds.

AUGUST 19

GOOD LEADERSHIP

"Take my yoke upon you and learn from me, for I am gentle and humble in heart, and you will find rest for your souls."
MATTHEW 11:29 NIV

It is within his right for Christ to be cruel to us. It is within his right to not be gentle, but out of the goodness of his heart, he shows us humility and understanding. On earth, there are numerous men who are cruel masters lacking in humility. They have no right to exercise their authoritarianism, but they do anyway out of pride and impatience.

What would it look like to follow Jesus' picture of leadership and manliness? Jesus wants to teach and lead us with grace and gentleness in his heart and by allowing us rest. We will find ourselves in positions of authority at times too, and this is the attitude we should have toward those entrusted to us. We should seek to be kind in our teaching and humble in every circumstance. This is the only mindset we are entitled to, and it is a righteous and Christlike one.

Dear God, please make me a good leader like you. I want to teach others with gentleness and give them rest as you give me rest.

AUGUST 20

HOLY DESIRES

May he give you the desire of your heart and make all your plans succeed.
PSALM 20:4 NIV

If our plans or desires are evil, God will not give them to us. He will not honor a sinful heart with fulfillment because he can't deny his own character. The first step toward receiving the desires of our hearts is having holy desires. Likewise, the first step to seeing our plans succeed is having plans in accordance with the will of God. He delights in granting blessings to his children and will ultimately bless us beyond measure.

An unbeliever is disappointed when he is denied the things he desires and when he watches his plans fall apart. A man who tries to follow God while making his own plans and living with old desires will also be disappointed. If we want happiness, we must set aside our old ways. We must place the foundation of our plans in Christ's plans for us and search out his will at every step.

Dear God, thank you for having a good plan for me. Please reveal it to me; help me

search out your will at every step. Make my heart, like your heart, desire the things of heaven.

AUGUST 21

LIVING IN FEAR

As high as the heavens are above the earth, so great is his steadfast love toward those who fear him.
PSALM 103:11 ESV

When the psalmist exalts those who "fear" the Lord, he does not have in mind a primal, animalistic fear akin to terror. This fear is condemned in 1 John 4:18, where it says, "There is no fear in love, but perfect love casts out fear" (NASB). The fear the psalmist praises is a fear of reverence. It is like fear in that it draws our attention toward something and makes us recognize its power and ability to destroy us, but it is a holy fear, not a fear of punishment (1 John 4:19), and it causes awe and wonder.

God reserves his unlimited love for those who fear him. He is ready to bless any and all who come in humility to him. He is more than willing to heap his love on us, and he requires only that we recognize his place and our small stature. This is not always easy for men, as we are creatures of pride, but it's the only way for us to come to our loving Savior.

Dear God, please fill me with reverence and a holy fear for who you are. May I be a righteous man who does not consider myself high or exalted but would rather exalt you.

AUGUST 22

OUR FIRST GOAL

"Seek the Kingdom of God above all else, and live righteously, and he will give you everything you need."
MATTHEW 6:33 NLT

To have a successful marriage, job, life in our community, or absolutely any good thing we desire, we have to seek God's kingdom first. If we search after love, fame, or fortune, we will be denied them. Our relationships will disintegrate, and our careers will degrade through insincerity and falsehood. Only by making God our first and primary goal can we realize any of our other goals. The throne of our lives was only intended for Christ, and he will not be placed second to anything.

In this passage, Jesus says, "Live righteously, and he will give you everything you need." The success Jesus gives us may not be the success we expect. We might find our goals and aspirations are washed away in light of the plan Jesus had for us all along. We will find his way is better than ours, but this realization might only come after some time.

Dear Lord, please work in my heart. I want to be a man who seeks your kingdom first and puts nothing else beside you.

AUGUST 23

ACCEPTANCE

"Everyone who asks will receive. The one who searches will find. And everyone who knocks will have the door opened."
LUKE 11:10 NCV

It is a great and glorious thing to receive what we work for. To put our time and energy into something and receive nothing in return is a great loss that is difficult to deal with. Humans naturally have a desire to pursue and attain. This desire leads us to God, and Jesus openly invites us in this verse to pursue him and be welcomed with acceptance. We can search, and we will find. We can knock on doors and have them opened to us. What we ask of him, we will receive.

Jesus desires our healing and redemption; he desires it more than we will ever understand. He is willing to give us every reason to come to him along with every promise of acceptance. What are we waiting for? What pride or fear stands between us and wholehearted, full redemption?

Dear Jesus, I will pursue you today. I will seek you in the little and big moments of this life. **With your promise of acceptance, I will seek your face.**

AUGUST 24

SACRIFICIAL LOVE

"I am the good shepherd.
The good shepherd lays his life down for the sheep."
JOHN 10:11 ESV

Love finds its meaning in sacrifice. Only through putting others' needs before our own can we find how much we truly love them. At its core, love is a choice often accompanied by emotion. Love is the choice to sacrifice our time and needs in favor of someone else's, and that's difficult to do. It becomes easier when we see the sacrificial love modeled for us by Christ on the cross.

In our lives, how can we choose to love others better than we currently do? Romantic partners, friends, and strangers are all good recipients of a man's sacrificial love. As men, we must learn how to become models of this love for others to follow. Our world does not prioritize love as the Bible does, but we are not of the world, and we don't need to follow our society's heartless model for manhood.

Loving Jesus, I need to be sacrificial as you are sacrificial. Remind me what a good

shepherd does and how I can do the same for those around me.

AUGUST 25

LETTING GO

"Forget the former things;
do not dwell on the past."
ISAIAH 43:18 NIV

The past can be an anchor that drags us into the oceanic depths of our emotions. The world is full of adverse experiences, and they accumulate in our memories. They pile up there, and if we carry the past on our backs, it will end up crushing us. Isaiah wisely says, "Forget the former things; do not dwell on the past." There is a time for reflection, but it's not an activity to partake in all the time.

One of the core truths of Christianity is that God forgets our sins. In a way, it is the process of him looking away from our mistakes. In his perfect forgiveness, God stands ready to forget the former things for our sake when we ask him. The real question is whether we are ready to forget them ourselves. Perhaps we are still attached to the past and are not willing to part with it as quickly as Jesus is.

Dear Jesus, help me let go. I don't want to be held down by the former things in my life. It's difficult to do, and I can't do it without you.

AUGUST 26

CONTINUING

Patient endurance is what you need now, so that you will continue to do God's will. Then you will receive all that he has promised.
HEBREWS 10:36 NLT

The easiest part of every race is the beginning and the end. At the beginning, we are full of energy and excitement. Having chosen to undertake the task at hand, we are eager to complete it, and fatigue and pain have not met us yet. At the end of the race, we can see the finish line and thus the completion of our efforts. The promise of relief is close at hand, and our physical exhaustion makes the thought of it all the better. But between these two highs is the middle.

The middle of the race is where doubts creep in. We start to wonder what we are doing, and we yearn for the relief that comes from giving up. We get impatient with the pain we are in. That is what the writer of Hebrews is encouraging us through. "Patient endurance is what you need now." If we want to reach the end, we need to continue. If continuing is all we can manage, that is sufficient.

Lord, give me the strength to continue in faith today. I need your help to endure the difficult stage of this race I am in.

AUGUST 27

HOPE IN TRIALS

I remain confident of this:
I will see the goodness of the LORD in the land
of the living.
PSALM 27:13 NIV

It is bold, almost dangerous, to hope. When darkness assails us and beats us down, leaving us broken and gasping for breath, what a daring act to remember the light. For David, this is a source of confidence. It's easier to give up and admit defeat, but that steals the meaning from our suffering. It makes it worthless. Only through enduring with hope do we conquer our suffering rather than being conquered by it.

Jesus wants men who suffer well. He wants men who can lock on to the promises of God with a vice grip. He wants men who can lead in suffering, stand in the crushing darkness, and shine a light to encourage those around them. It's an overwhelming standard to aim for, yet we have the strength of the almighty God on our side. We have the support of a god who will not let us suffer forever.

Bright Jesus, give me hope in troubles. I will see the goodness of the Lord again. Of that, I am sure.

AUGUST 28

ALREADY PERFECT

By that one offering he forever made perfect those who are being made holy.
HEBREWS 10:14 NLT

Can it be true that we are already perfect? It's difficult to imagine, but by Christ's death, we are perfect. We are forgiven our debts and made righteous before God. God will not accept a half measure of righteousness, so in his eyes, we are perfect in righteousness because of the death of his Son. It is also true that we are "being made holy." We are still learning the character of God and how to honor him in our hearts and conduct.

Christ's death was the ultimate offering. He did not have to offer himself up repeatedly the way offerings were sacrificed in the Old Testament. It was once, and it was for all. No one can question the efficacy of this sacrifice because Christ was and is the perfect lamb of God. He has proven himself both as a worthy object of worship and as a worthy object of sacrifice.

Lamb of God, I don't deserve the sacrifice you made for me. Thank you for making all

things right and for forgiving me my sins. Please continue making me holy.

AUGUST 29

SURRENDERED

Continue to walk surrendered to the extravagant love of Christ, for he surrendered his life as a sacrifice for us. His great love for us was pleasing to God, like an aroma of adoration—a sweet healing fragrance.
EPHESIANS 5:2 TPT

Being a man is a dichotomy of surrender and refusing to surrender. In the face of darkness and temptation, we learn to hold on and never surrender. In the face of Christ's extravagant love, though, we learn to let down our guard and surrender. We learn to let go of our pride and identity and accept the love of God. This love, this "sweet healing fragrance," has the power to transform us.

If we find ourselves often discouraged, never living up to the standards we have for ourselves, we likely have not surrendered all to Christ. Maybe we are still trying to do things by our strength and have not learned the futility of doing so. God doesn't need a kingdom of people trying to do things on their own. He needs people who will surrender to his loving, all-encompassing power in their lives.

Dear Jesus, how glorious is your extravagant love. Let the fragrance of it heal the wounds I have received from this life of tribulation.

AUGUST 30

UNCONTROLLED SPIRIT

> Be not quick in your spirit to become angry, for anger lodges in the heart of fools.
> ECCLESIASTES 7:9 ESV

Ecclesiastes is a somber book of wisdom. Solomon does not mince words, and he is willing to verge toward pessimism for the sake of accurately depicting the sorrow of the world we leave in. In his survey of the human spirit, he chooses to point out anger and warn us of its danger. He ties it to a lack of knowledge, saying "anger lodges in the heart of fools." This is a serious warning and not to be glossed over.

We are warned, "Be not quick in your spirit to become angry." Often the search for success, love, or meaning makes us impatient when things don't go our way. By trying to control our circumstances, we lose control of our spirits. They become controlled by whether or not we feel in control. God is warning us through this verse that the only thing we can control is our spirits and not the world around us. That is his to control, and it is not a legitimate reason for us to be angry.

Oh Lord, please make me a man of patience who seeks to control himself before controlling anything else.

AUGUST 31

OUR FINAL TRIUMPH

Those who sow with tears will reap with songs of joy.
PSALM 126:5 NIV

We may never see the sun rise on our happiness in this life. We may be surrounded by heartache or given love only to see it taken away. Life may be hard beyond all reckoning and fill us with unfathomable brokenness. Every moment may be a choice between bitterness and hope; to choose hope might be an uphill battle every time. Little in the way of blessing may come to us while we are alive on earth, but "those who sow in tears will reap with songs of joy."

Yes, no matter the pains of this life, we have our final triumph in death. If we continue to hope in the Lord, we will be joined to the Father and joys unimaginable. We will be given a place in a kingdom-sized family where we belong, and every tear is wiped away. The heartache of life will be ended, and we will find we are, for the first time, in perfect peace.

Dear Lord, please give me hope for the final triumph that awaits me. Help me see that the circumstances of this life are fleeting and will not continue into eternity.

SEPTEMBER

He applies his justice morning by morning;
he does not fail at dawn.
ZEPHANIAH 3:5 CSB

SEPTEMBER 1

MEN OF VIGILANCE

Devote yourselves to prayer with an alert mind and a thankful heart.
COLOSSIANS 4:2 NLT

God wants us to be vigilant. He wants us to search for him in our prayers and with our hearts and desire the kingdom as our first and greatest love. He wants us to be devoted to him with the noblest of intents and seek his glory beyond the pleasures of being his servant. That is why Paul tells the Colossians, "Devote yourselves to prayer with an alert mind and a thankful heart."

What does it look like to have an alert mind and a thankful heart? What kind of transformation would we have to undergo to be found thankful in our hearts? Perhaps there is something in our past we hold against God, and we still don't understand how he allowed it to happen. Whatever the barricade between us and thankfulness and an alert mind, it must be brought to God. He is perfect in understanding and will not turn us away for our complaints.

Dear Lord, please make me attentive to your will in my prayers. Make my heart perfect in thanksgiving.

SEPTEMBER 2

HOLY GUARD

> It is God who arms me with strength and keeps my way secure.
> PSALM 18:32 NIV

Where do we go when we are afraid? What do we look to for comfort as well as strength? Maybe we have a host of coping mechanisms like food, television, or our phones. Maybe we numb ourselves to the pain or difficulty rather than letting it grow us. God arms us with strength and keeps our way secure, but he can only do so if we take tribulation and turn it into prayer.

Jesus is our holy guard. He is there to protect us when all our friends turn on us and nothing but our conscious minds are left to us. He makes our way secure as he sees fit. He is willing to work in us but only if we are willing to accept his help. As long as we push him away or try to make it on our own, he will let us flounder.

Dear Jesus, I don't want this to be another day where I rely on my own strength or just numb myself to life's difficulty. Please use the difficulty to push me toward you and your strength.

SEPTEMBER 3

MEN OF WISDOM

*Listen to advice and accept correction,
and in the end you will be wise.*
PROVERBS 19:20 NCV

When we reach a point where we prefer to give answers rather than receive them, we are in danger. We have reached a point of blind arrogance, and nothing but trials and the love of God can return us to humility. For us to be the men we think we are in our arrogance, we must accept correction. The correction of our friends is the most valuable, but the vindictive correction of our enemies also holds a kernel of truth.

The writer says, "In the end you will be wise." At the end of a conversation, we can gain wisdom through listening. At the end of a disagreement, we can gain wisdom through humility. Finally, on judgment day, we can look back and see either a life lived in the wisdom of humility or squandered through proud stupidity.

Dear God, please open my ears to what other people have to say today. I want to be a man of wisdom who would rather hear

than speak and accepts correction than spurns it.

SEPTEMBER 4

VICTORIOUS

*The LORD takes delight in his people;
he crowns the humble with victory.*
PSALM 149:4 NIV

The man who thirsts for victory above all things will not receive it. He will receive disappointment and find himself continually crushed. Jesus has found it right to give victory to those who feel the least entitled to it. The humble Christian who puts his greatest effort into everything he does, for no other reason than to please his Savior, is the one God bestows his greatest honor on. He wishes to exalt the humble spirit so others may see it and appreciate its righteousness.

It is strange to think of God delighting in us. We are just pawns in his hand, yet our righteousness pleases him, and he is happy to call us his own when we reflect his character and righteousness. True masculinity, founded in humility and strength, is a thing most pleasing to Christ as he sits on his throne.

Dear Jesus, make me humble both in defeat and victory. Make me righteous, Lord, just as you are righteous, and may others be

able to look to me as a role model of Christian masculinity.

SEPTEMBER 5

PERFECTION MINDSET

Do not be shaped by this world; instead be changed within by a new way of thinking. Then you will be able to decide what God wants for you; you will know what is good and pleasing to him and what is perfect.
ROMANS 12:2 NCV

The mindset of this earth is okay with imperfection and wrongdoing. Earthly men settle for a half measure of purity, purpose, and honor. They don't waste time on what they consider idealistic. Yet Paul warns us, "Do not be shaped by this world; instead, be changed within by a new way of thinking." What is this new way of thinking Paul is pushing us toward?

Paul wants us to have perfection in our minds. He wants us to be men who don't settle for imperfect purity or righteousness but push further into the heart of God. He also wants us to set aside a works-based religion and acknowledge that our best efforts are far from perfect; only Jesus' blood is sufficient. Yes, Paul wants us to have a mindset of perfection.

Oh Jesus, please stop this world from shaping me into its image. Transform me from

within and make me into the man you have in mind. Craft me in your image of righteousness and tender humility so others would see me and give you glory.

SEPTEMBER 6

COST OF SIN

> Let my passion for life be restored, tasting joy
> in every breakthrough you bring to me.
> Hold me close to you with a willing spirit that
> obeys whatever you say.
> PSALM 51:12 TPT

David sang this refrain following his manipulative adultery with Bathsheba. Yes, David's sin didn't destroy his salvation. Yes, he remained a man after God's own heart. But in this verse, we see one of the prices David paid for his sin. His "passion for life," "joy," and "willing spirit" had all deserted him, and he could feel dryness and apathy creeping over his soul. He had poisoned himself, and while he was still alive in the Spirit, he was severely damaged.

We live in a world of temptation. We are tempted to give in to false desires with the promise that they will not sever us from the love of God, so what damage could they cause? Yet every time we give in, the ability to resist weakens, and our passion for God is slaughtered. Wrongful desires rewire our minds with every mistake we make.

Oh Lord, let my passion for life be restored. Please renew my mind and guard me from the world of temptation. Make me righteous beyond my own ability so I can stand firm against the assaults of the devil.

SEPTEMBER 7

BEING CONSCIOUS

"I tell you the truth, anything you did for even the least of my people here, you also did for me."
MATTHEW 25:40 NCV

Are we conscious or simply living in a dream? The devil would like us to forget about compassion, mercy, and loving the forgotten and downtrodden. He wants us to get caught up in delusions brought on by empty goals, monetary reimbursement, and earthly pleasures. But this is not the real world. The real world is made up of meaningful actions, spiritual growth, and a Christ-centered life. We are conscious of the real world when we live by the truth of the gospel.

In this verse, Jesus says, "I tell you the truth." We must remember he tells us the truth throughout the entirety of Scripture. He preaches a radical lifestyle of love, selflessness, and forgiveness. The level of devotion Jesus calls us to does not conveniently fit with our typical day. It involves restructuring how we spend our time and emotion, and this is only possible through faith, devotion, and trust.

Dear God, make me conscious of what matters in this life. May I not pass up on opportunities to further your kingdom. Help me show your love to those around me.

SEPTEMBER 8

NOT FOREVER

> "Now is your time of grief, but I will see you again and you will rejoice, and no one will take away your joy."
> JOHN 16:22 NIV

The promise Jesus gives us in this verse is "no one will take away your joy." This is a high-stakes promise. The death of someone close to us, the loss of a valued friendship, or the onset of a serious disease all have the power to crush spirits and steal joy. Jesus promises us the opposite, and it is our blessing to explore this promise.

Thankfully, Jesus is not blind to our pain. He does not gloss over the importance of grief but gives it a place to exist. He says, "Now is your time of grief." It is okay to live with pain and fully experience the sorrow that life events might bring to us. There is nothing unchristian about being in grief or feeling hopeless. These are natural emotions, and Jesus himself felt them. But no matter how dark life gets, Jesus wants to walk with us through it. He wants to be there so he can remind us that our grief is not forever and his love for us endures.

Dear Lord, I pray for those dealing with a heavy load of grief. Be near to them and walk with them through their tribulation.

SEPTEMBER 9

THE GREATEST MAN

> He was pierced because of our rebellion, crushed because of our iniquities; punishment for our peace was on him, and we are healed by his wounds.
> ISAIAH 53:5 CSB

A man is seen as noble when he bears others' burdens. When a father bears responsibility for his family, or a single man shoulders the burdens of his community, he gains respect for his virtue. Jesus bore the greatest burden of any of us. He took our wounds, iniquities, and punishment on himself. His heart bleeding divine love, he walked the way of pain we were meant to walk. No man has demonstrated masculine compassion better than Jesus Christ.

We have a perfect role model to look up to. As he is perfect, there is no measuring up to his standard. He forever deserves to be exalted in our hearts as our standard of perfection. We are to aim for his example every day but also rest in the assurance that he makes up for our imperfection.

Dear Jesus, thank you for hanging on the cross to defeat my sins. Thank you for your great compassion. Nothing can lessen the cost you paid for me. May I forever exalt you for it.

SEPTEMBER 10

SUSTAINED IN CHRIST

The LORD is my shepherd;
I have everything I need.
PSALM 23:1 NCV

Self-reliance is often championed as a desired characteristic. People respect a man who can be dropped anywhere find a job, make his own community, and start a family. Even greater than the self-reliant man is the man who relies intensely on the Lord. This does not mean he is inactive; instead, he searches for the Lord's plan and seeks to be the agent Jesus uses for his purposes. This is how God makes men greater than they can be on their own.

A shepherd protects, sustains, and guides the sheep. Likewise, Christ holds back the devil's onslaughts against us while giving us the spiritual food we need and lighting our path. He is the greatest shepherd who wants us to have the humility of sheep and the wisdom of serpents. He desires people who are equipped for every good work by relying on the Savior and Redeemer of this world.

Dear God, please guide me and sustain me today. I will listen for your will.

SEPTEMBER 11

WITHOUT SHAME

Hope does not put us to shame, because God's love has been poured into our hearts through the Holy Spirit who has been given to us.
ROMANS 5:5 ESV

We have numerous reasons to abandon our hope in the Lord. The pleasures of sin call to us, and reckless coping mechanisms are always tempting us to take refuge in their arms. Without God, we could put our hope in a career or our strength. We could be gods of our own making and stop fighting the difficult fight. All these reasons, however, are unreasonable. As Paul declares, "Hope does not put us to shame." Every time we push aside these temptations, we will live to see it was worth it. Every time we choose to hope in the Lord, we will discover he fulfills our hope.

If only we could measure the love of God now rendered to us through the Holy Spirit within us. If we could only see in a moment the difference in our lives with and without God. We can draw from the deep well of God's love whenever we please, and this love holds our hope secure within us.

Dear Jesus, my hope is all in you. Your love has sealed it, and I have entrusted my future to you. Only you are worthy of my trust.

SEPTEMBER 12

REMEMBRANCE

"Don't be afraid, for I am with you.
Don't be discouraged, for I am your God.
I will strengthen you and help you.
I will hold you up with my victorious right hand."
ISAIAH 41:10 NLT

What a picture of triumph! The words God speaks through Isaiah are words of remembrance that bring to light the past acts of the Lord and his fresh promises. For fear, God gives his presence. For discouragement, he gives us himself. He promises to strengthen, help, and finally reign in victory and hold up the man of God. When every negativity assails us and we struggle, we must remember the promises God has given us.

When we root our peace in God's strength rather than our circumstances, everything changes. We are no longer tossed about by the cares of this world, and we stand out among our fellow men as unshakeable. God's strength is eternal and his victory unstoppable. When these things are our peace, we never have to worry about them changing. We are made both righteousness and happy by putting our hope and trust in the Lord.

Victorious God, you reign mightily in the clouds. You are eternal in your power and station. Nothing can stand against you, and I exalt you with a heart full of awe.

SEPTEMBER 13

MERE PEOPLE

We can say with confidence,
"The Lord is my helper, so I will have no fear.
What can mere people do to me?"
HEBREWS 13:6 NLT

Do we worry about people's opinions of us? Many men give off an attitude that no one's opinion matters to them even though it secretly does. Other men are visibly crippled by the words of an insensitive friend. Every man, no matter his personality, processes the opinions of others. The writer of Hebrews knew this when he said, "What can mere people do to me?" Beyond opinion, even the actions of others have no power over us anymore. Direct persecution and the destruction of our flesh have no power to take us away from our God.

What problem do we need to declare this truth over? What can mere people do to us at work, in our family, or among our friends? Over what situation should we say this with confidence? Nothing in this physical world can topple the spiritual King of truth off his throne. He is without weakness, soft spot, or insecurity. He is perfect in strength and tender love.

Oh Lord, I declare your power over this day with confidence. I see you, perfect in power and gentleness, as King over my life.

SEPTEMBER 14

MAKING ALLOWANCE

Always be humble and gentle. Be patient with each other, making allowance for each other's faults because of your love.
EPHESIANS 4:2 NCV

How can we make allowance for someone's faults when they are inherently wrong? Why would we not correct them if they are wrong? The truth is, we can't force the evil out of our friends just like we can't beat lust out of our minds through legalism and anger. Only through surrender to God, and being empowered by him, can we overcome any sin. In the case of others and their faults, the choice has to be made by them. We can encourage them in the right direction and pray God's power over them, but we can't do more than this.

Paul says, "Always be humble and gentle." This is a great commandment for us to take to heart because humility is one of the most difficult virtues for any man to fake. We can be subservient or self-deprecating, but true humility is impossible to produce without the Holy Spirit. When we find ourselves bothered by our brothers' faults, it often says just as much about us as it does about them.

Oh Lord, teach me to make allowance for others' faults just as you make allowance for mine.

SEPTEMBER 15

EVERY SORROW

*You keep track of all my sorrows.
You have collected all my tears in your bottle.
You have recorded each one in your book.*
PSALM 56:8 NLT

Every man is wounded. In one way or another, whether he has the power to see it or not, he carries scars on his heart that are unique to him. It might be the disapproval of a parent, rejection from a partner, or the pain of defeat, but each man has a wound deep in his soul. Jesus carries them on his heart too. Every hurt his spiritual family has experienced equally wounds him, and he has shed the tears we have shed. He feels our pain in equal measure.

Even when we forget a pain, the Lord does not forget. No one is as worthy of our trust because no one understands us the way Jesus does. No one, absolutely no one, loves us like Jesus loves us. No one else was willing to take our pain on his back and bring us into his family. Only Jesus continues to feel our wounds with us and has the power to heal them.

Loving God, I need you desperately. No one knows me like you do. Please show me your mercy and love today.

SEPTEMBER 16

LIVING IN DARKNESS

"I am the light of the world. Whoever follows me will not walk in darkness, but will have the light of life."
JOHN 8:12 ESV

There is no other way to see or be aware other than Christ. There is no light of reason but Christ and no way to see the world as it truly is except through Christ. When he says, "I am the light of the world," he is saying those who don't walk with him are darkened in their understanding and in their hearts. Their minds are inaccurate because of the lies they have accepted, and their hearts are likewise broken.

Would those around us describe us as the light in their world? Christ's light within us should shine for others to see and not be hidden or concealed. If we act like the men of this world, talk like them, and hide our Christlike differences, what impact will our lives have? The light of life shining within us is to be a blessing to the world.

God of Light, I can do nothing apart from you. Please set me ablaze and make me a beacon of your truth and godliness.

SEPTEMBER 17

EVER-WAKING FRIEND

> He will not let you stumble;
> the one who watches over you will not slumber.
> PSALM 121:3 NLT

Today's psalm promises us, "The one who watches over you will not slumber." When Jesus and the disciples went to the garden of Gethsemane, he instructed his disciples to stay awake. Even though they were Jesus' closest friends, and even though it was the most crucial point in history, they couldn't keep their eyes open. They couldn't stop themselves from dozing off.

If we were to rely on a friend or any human being for constant support, we would be in a dire position. Thankfully, we have the Holy Spirit to watch over us. We can never wander from his gaze. No matter the state of mind we are in, the Spirit is watching over us with perfect attention and the power to rescue us no matter the situation. He does not slumber, and he will not let us stumble. As men faced with constant temptations and fears, this is a comfort.

Holy Spirit, I will rely on you every waking hour. In my sleep, I will know you watch me.

SEPTEMBER 18

OUTSIDE OPINIONS

Let patience have its perfect work, that you may be perfect and complete, lacking nothing.
JAMES 1:4 NKJV

Who would describe us as "perfect and complete, lacking nothing?" Hopefully nobody, and if someone does, we should probably discuss our faults with them. James is not telling us that just by being patient we can become perfect. He is telling us that with patience in tribulation, we can learn every virtue and kind of righteousness. So long as we stay in tribulation with contentment and patience, we will continue to grow toward perfection and completion until we reach heaven and lack nothing.

There is not a soul on this earth who does not need to work on patience. We are impatient creatures, and patience is a learned discipline more than anything else. This patience, James promises us, has untold benefits for our eternal souls. If we want to be the men that those around us hope we will become, we must dive into patience through prayer and meditation.

Dear Jesus, please be at work in my soul during trials. Make me patient and content when I would rather do things my own way.

SEPTEMBER 19

PROMISE OF DISCIPLINE

No discipline is enjoyable while it is happening—it's painful! But afterward there will be a peaceful harvest of right living for those who are trained in this way.
HEBREWS 12:11 NLT

The promise of discipline is that "there will be a peaceful harvest of right living for those who are trained in this way." This is the truth we hold on to when the Lord's hand lays heavy upon us. Discipline is the Lord's testing of our spirits, and we have the option to break instead of growing stronger. When a hot sword is quenched in water, it is either hardened and perfected or it shatters. If we endure in the Lord's hope, we will reap a peaceful harvest.

Can we be trained in this way of discipline? Are we willing to endure the Lord's good sorrow and trial for the sake of growing closer to him? If we are willing to be perfected in this way, we will reap reward beyond measure. If we are unwilling, though, our lives will be crippling.

Oh Lord, perfect me in hope. Give me strength to endure your discipline, embrace the pain, and trust in you.

SEPTEMBER 20

SURROUNDED IN VICTORY

You are my hiding place;
you protect me from trouble.
You surround me with songs of victory.
PSALM 32:7 NLT

Life can be unspeakably defeating. Maybe it is a job promotion you work toward for years only to be denied. Other times, it's the death of a friend or something similarly serious. We all need a "hiding place to protect us from trouble." No matter the number of times we are kicked while we are down, no matter the number of times we are dismayed, we are victorious in Christ's death for our sins. We are surrounded by songs of victory flowing from the cross.

We might scorn the idea of a protector. Men are crafted by this world to strive for self-sufficiency and to push aside ideas of weakness or help. Christ, however, will not accept any of us until we reduce ourselves to the station of a child. We are to look to him as our protection and hiding place, but if we are too proud to take it, then we surely will not be given his salvation.

God my refuge, please be my shelter from the storms. Be my peace in failure and my victory in defeat. I am nothing without you, Lord Jesus.

SEPTEMBER 21

WORK HAS MEANING

Don't allow yourselves to be weary or disheartened in planting good seeds, for the season of reaping the wonderful harvest you've planted is coming!
GALATIANS 6:9 TPT

The harvest is coming, Paul promises. For farmers, every year has a cycle of planting seeds and harvesting the fruition of their toils at the end of the season. They have years of past farming to look back on, and this assures them that when they plant seeds in the spring, they will grow. They know by experience that, even in the oddest season, it is not foolish to expect plants to grow from seeds. For Christians, though, the harvest is less predictable. We might spend our entire lives planting seeds before seeing any of them begin to grow.

This is why Paul's promise is important for us. What we do must be done because it is right and not necessarily because of what it will produce. We must be kind to others not so they will repay us but because it is what Jesus did. If we do everything out of good cheer, knowing the harvest will come eventually, we will be far less disheartened.

Dear Jesus, please give me faith in the harvest. Though today may be filled with discouragement, I will one day see the fruits of my labor.

SEPTEMBER 22

UNTOLD GLORIES

With God's power working in us, God can do much, much more than anything we can ask or imagine.
EPHESIANS 3:21 NCV

There is no telling what God is going to accomplish with us in our lifetime. No one in this world can foresee what God will accomplish with the most ordinary and most broken men. Jesus likes to make this world's wisdom foolish and its strength weak. He likes to take men whom society calls ordinary or unlikely to succeed and make them extraordinary cases of success. He has no qualms with our sense of insufficiency; it makes us aware that success is not ours but his.

What does it take to have "God's power working in us?" As long as we are weak in ourselves, Jesus will be strong in us. As long as we consider ourselves insufficient, we will learn to rely on God for our sufficiency. It is the proud man whom God will refuse to use. The man who is able to stay humble despite success and triumph is the man God will continue work through to do "more than anything we can ask or imagine."

Dear Jesus, make me humble. May your power work through me.

SEPTEMBER 23

GOD OF EMPATHY

I will be glad and rejoice in your love,
for you saw my affliction and knew the anguish
of my soul.
PSALM 31:7 NIV

God has no obligation to be kind to us in our affliction. Without him, we are infused with sin down to the bone, and nothing in us evokes feelings of mercy or tenderhearted love. Still, God has chosen to find us lovable. He has chosen, out of the depths of his heart, to truly love us for who we are. He has chosen to be kind to us in our affliction, see us, and rather than despising us, reach down and touch our hearts out of love and mercy.

We worship a god brimming with empathy. We have every reason to be men of mercy and compassion because he has been this way to us. He has given us every reason to be gentle and to feel the pain of the weak. Are we willing to act this way? Are we willing to be kind when others are gruff and coarse? God desires men of gentle strength who show the empathy which pours from the cross at Calvary.

Dear God, please make me an empathetic man of mercy. Give me a heart for the affliction and struggles of others so I can be more like you.

SEPTEMBER 24

UNFATHOMABLE DEPTHS

Oh, how great are God's riches and wisdom and knowledge! How impossible it is for us to understand his decisions and his ways!
ROMANS 11:33 NLT

God is infinite in many ways. In time, his existence is infinite because it has no start and no end. In virtue, wisdom, and power, he is also infinite. When we describe him as such, though, we don't really know what we are saying. We can't understand how perfect or glorious he is. Paul speaks accurately when he says, "How impossible it is for us to understand his decisions and his ways!"

A great deal of wisdom can be gained by knowing just how ignorant we are. We must be willing to accept that God's wisdom truly is unfathomable, and we will spend our entire lives trying to understand this world and the God who created it. None of us should count ourselves wise as long as the decisions and ways of the Lord remain as complex and beautiful as they currently are.

Dear Jesus, how unsearchable are your ways! May my interactions with others be humble and acknowledge the limitations of my own wisdom.

SEPTEMBER 25

GOD OF GOODNESS

Whatever is good and perfect is a gift coming down to us from God our Father, who created all the lights in the heavens. He never changes or casts a shifting shadow.
JAMES 1:17 NLT

Today's verse expresses the mystery of God's providence. Not only does he provide for us materially, supporting our physical bodies, but he also provides for us morally. James says, "Whatever is good and perfect is a gift coming down to us from God our Father." He attributes "all the lights in the heavens" to God who is the Father of lights and casts no "shifting shadow."

There are a lot of good things in this world such as the glory of creation or the wealth of cultures on our planet. Without acknowledging that their goodness originated in God, we can struggle to appreciate these things. For example, a beautiful woman does not have to be an idol if we can appreciate her as an expression of God's beautiful design. Through this verse from James, we have a framework for understanding earthly goodness.

Dear Jesus, thank you for being a god of goodness and for expressing your goodness in a number of ways. Thank you for this beautiful world full of gifts.

SEPTEMBER 26

GIVING IN POVERTY

Our hearts ache, but we always have joy. We are poor, but we give spiritual riches to others. We own nothing, and yet we have everything.
2 CORINTHIANS 6:10 NLT

There are many kinds of poverty. There is the material poverty which Christians often seek to remedy, but there is also poverty of the spirit, poverty of relationships, poverty of experiences, and a host of other versions. In this verse from 2 Corinthians, Paul recognizes his cohorts' spiritual riches despite their physical poverty. He declares, "We are poor, but we give spiritual riches to others." The spiritual wealth they have is multipliable, and they can share it without losing any themselves.

In what ways are we wealthy? Perhaps we have a strong group of Christians we can rely on, phenomenal success at work, or experiences most people do not share. No matter how we are blessed, each of us is blessed with some kind of riches from Jesus for the sake of furthering his kingdom, and all of us are to seek the spiritual riches Paul speaks of.

Dear God, thank you for the spiritual riches you have offered to me. Please make me a rich man spiritually even if I am poor in other ways.

SEPTEMBER 27

LEAVE THEM

Pour out all your worries and stress upon him and leave them there, for he always tenderly cares for you.
I PETER 5:7 TPT

A holy relaxation is found in this verse. We do not just talk about our worries; we do not just give them to him. We pour them out. A mighty monsoon of fears and anxieties rushes upon Christ, and he takes the brunt of it without budging an inch. The flood of our anxiety and stress has the power to crush us, but they are no match for Christ.

For some of us, the difficulty is not in giving our stress and worries to Christ but in leaving them with him. We spill our stress on him, but once we have given him all our worries, we take them right back into our minds. It takes purpose and dedication to leave our anxieties with Jesus. He will take them and deal with them, but we sometimes have to let them go for him to work. He can't do anything with what we will not release.

Jesus, I can't be the man I should be with all the worries I have. Help me let them go.

May I give them to you and not hold on to them.

SEPTEMBER 28

OUR PUREST FAITH

I trust in the all-sufficient cross of Christ alone.
I CORINTHIANS 1:17 TPT

If we want to be happy, content, and filled with all the virtues we desire for our character, we must learn to follow the words of this verse. These nine words express the purest form of our faith. Setting aside long doctrines, spiritual disciplines, and coping mechanisms, we look to "the all-sufficient cross of Christ alone" for our sustenance. The Christian who has learned to trust in Christ's cross alone has learned this lesson through many tribulations and trials.

What do we trust in? It may take self-honesty to recognize it. Perhaps our morning coffee, or our financial security, or some form of relaxation is so necessary for our peace we can't imagine our lives without it. Whatever it is, we can simply choose to acknowledge it and ask God to help us appreciate it but never need it like we need him.

Dear Jesus, teach me to trust in your all-sufficient cross alone. Make me a man of holy dependency and pure faith with no strings attached. Once I have nothing to cling to but your cross, I will have all joy.

SEPTEMBER 29

TRUE WORK

Encourage one another and build one another up, just as you are doing.
I THESSALONIANS 5:11 ESV

A man who shepherds the flock of God with anger and discouraging remarks is doing worse than the average Christian who builds people up throughout his day. The true work is not a checklist of to-dos that must be completed at any cost. The true work is not found in the task but in the process. Jesus did nothing efficiently; he walked everywhere, he stopped all the time, and he never had a day job once he started his ministry. The true work is in the process, and it is more rewarding than any completed checklist.

When we encourage others, we gain encouragement in return. Their respect, trust, and admiration are placed on us like holy robes. A man who learns to spend his energy building others up instead of focusing on himself will achieve beyond his measure and be blessed in miraculous ways.

Jesus, I pray for those around me today. Please bless them and build them up in

beautiful ways. I want to see them filled with life and given abundance through you.

SEPTEMBER 30

SHINING FRAGILITY

We now have this light shining in our hearts, but we ourselves are like fragile clay jars containing this great treasure. This makes it clear that our great power is from God, not from ourselves.
2 CORINTHIANS 4:7 NLT

The truest and greatest strength shines through weakness. A great wealth of this is found in older men. They have decades of wrongs they could choose to hold against people, but they instead have the grace to play with children and smile on their enemies. Their bodies are broken and aging, but their spirits are strong and alive within them. God has made us his "fragile clay jars" so his own power can shine all the brighter.

The greatest place we can be is bending beneath the weight of God's glory. When we feel our hearts pouring over in wonder and deep appreciation, when the glory of God's handiwork leaves us wondering how we can live in light of it, then we know we are where God wants us. God made us to be stretched, to grow, and to have the clay of our jars crack so his light might shine through.

Great Creator, what a great blessing to have your power pouring through my weakness. May my life be an altar where your power can shine.

OCTOBER

The LORD is good, a refuge in times of trouble.
He cares for those who trust in him.
NAHUM 1:7 NIV

OCTOBER 1

TO KNOW GOD

> By his divine power, God has given us everything we need for living a godly life. We have received all of this by coming to know him, the one who called us to himself by means of his marvelous glory and excellence.
> 2 PETER 1:3 NLT

"Everything we need for living a godly life." That is a heavy list. There is a sea of books on living the Christian life. Many Christians have shelves brimming with volumes that detail all sorts of aspects of our walk with Christ. How is it that "everything we need for living a godly life" can be found in whatever Peter is claiming?

According to the apostle, it is through God's divine power and "by coming to know him" that we gain what we need for godliness. God is rich beyond all measure both in power and wisdom, and his marvelous grace and excellence spill over in abundance. In his endless grace, he desires to impact us through our relationship with him. He wants us to be close to him and, through this, to be like him and thus righteous. In essence, the more we come to know Christ, the more we become like him.

Lord, bring me into sweet relationship with you so I might learn to be like you. I will bask in your glory and excellence and rejoice in your grace.

OCTOBER 2

SOLE DESIRE

One thing I ask from the LORD, this only do I seek: that I may dwell in the house of the LORD all the days of my life, to gaze on the beauty of the LORD and to seek him in his temple.
PSALM 27:4 NIV

In the words of David, "This only do I seek." He wanted only one thing: to know God's love for him and to bask in his glory. If someone looked into the heart of a perfect man, they would find a sole desire to be near to Jesus. This purity is beyond comparison. It is perfect gold refined through numerous fires. Just to gaze, just to seek him in the recesses of his heart, was David's sole desire.

What do we ask from the Lord? What bogs down our hearts and minds? Perhaps the answer to our prayers is not what we want but another prayer. When our desire is just to be near to God, just to love him, we will find the rejuvenation we long for. Jesus is the healing balm our souls crave.

Dear Jesus, I only want you. I just want to be near you and know you will never

leave. I want to see, truly and wonderfully, the glory of your face for all eternity.

OCTOBER 3

CHAINED DOWN

I don't depend on my own strength to accomplish this; however I do have one compelling focus: I forget all of the past as I fasten my heart to the future instead.
PHILIPPIANS 3:13 TPT

Within this single verse, Paul gives us a wealth of encouragement. He begins by reminding us of our holy dependence on the Lord and goes on to dismiss the power the past has on us. Paul faced great tribulation, and his faith faced more opposition than any of us will probably ever experience. He could not fool himself into thinking his own strength was of any use to him. There was too much to do, and only a holy passion animating his soul could accomplish anything meaningful. The same is true of us; our strength is only from the Lord.

Paul was once the greatest persecutors of Christians. That was his past. If he let his past drag him down, he would be crippled. He would have to battle guilt over his actions and fight the pride that came with his Jewish legal training. Instead, he says, "I forget all of the past as I fasten my heart to the future." What about the past do we need to let go?

By your strength and only your strength, oh Lord, help me let go of the past.

OCTOBER 4

FULLNESS OF JOY

You make known to me the path of life; you will fill me with joy in your presence, with eternal pleasures at your right hand.
PSALM 16:11 NIV

In the Lord is fullness of joy. Our minds are surrounded by mental stimulants, shows and movies, sex, and other experiences that give us an unearthly level of elation. In the momentary high, we give ourselves a false hope that maybe, just maybe, eternity is found in them. Maybe that high can fill our soul or heal our past. Maybe it can last forever. No; only in the Lord is there fullness of joy.

Some might say God brings happiness at the expense of pleasure, but the psalmist goes so far as to ascribe "eternal pleasures" to God's right hand. Heaven will not be the sacrifice of pleasures but their perfection. We give our hearts to the Lord rather than earthly pleasures, not because they are bad, but because they are only faint reflections of the real thing. God is what our whole being longs for.

Lord of all joy and all pleasures, please sanctify this poor life of mine and raise me

from my grave of death. I am nothing without you, and I need you.

OCTOBER 5

JOY HOPE PATIENCE

Be joyful because you have hope. Be patient when trouble comes, and pray at all times.
ROMANS 12:12 NCV

In quick succession, Paul lists several virtues he wants his readers to practice. He says to be joyful, but this is a surprisingly difficult commandment to follow. Faking joy is vain, and God is not pleased by forced emotions. Joy is the product of hope. Hope is necessary because our world is full of brokenness and heartache, and it's not possible for us in good conscience to be at peace with it. We need hope to reconcile ourselves to the current state of things and make room for joy.

In light of this world of troubles, Paul says to be patient through prayer. Often, patience means lasting one more second or taking one more step when we would not like to. Patience means setting aside our discontent and adopting a mild temperament instead. This is done through prayer as we voice our thoughts to Jesus every moment. God wants us to be heavenly men displaying the fruit of the Spirit as a testimony to our Savior.

Dear Jesus, please work slowly but surely in my heart today to produce the joy, hope, and patience I lack.

OCTOBER 6

BURDENED BEYOND MEASURE

When the cares of my heart are many,
your consolations cheer my soul.
PSALM 94:19 ESV

It's normal to feel trapped under the weight of life's cares. Between caring for loved ones, hobbies or jobs we are invested in, and global affairs, we will likely experience the anxiety of having too many cares resting on our minds. This can overwhelm us and make us feel unable to escape, which can lead to desperate coping mechanisms. Jesus wants to lift our burdens right off our backs, though, and console and cheer our hearts.

The psalmist says, "Your consolations cheer my soul." Oh, to be cheered in times of trouble! What a glorious idea to have our bare souls consoled by Jesus himself. Perhaps food, alcohol, or sex are not what we need tonight to feel at ease. Perhaps it's time to lift our cares to Jesus so he can carry them as we strive through our troubled world.

Dear Jesus, please be at work in my situation. Lift the cares off my back and cheer up my soul by your consolations. May I likewise be a consolation to others through you.

OCTOBER 7

FOLLOWING JESUS

"Teach them to faithfully follow all that I have commanded you. And never forget that I am with you every day, even to the completion of this age."
MATTHEW 28:20 TPT

In this passage, we see Jesus' farewell blessing to his disciples. He admonishes them to not just follow his example but also teach others to follow his example. Later, Paul would make the same point by saying people should not seek to follow someone like himself but should always keep their eyes on Jesus. No man of Christ is the crucified Savior himself. No matter the respect we give them, we can't have any role model whom we hold above our Lord in honor.

Teaching others to follow Jesus also means teaching them to not follow us. Our friends, mentors, and those who look up to us are going to do things differently than we do. We might not like their way, but as long as they do it in honor of Christ, it is valid. We should encourage Christ's way and not our own. If, in following Christ's commandments, they have differences with us, that can be reason for rejoicing. We can still find unity in our differences.

Oh Jesus, make me a good teacher. Help me avoid teaching others my ways; may I instead teach them your ways.

OCTOBER 8

APART FROM CHRIST

"I am the vine; you are the branches. If you remain in me and I in you, you will bear much fruit; apart from me you can do nothing."
JOHN 15:5 NIV

There is unity in the Holy Spirit. Jesus will not give his Spirit to those who are against him. He will not bear fruit through those who deny his character. Remaining in Jesus enables us to do much both in the world and in ourselves. With him, we can change lives through love, experience healing, and grow in ways we can't without Jesus. He is the vine giving us the lifeblood we need to spiritually breathe.

Remaining in Jesus can be difficult without others to keep us accountable. By having fellow brothers and sisters in Christ who turn our eyes to our Savior, we can remember Jesus' salvation and the cross he bore so we could have salvation. Without a spiritual family, it is incredibly difficult to remain in the vine of Christ. We need continual reminders of the light of the gospel for it to remain burning bright within us.

Oh Savior, how I long to never be apart from you. Keep me near to you and let me bear fruit through your Spirit.

OCTOBER 9

DISPLAYING WISDOM

Who is wise and understanding among you? By his good conduct let him show his works in the meekness of wisdom.
JAMES 3:13 ESV

If we understand a subject or are qualified at something, it's good for people to know in case they need our services. In the case of wisdom and character, however, to give ourselves accolades would negate our wisdom and character. Instead, James instructs us to show our understanding by meekness and good conduct. Through good conduct, we display our biblical wisdom modestly and humbly.

James speaks of "the meekness of wisdom." How many of us grow in meekness when we learn something? Our knowledge is often used as ammunition to defeat others in arguments. To take knowledge and wisdom in a spirit of meekness is virtuous but not easy. We must practice being men of meek wisdom, so it's not soured by our pride. If we speak wisdom out of pride, we will give a bad name to the wisdom we speak.

Dear Jesus, please make me a man of wisdom and humility. Take me and make me wise and understanding. May I display myself to others with good conduct and meekness.

OCTOBER 10

FEARLESS GLORY

The LORD is my light and my salvation; whom shall I fear?
The LORD is the stronghold of my life; of whom shall I be afraid?
PSALM 27:1 ESV

This psalm is bold. David is singing to his God with fearless trust. It is a unique psalm because it is not making a request or praising the Lord for something he has done. Instead, it is a statement of the truth David knows needs to be heard. We sometimes make prayers of truth too; they remind us of our salvation, life, and hope we have in Christ.

David does not hide from his demons as he declares, "Of whom shall I be afraid?" It is as if he is shouting out to the darkness and seeking a foe worthy of the Lord's strength. David is a man drenched in fearless glory. It is not a glory of his own, but it is a glory of trust in Christ's power and light. He is willing to shout out his testimony of faith because he knows when the world looks at his life, they will see the hand of God at work.

Oh God, why am I so timid? What am I afraid of? May the glory of your presence surround me in every battle I encounter.

OCTOBER 11

CHOOSE THE UNSEEN

We set our eyes not on what we see but on what we cannot see. What we see will last only a short time, but what we cannot see will last forever.
2 CORINTHIANS 4:18 NCV

Will we be controlled by our surroundings or rise above them? Paul says, "We set our eyes not on what we see but on what we cannot see." It's impossible to put our eyes on something we cannot see, but our eyes have a role in gathering information and determining our actions. Rather than seeing the circumstances we are in and judging our course of action off them, we instead gather information from God's voice and act based on him.

A good man is not controlled by what his eyes see. He is not led into lust, gluttony, or laziness by every stray image that catches his attention. To be good men, we must rise above our senses and control them. This isn't easy, but it is incredibly rewarding. It is the difference between bondage and freedom or crouched apathy and noble determination.

Heavenly God, let me not be controlled by the visible world. Teach me to rise above it and search for you as my source of wisdom and mission.

OCTOBER 12

MEN OF CARE

Warn those who are lazy.
Encourage those who are timid.
Take tender care of those who are weak.
Be patient with everyone.
1 THESSALONIANS 5:14 NLT

In this passage, Paul tells us to treat others ethically and with care. He calls us to tailor our words to others based on their spiritual need whether it be laziness, timidity, weakness, or something else. We can't use the warning we would use for the lazy on someone else; it might have the effect of saltwater on a thirsty plant. It's good to be "patient with everyone" because everyone's situation is different, and it takes time to understand fully.

How can we be better men of care? How can we be more encouraging or wake someone from a current spiritual slumber? It takes time and practice to see the needs of those around us, but developing this skill makes us more Christlike in the end. Christ, while on earth, was a man of deep care who watched over the needs of anyone who crossed his path. He neglected no one and saw both spiritual and physical needs. He still does.

Dear Jesus, please make me kind and loving like you. Teach me to be a man who cares about those around him. May I see and respond to their needs.

OCTOBER 13

EMPTY DARKNESS

A light shines in the dark for honest people, for those who are merciful and kind and good.
PSALM 112:4 NCV

No light follows those who readily sow seeds of darkness. If we are dishonest and cruel, no light will search us out when darkness enfolds us. That light searches out those who, while in the light, acted kindly and sowed goodness. Or perhaps while we were in the light, we had no appreciation for virtue or goodness, but when darkness came, we saw the error of our ways. We longed for a spark of light to lead us.

Isaiah says those who walk in darkness have seen a great light (Is. 9:2). This is the good news; even if we are in darkness today without a speck of mercy or kindness in our past, the light will seek us out. We belong to the darkness because of all the wrong we have done and the people we have hurt, but the light does not care. The light knows our sin and our darkness and will find us anyway. The light wants to shine on us, and it will if we ask it to.

Oh God in heaven, shine your light on me today. Show me the love I desperately need and flake the scales off my heart.

OCTOBER 14

IN AND OUT

"I am the door. If anyone enters by me, he will be saved and will go in and out and find pasture."
JOHN 10:9 ESV

Jesus is the door we are looking for. Are we trapped at work? Are our relationships going nowhere? Jesus is the one we need. Our repentance through him, baptism in him, resurrection with him, is the path we seek. There is no other way that works and no other method of escape. However, Jesus is not just an escape. According to him, the man who walks through his door "will go in and out and find pasture."

When we repent and are saved through Christ, we do not immediately ascend to heaven. Jesus expects us to enter his fold, but he also expects us to go out into the world and bring more sheep to the pasture. Jesus wants men in business, in education, at home, and in every corner of the world bringing back the lost sheep of God. Through Jesus, we enter into salvation; through him, we go out into the world.

Dear Lord, may I humbly live for you and bring others into your salvation. Please be with me as I go out and bring me back in when the day ends.

OCTOBER 15

EYES OF FAITH

Faith empowers us to see that the universe was created and beautifully coordinated by the power of God's words! He spoke and the invisible realm gave birth to all that is seen.
HEBREWS 11:3 TPT

Our world, though fallen, contains a remnant of the glory of God. Like an eggshell with the yoke drained from it, we can still see in its design the intelligence of our Creator and his desire for wholeness and perfection. This is not visible to unredeemed eyes. The writer of Hebrews says, "Faith empowers us to see."

This is the important contribution a Christian man makes to his community. The chaos and disorderly mess found in society and nature have meaning to us, and we can explain it to those who ask and thus testify to them. In the structure and design of creation, we see the power of God's words. That same power called us to our Savior and washed us free from our sin. The universe is beautifully coordinated, and we must recognize it.

Dear Jesus, please open my eyes to the meaning of the universe. Show me its beauty and brokenness so I have an explanation for those who ask. You have displayed your power in the world around me.

OCTOBER 16

BE STILL

"The LORD will fight for you, you have only to be still."
EXODUS 14:14 NIV

Life is like a crushing weight that tests to see what it takes before we break. When will we snap? How long will we last? No matter how long we fight, it can feel like the onslaught of problems never abates. We land in times when it feels like a sin to stop and breathe. This mindset is a lie. God wants us to be constant in obedience and trust, but he never meant for us to burn out by working for what only God can secure.

The verse says, "The LORD will fight for you, you have only to be still." We have only to be still. That is what it takes to conquer our greatest battles. For those fighting temptation, the moment of triumph is more often a moment of still trust than it is a high-spirited battle. God wins our battles when we rest in him. The industry of manhood is built on faith and doesn't try to do God's job for him.

Oh Lord, please fight my battles. Please be the strength no man has in himself.

OCTOBER 17

PRAYING OPENLY

I spill out my heart to you and tell you all my troubles.
PSALM 142:2 TPT

The prayers heard in church might not be the most sincere. Christians don't like to talk openly about addictions, personal accounts of lust, alcoholism, or even depression. Going into church as we are, with all our messy emotions apparent, takes a lot more bravery than most men have. But this is the exact honesty God wants us to have with him and hopefully with those close to us. He wants us to spill our hearts out to him and share our troubles so we can grow close to him.

The first step we can take to lead us away from God's presence is to resort to prayers of formality and insincerity. God is a friend to confide in, a captain to follow, and a father to hold us in our brokenness. If we treat him like a stranger, we will estrange ourselves from his glorious presence.

Oh Jesus, please teach me to pray openly. I want to pray sincerely and without pride or haughtiness. I can't do anything without you, so please give me the words I need to pray.

OCTOBER 18

EACH OF US

Remember that the Lord will reward each one of us for the good we do.
EPHESIANS 6:8 NLT

Following this, Paul continues, "whether slave or free." No matter our life circumstances, the good we do has meaning. Whether we are in a dead-end marriage or a fulfilling relationship, whether we work at a gas station or own billions in oil stocks, the good we do toward others is noticed. Jesus is careful to notice our every good deed, and it pleases him. Our heavenly reward from him awaits.

What a blessing it truly is to have an attentive and gracious savior. We don't deserve the kindness Christ lavishes on us, yet we can expect it and rejoice in it. Even better, we can now spend our days focusing on doing what is good and gracious rather than simply avoiding mistakes. We can seek reward rather than fear failure, and that is a freeing thought in the mind of any man.

Dear Jesus, please work in my heart. Bless me with many opportunities to seek your

good works knowing it will one day bring reward.

OCTOBER 19

TIRELESS HEART

Never become tired of doing good.
2 THESSALONIANS 3:13 NCV

Can we truly be tireless of doing good? Can we truly have hearts that "never become tired of doing good?" Although only six words long, this commandment is daunting. The truth is, we can't follow this commandment without God's Spirit doing it for us. If we try, through personal effort, to not grow tired of doing good, we will be quickly disappointed. God delights in giving us commandments we can't follow without him.

We are right to master our tiredness. We should learn to rest in peace and rise with energy. Further, we should learn the things we can never rest from such as doing good. A good man is a role model for those around him. He takes the Lord's commandments ever seriously and is not satisfied with carnality in his heart. He pushes into the heart of God with continual energy and purpose.

Dear Jesus, please work tirelessly in me. I am weary and unable to do any good on my own. Make me your man.

OCTOBER 20

PATH OF THE LORD

Lead me by your truth and teach me,
for you are the God who saves me.
All day long I put my hope in you.
PSALM 25:5 NLT

A heart's greatest joy and contentment comes from being near the Lord with a spirit of seeking. The purest, happiest psalms are those with a deep desire to be near God and to enjoy him. This psalm is no different, and the writer is filled with a holy desire worthy of imitation. He prays, "Lead me by your truth and teach me." He doesn't presume the wisdom to lead himself, nor does he think there is any other source but God. He is the King of truth and mercifully gives that truth to those who ask.

What are we seeking? If we could be given anything we want, what would it be? Our hearts are idol factories, and unless we turn our eyes to the Lord every day, we will revert to that state. The reason for the psalmist's urgency is the importance of his quest, and our quest for the Lord is equally important. Men were made to seek and pursue the Lord.

Dear Lord, be my sole pursuit today. Be the greatest desire of my heart and never leave me.

OCTOBER 21

FEAR

God gave us a spirit not of fear but of power
and love and self-control.
2 TIMOTHY 1:7 ESV

Fear is a primal instinct created to alert a man as to danger in his immediate surroundings. It sends a message to the nervous system immediately before it is too late. In a fallen world, fear is often projected onto events so far in the future they need not be feared. Imagine not being afraid of losing your job, of not being able to provide, or of disease? Imagine the freedom of looking at possibilities with either optimism or trust in the Lord's outcomes.

This is more than a dream; it's the mindset God intended for us. "Be not afraid" is one of the most repeated commandments in the Bible. God intended for men like us or Timothy to be characterized by "power and love and self-control."

Oh Jesus, be first in my mindset. I want to rely on you first before falling into fear. Give me the heart to seek self-control before I worry about losing control of my situation.

OCTOBER 22

ALMIGHTY HELP

> Our help is in the name of the LORD, the Maker of heaven and earth.
> PSALM 124:8 NIV

In every fight, the odds are in our favor. We have almighty help against every opponent. He is ready to be our courage and shield in battle. When Satan lays fires at the walls of our souls, Jesus is there to dowse water on them and fortify our defenses. He fears nothing because he is "the Maker of heaven and earth" which makes him the maker of all things. Only the almighty God can bring all things into being, and this is the God who is there for us at a moment's notice.

Where have we been pushing away the help of God? Where have we been working alone and fighting through effort instead of faith? It's difficult to surrender to the Lord while fighting the devil. Many men have not been able to do this, but if we are to experience God's healing power working in us, we must learn how to give our lives to him.

Oh Lord, you are my help in times of need. You are there for me when it counts,

and nothing can stand against you. Help me trust you.

OCTOBER 23

FLESH OR SPIRIT

The Lord is the Spirit, and wherever the Spirit of the Lord is, there is freedom.
2 CORINTHIANS 3:17 NLT

The Lord's mission is to free sinners from the prison walls surrounding their souls. Men are flesh and bone, like animals, and the only god they have to worship is their appetite. Despite the eternity in their hearts and the desire for meaning, men are incapable of pursuing it because they have no Spirit to empower them. But "the Lord is the Spirit," and wherever he is, he brings freedom.

In Romans, Paul describes us as enslaved to either the flesh or the Spirit. Being enslaved to the Spirit, though, means freedom because we are bound to the noblest desires of our hearts. To be free in the Spirit means putting aside lust, greed, and ambition because we know of holy pleasures far greater. To be a man of God is to be filled with the Spirit and thus live in freedom. Our earthly counterparts follow their appetites with no ability to rise above it.

Oh God, fill me with your Holy Spirit today. Free me from the flesh and the world and be the deepest desire of my heart. I am nothing without you.

OCTOBER 24

LOVE INCOMPREHENSIBLE

Your love is so extravagant it reaches to the heavens,
Your faithfulness so astonishing it stretches to the sky!
PSALM 57:10 TPT

    The love of God is beyond human understanding. We are miniscule and broken compared to Jesus, and the best we can manage is to stand in wonder at the depth and breadth of his love and faithfulness toward us. The psalmist uses physical measures to describe the immeasurable Spirit of God, saying it "reaches to the heavens" and "stretches to the sky." What can we do but worship him? Even with our limited human spirits, we can shout praises to God.

    As Christians, God pours a portion of his eternal love and faithfulness into our hearts. He makes us his image bearers, and those around us learn to recognize him by first seeing us. Do people see the incomprehensible love of God in us? Do we love our neighbors boldly or just to the extent anyone else would? Do we have character beyond earthly explanation, or are we living with old limitations?

Dear God, please make me a man of love and character beyond earthly explanation. Let others look at me and see your eternal virtue.

OCTOBER 25

BEYOND FALSEHOOD

Little children, let us not love in word or speech, but in action and in truth.
I JOHN 3:18 CSB

Christian conduct is important to us for a lot of reasons, but that can easily translate into pretending to be something we are not. Knowing the importance of being a Christian can make us fake ones if we don't have a sincere desire for the Lord in our hearts. We become hypocrites who turn away the poor with a verbal blessing. This is the danger John warns of, and he uses the truth and our actions to indicate where our hearts are.

To love in word or speech but not in truth and action is worse than not loving at all. It makes us sin through lovelessness but also through lying because we are pretending to be something we are not. What is the true condition of our hearts, and what are our actions testifying about us? Through turning to God in repentance, we can put aside hypocrisy and become sincere, passionate believers of Jesus' example.

Dear Lord, please work in my heart and make me love others both in truth and action. Make me a man who cares about others not because I feel like I should but because I want to.

OCTOBER 26

RUNNING FOREVER

Don't you know that the runners in a stadium all race, but only one receives the prize? Run in such a way to win the prize.
I CORINTHIANS 9:24 CSB

Every good runner looks to their goal while pushing the pain out of mind. They decide pain and exhaustion are not worthy of their respect the same way the goal is, and this drives them forward. This is the spirit Christ desires for us. He wants us to be indefatigable and set aside pain in a holy kind of ignorance. Our prize, a welcoming heaven, lies before us, and we can push forward every day.

If we act as if we care about our faith but are unwilling to sacrifice, we expose our true nature. We are Christians in word and speech but not in truth and action. We have convinced ourselves we love Christ even though his sacrifice and faithfulness are foreign concepts to us. If we are to be sincere in the faith, we will demonstrate we value our Lord by a spirit of sacrifice and grace.

Dear God, give me the strength to run this race. My legs are giving out, and I need your passion. Please enlarge my heart.

OCTOBER 27

WHY TRY

Without faith living within us it would be impossible to please God. For we come to God in faith knowing that he is real and that he rewards the faith of those who give all their passion and strength into seeking him.
HEBREWS 11:6 TPT

Do we give all our passion and strength to seeking God? Passion and strength only have value if they are God's passion and strength. If we try to please God on our own, we might as well give up. We are like filthy rags before him, and our most noble acts are nothing without him. "Without faith living within us it would be impossible to please God," the verse says. Until we give our lives to him in holy dependency, our efforts are in vain.

The verse says, "He rewards the faith of those who give all their passion and strength into seeking him." This kind of passion and faith is possible when we lean on Jesus for every ounce of our strength. When we passionately seek his help, believing he will give it, we find our true strength.

Dear Lord, work in me to produce faith that brings action. I can do nothing without you, so please give me the faith and the strength to pursue you wholeheartedly.

OCTOBER 28

FLEEING AND FIGHTING

Submit yourselves, then, to God.
Resist the devil, and he will flee from you.
JAMES 4:7 NIV

Part of becoming a man is learning when to fight and when to flee. In this passage from James, he gives us specific instructions to "resist the devil, and he will flee from you." It is important to note we do not chase after him. If he leaves us alone, we let him be. In other passages from the Bible, we are told to flee from immorality. In the case of some sins, our plan of attack is more of a retreat.

It may sound unmasculine to run away from a fight, but it is the wisest thing we can do. Even Joseph, a man of great godliness, ran from Potiphar's wife when she sought to seduce him. There is no shame in running away sometimes. As long as we submit ourselves to God, we will know when it is right to do so.

Dear Jesus, please teach me the wisdom to know when to run and when to fight. Give me a heart that avoids immorality and does not submit to it. Make me wise in you.

OCTOBER 29

IT MAKES SENSE

> How great is our God!
> There's absolutely nothing his power cannot accomplish, and he has infinite understanding of everything.
> PSALM 147:5 TPT

Is your soul downcast within you? At times, it feels like God has left us to our troubles, and his plan is concealed from us. To lose faith in God's plan leaves us in a desperate and lonely place. It's difficult to regain a sense of purpose after losing it. No matter the trials or difficulties, though, God's plan remains. His power remains. His understanding of our situation remains stronger than ours.

Yes, "how great is our God!" Life may be out of order, but it still makes sense to him. We may have lost hope, but he remains hopeful. We may feel weak and helpless, but there is still "nothing his power cannot accomplish." No matter the difficulty, his ability exceeds it. It's hard to understand at times, but God really does have a plan no matter how terrible life is. He remains true to us.

Dear Jesus, show me your power and infinite understanding. You do not watch over my life lightly, and you understand it far better than I do.

OCTOBER 30

SINCERE LOVE

Love each other with genuine affection and take delight in honoring each other.
ROMANS 12:10 NLT

God doesn't want us to be good out of compulsion, and he doesn't want us to fake our love for fellow brothers in Christ. He wants us to be sincere, to love because we can't help ourselves, and to show this love in brotherly affection and honor. David said his friendship with Jonathan was better than a woman's love. Most people today scoff at this because they have never felt it. The genuine affection God can create between men is so powerful, Satan lays every trap to subvert it.

Paul also says, "take delight in honoring each other." We know we love our brothers in Christ when we take more delight in them being honored than in our honor. When we gladly step to the side so a brother can be in the spotlight, we are living in love.

Oh God, I praise you for the love that exists between brothers in Christ. Make me a loving brother who puts others' needs and honor before my own.

OCTOBER 31

BEAUTIFUL PRAYER

Fill us with your love every morning.
Then we will sing and rejoice all our lives.
PSALM 90:14 NCV

To be filled with God's love is a joy beyond description. It is a holy ecstasy and elation we can't comprehend. When it crashes over us, it leaves us breathless and enraptured by our Savior. His love can sustain us through every trial, and without it, there is not a comfort in the world. Yes, we should readily cry out, "Fill us with your love every morning."

A man can run on many types of fuel. He can make alcohol, sex, or work into the thing that gets him up every morning. We have to be aware of this and let these things be ruled by God's love. Even if we have no work, no sexual partner, or no earthly comforts, the love of God can drive us every morning.

Dear Lord, please give me the strength that can only come from your love. Make me holy, righteous, and completely dependent on your support. Your love is greater than life, and it's all I want.

NOVEMBER

Because of the LORD's great love we are not consumed, for his compassions never fail. They are new every morning; great is your faithfulness.
LAMENTATIONS 3:22-23 NIV

NOVEMBER 1

PRIVATE CONDUCT

"When you pray, go into your room, close the door and pray to your Father, who is unseen. Then your Father, who sees what is done in secret, will reward you."
MATTHEW 6:6 NIV

Goodness is most visibly seen in how we treat others. Someone who treats their coworkers, family, friends, and strangers well is seen as a good person. What we do in private, where only our minds and souls are affected, is often seen as outside the impact of morality. Pornography, online cruelty, and even loneliness are difficult because they find us while we are alone and mask themselves as harmless. These secret acts are conditions of brokenness and ripple out into our lives like stones in a pond.

Jesus Christ has a standard of conduct for what is done and felt in secret. In this passage from Matthew, he commands his disciples to "close the door and pray to your Father, who is unseen." He comforts them with the thought that God "who sees what is done in secret, will reward you." Jesus knows where the material of a man's soul is produced: in secret.

Lord, the condition of my soul is produced in secret. The private areas of my life make me who I am. Work in those private moments.

NOVEMBER 2

FIGHTING SURRENDER

"Don't worry or surrender to your fear. For you've believed in God, now trust and believe in me also."
JOHN 14:1 TPT

Jesus wants us to surrender to the force we feel pulling us toward him. He doesn't want us to surrender to anxiety and fear pulling us down. He wants us to surrender our souls to the right choice: him. When life beats us down and leaves our insides cold, we must know what to give in to and want to shun. Jesus puts difficulties and trials in our path, things we fear, so we learn to run to him. He doesn't want us to blindly run in fear.

The difference between good and bad surrender is faith. Jesus says, "Trust and believe in me also." Bad surrender involves chains to fear and worry; good surrender involves the freedom of faith in Christ which comes from trusting and believing in the only Savior who can dispel our every fear. Jesus reminds his disciples of this trust and belief to comfort them in the midst of their fears.

Lord, please work out my fear and worries. Build in their place the trust and belief I need to rest in you.

NOVEMBER 3

BROTHERS AND SISTERS

I appeal to you, brothers and sisters, in the name of our Lord Jesus Christ, that all of you agree with one another in what you say and that there be no divisions among you, but that you be perfectly united in mind and thought.
1 CORINTHIANS 1:10 NIV

Paul gives a strong request to his brothers and sisters in Corinth. He requests their unity and that they agree with one another rather than being divided. He demanded that "all of you agree with one another in what you say." He further requested this unity bleed into the realm of "mind and thought." This is a supernatural level of unity where people of different backgrounds and personalities are brought together through shared purpose and belief.

Where is there disunity in our lives? If we are disconnected from our brothers and sisters in the faith, this preempts any possibility of disagreement, but not in a good way. Christ wants us to live closely alongside our fellow Christians and to do so in unity. Are we willing to put in the work to achieve this unity, or have we resigned ourselves to disagreement and bad blood?

Oh Jesus, please teach me how to be a brother of unity. Teach me to communicate with humility and love and to listen before I speak.

NOVEMBER 4

PROTECTED IN WAR

Put on God's complete set of armor provided for us, so that you will be protected as you fight against the evil strategies of the accuser!
EPHESIANS 6:11 TPT

Men were created to fight the good fight. This is not always a physical war, but it is a war nonetheless. Satan lays traps for us hoping we will fall away from God. He hurtles his arrows of death in our direction with accurate aim, and he will hit us where it hurts most. Only by the "complete set of armor provided for us" can we endure the war. Jesus must protect our minds, souls, and hearts if we are to endure the attacks of the devil.

Where is your weakest point? Where can Satan hit you most easily? Every man bears on his heart the wounds of past experiences, and some of them are not fully rendered to God. These are sore spots, and they can easily trigger our defenses and make us feel powerless. Our weak spots and wounds must be rendered to God, so they don't destroy us.

Dear God, please work inside my heart. Please armor weaker areas of my life and keep me strong. Do not let Satan into my heart.

NOVEMBER 5

GOOD AS DONE

*Faith shows the reality of what we hope for;
it is the evidence of things we cannot see.*
HEBREWS 11:1 NLT

God desires for us to hope. He knows we are best when we hold to pure hopes of a reality far better than ours. Hoping in his redemption and healing and not seeing it can lead us to be cynical, however, so he places in our hearts a way to know our truest hopes are accurate. He gives us faith so strong we know it is not of our doing. This faith proves to us the higher power of God and makes us sure that if he is there, his promises will surely come to pass.

We can be sure of God's promises because he is always faithful to what he says he will do. Can the same be said of us? Do our friends and family consider us reliable men? If we are to be like Jesus, we will become structures of support for those around us.

Dear Jesus, please remind me of the faith planted in my heart. I only believe because you make me believe; let that be the assurance of my hope.

NOVEMBER 6

IT IS DONE

"No one can undo what I have done."
ISAIAH 43:13 NLT

What God does, his creatures cannot undo. They can't reverse his decisions or alter his plans. Since eternity, God has planned his actions, and they are all irreversible. Sometimes, we would like to undo what God has done or alter the fate of our lives, but this is not in God's will, so it cannot happen. Just as he says in Isaiah: "No one can undo what I have done."

Where would we like to reverse God's plan? What fate do we know is his work, but we would like to deny it? As long as we are trying to undo what God has done or plans to do, we will always resent him. We will pit ourselves against the Savior of the universe in a petty battle for autonomy we can't win. He reigns supreme, and he alone decides our path. Man can surrender to his God or be destroyed by him.

Oh God, make me a man who does not fight you. I want to trust your plan and not try to undo it. I believe in your will.

NOVEMBER 7

INCOMPARABLE LIFE

To know you is to experience a flowing fountain,
drinking in your life, springing up to satisfy.
In your light we receive the light of revelation.
PSALM 36:9 TPT

We don't know something until we experience it. We can't know what it is like to be a lover, a father, or a widower unless we have experienced it for ourselves. If we view experiences as an outsider, we need to recognize it and not pretend otherwise. "To know you is to experience a flowing fountain, drinking in your life," this psalm declares. Think about those words: drinking in your life.

We can drink in God's life. God is not a lofty goal pitted against the greater pleasures of sin; he is the ultimate pleasure, and when we pursue him and experience him, he reveals all we missed when looking to other idols and gods. He is the light of revelation because he reveals himself to be the greatest source of pleasure, life, and abundance.

Eternal Jesus, how sweet is your love. How sweet it is to know you and your kindness. I pray for your presence over this day, and I want to experience the fountain of your flowing love.

NOVEMBER 8

LITTLE WHILE

You know that the testing of your faith produces perseverance.
JAMES 1:3 NIV

Only after our faith is tested do we see the value of the experience. Metal is tested with hammers, fire, and heat, and we are tested through the fiery ordeals of life. Christ only asks us to be faithful through the trial by leaning on him and growing in faith. If we deepen our faith through trial, we will have the perseverance he promises here in James. If we instead rely on other ways to cope, or turn away from God, the testing and tribulation will be for nothing.

This is God's will for us: that we become the perfect versions of ourselves. We will not reach this goal while alive on earth, but every trial and situation put in our paths to test us has the potential to make us a little more like him. It can make us men that others can look up to, rely on, and benefit from.

God, this testing I am in only lasts a little while. Please help me endure with perseverance rather than break down and look to the world to save me.

NOVEMBER 9

MEANINGFUL WORK

"You did not choose me; I chose you. And I gave you this work: to go and produce fruit, fruit that will last. Then the Father will give you anything you ask for in my name."
JOHN 15:16 NCV

The Christian walk is not made up of personal choices and developing our virtues. Our walk is God's story and made up of his actions in our lives and how he uses them to shape us for his purpose. He did not create us to have a bunch of people in charge of their own lives; he created us as image bearers and stewards of his kingdom. Once we come to understand this, God will entrust us with his kingdom and give us anything we ask for in his name.

It is all in Jesus' first statement: "You did not choose me; I chose you." Jesus chose us specifically. We didn't choose a path that many others were choosing, but Jesus chose each and every one of his children specifically and with a purpose in mind. It's easy to lose sight of how special we are but not when considering this verse.

Dear Jesus, you chose me. Remind me that I am yours, created and chosen for a purpose, and I have value to you.

NOVEMBER 10

COMMON NEED

"People everywhere seem to worry about making a living, but your heavenly Father knows your every need and will take care of you."
LUKE 12:30 TPT

Every man knows the pressure to provide for himself, yet few of us will admit that daily provision is common need Jesus has never refused. We wake up early to work and stay up late to make a living, but once it stops being done for Jesus' honor and starts being done out of fear, work is pointless. Work exists for men and women to do meaningful tasks and better themselves, but when Jesus finds it right, he removes us from our jobs and provides for us himself. It might feel like a thin provision, but it is provision.

Jesus says, "Your heavenly Father knows your every need." It's incredible that the Father knows our individual needs better than we do. There is never a time when we must explain to God what we need or how he is failing us. In reality, we are failing to understand. He is worthy of our trust.

Dear Lord, thank you for being a god of provision. Please watch over me and those around me this day and show your loving hand in simple ways.

NOVEMBER 11

STEADFAST IN THE STORM

LORD, you do not withhold your compassion from me.
Your constant love and truth will always guard me.
PSALM 40:11 CSB

This psalm is an intimate picture of a believer with his Savior. The writer cries out to God, pleading for his mercy not to be withheld, and it almost makes us wonder if God would do such a thing. The truth is, this writer likely had faith in God's merciful presence, but he knew the value of voicing his fears to the Lord anyway. He knew the value of speaking openly to God and not hiding his feelings.

God's love is steadfast in the storm, and we don't need to question it. Nothing can separate us from it, but it is still valuable to recognize when we are afraid. Men are pressured into not showing fear, but this is not the biblical picture of manhood. David brought his fear and anxiety to the Lord constantly and showed what it looked like to trust God when circumstances are confusing, frightening, or sorrowful.

Dear God, please teach me your faithfulness and mercy. Remind me that you are steadfast and not liable to change like I am. Give me faith.

NOVEMBER 12

HIS MIND FOR US

> May the God who gives endurance and encouragement give you the same attitude of mind toward each other that Christ Jesus had.
> ROMANS 15:5 NIV

Christ has an opinion of us. It's weird to think about, but he does. Most of us, unless we have enormous egos, care too much about what other people think of us. We will obsess over an opinion and not let it go. Do we care about God's opinion of us? What was his "attitude of mind" toward humans while on earth? He knew everything about us, all our flaws and weaknesses, but he was gracious to us anyway and treated us kindly. He still walks alongside us as we fight through our issues.

Can we not do the same for others? Can we walk in encouragement and forgiveness and give our brothers and sisters in Christ the space they need to grow? A man's words carry a lot of power, but even more power is found in his opinion of people. If we look down on someone for their weakness, even if we do not tell them, they will know. Our opinion has to be Christlike and filled with encouragement and kindness.

Dear Jesus, you have been kind to me in my weakness. Teach me to do the same for those around me.

NOVEMBER 13

UNSHAKEABLE FAITH

"The rain came down, the streams rose, and the winds blew and beat against that house; yet it did not fall, because it had its foundation on the rock."
MATTHEW 7:25 NIV

How would you describe your faith? Is it worn, exhausted, being tested? God is not frightened by our honesty, and it is no use faking where we are spiritually. A strong faith is only reached through honesty with God and learning to trust him with problems we would rather leave unaddressed. Once our faith has been built on an intimate, accepting relationship with Jesus, no storm or wind can tear us from our foundation.

What is our foundation set on? Is our faith built on emotional experiences or ambitions? If we make God just a part of life, a building block, then he will not be part of our lives at all. He wants it all; he wants our plans, our ambitions, and he wants to be our foundation. Nothing else will do for him.

Dear God, I set my heart on you. Make me a man who does not give up his faith easily but stands in humility and patience to uphold your name.

NOVEMBER 14

STRENGTH AND SHIELD

The LORD is my strength and shield.
I trust him with all my heart.
He helps me, and my heart is filled with joy.
I burst out in songs of thanksgiving.
PSALM 28:7 NLT

Only God can protect us from the evil one. Only he can uphold us in times of trial and encourage us when we are weak. He is our ultimate helper and a real person whom we can talk to and share with at every moment. When the psalmist says, "The LORD is my strength and shield. I trust him with all my heart," he declares the mighty presence of God over his problems and trials. He will not look to work, sex, or anything else to cope; he will trust in the Lord's almighty ability to conquer every trial.

The psalmist also says, "He helps me, and my heart is filled with joy." When we look to other things to satisfy the God-sized hole in our hearts, they don't fill us with joy. They are unsatisfying as if we're eating sand instead of food. Only God, who can help us in every way, will fill us with the joy of gratitude and thanksgiving.

Dear God, I want to be a man who rejoices in your strength and exalts you in my heart. Help me rely on you through every storm.

NOVEMBER 15

BROTHERLY ACCOUNTABILITY

Look after each other so that none of you fails to receive the grace of God. Watch out that no poisonous root of bitterness grows up to trouble you, corrupting many.
HEBREWS 12:15 NLT

Accountability is not for the weak but the strong. No man is an island, and no man was made to walk alone. He was made to live in a community with brothers and sisters to walk alongside and run the race with. The individualist man lacks encouragement and affection. His habits are to his own detriment, and he separates himself to his own discouragement. The verse says, "Look after each other so that none of you fails to receive the grace of God." It's less about being accountable to one another so we don't sin and more about being accountable, so we don't forget the grace God offers every morning.

Bitterness is a poisonous root because it severs us from our siblings in Christ. It isolates us and takes away the support structure of our faith. We are made to be holy in God, and this is a difficult task to do alone. We should pray against bitterness whenever it arises.

Dear God, please cast out the bitterness between my brothers and sisters and me. Make us into scaffolding so we rely on each other for every need.

NOVEMBER 16

FAITH AND BOLDNESS

Because of Christ and our faith in him, we can now come boldly and confidently into God's presence.
EPHESIANS 3:12 NLT

When we are unsure, we cannot be bold. If we are unsure of our security, we will be afraid. If we are unsure where we will find the strength to fight our battles, we will be timid. Boldness comes from faith which is trust in what we can't see. Paul says that "because of Christ and our faith in him," we can be bold even in the presence of God. Our every sin and grievance is outweighed by the blood God's Son shed on the cross. By this blood and by trusting in him, we can be bold to lay our cares and worries before the throne of God.

If we can come boldly and confidently into God's presence, is there anywhere we cannot be bold in going? A man, through his boldness and courage, can encourage those around him. We are specially equipped to encourage others through our boldness and faith, and this is accomplished solely through trust in Christ's power.

Dear Jesus, you alone are my source of courage. You alone have given me access to the throne of grace. I praise you!

NOVEMBER 17

STRONG AND BRAVE

*All you who put your hope in the LORD
be strong and brave.*
PSALM 31:24 NCV

It's difficult to live in light of the image of God. He was perfect in strength and bravery as well as humility and meekness. We can easily feel like failures compared to Christ's example, but this was not Christ's intention when he lived a perfect life. He doesn't expect perfection from us even in light of his own perfection; he only requires our hope, love, and faith.

It is God's greatest glory to choose the weak and the least brave and make them his mightiest heirs. He is exalted through our weakness, and we are only strong and brave because of his strength living in us. We are made sufficient through walking in faith and not in being perfectly brave or perfectly strong. He abounds in grace for our weakness and infirmities, and out of this abundant grace, he encourages us: "Be strong and brave."

Mighty Lord, thank you for your encouragement amid my insufficiency. Thank you for the strength and bravery you give

which I can't find on my own. I am nothing without you, Jesus.

NOVEMBER 18

EQUAL MEASURES

"In the same way you judge others, you will be judged, and with the measure you use, it will be measured to you."
MATTHEW 7:2 NIV

We can't expect to get what we do not give. When we do, that is the grace of God, but tempting his grace repeatedly is a sure way to land ourselves in trouble. When we treat others harshly, discourage those close to us, and don't put work into our lives, we will receive the same treatment in return. We will not find grace by giving judgment. Jesus says, "In the same way you judge others, you will be judged." This often how the world works too. When we treat others badly, they will be embittered and treat us badly in return.

Priorities are all around us. Our careers, significant others and friends, and our churches all ask for a portion of our lives. If we put the things of this world first, like pay raises and pleasure, we will likely be blessed with them. But if we pour a great measure of ourselves into relationships, acts of compassion, and kindness, we will receive the same in return.

Dear God, teach me to use the measure of my life for good. I want to be man who gives abundantly; may I be fit to receive the same.

NOVEMBER 19

GENEROSITY AND FAITH

God is able to make every grace overflow to you, so that in every way, always having everything you need, you may excel in every good work.
2 CORINTHIANS 9:8 CSB

Generosity is an act of faith. We give away what we have with the thought that it's not up to us how much we have on this earth. God is the one who determines our abundance. In this verse, Paul says we should give out of generous hearts. We should not give out of compulsion or fear, and we are able to conquer these emotions by the truth of God's generosity toward us. As he says, "God is able to provide you with every blessing in abundance."

The joy of our hard work is only found through sharing. Men are positioned to be productive and work hard, and the dangers of workaholism and apathy threaten us on either side. That is why we must "share abundantly in every good work" and, by our generosity, bring together a community around us.

Dear God, I want to be a man of generosity. Please teach me to bring others together through work and a sense of selfless community.

NOVEMBER 20

PRIESTS OF LIGHT

You are God's chosen treasure—priests who are kings, a spiritual "nation" set apart as God's devoted ones. He called you out of darkness to experience his marvelous light, and now he claims you as his very own. He did this so that you would broadcast his glorious wonders throughout the world.
I PETER 2:9 TPT

Peter tells us we are "set apart as God's devoted ones." Humanity is drenched in darkness and unable to comprehend the fog hanging over their minds and darkening their understanding. As God's priests, his holy nation, we bring light into the world around us. Jesus has called us out of the dark, and we are not to recede into those shadows trying to consume us. We are to live boldly as priests of the light and bring the presence of God to those who don't know it.

The verse says we are to "broadcast his glorious wonders throughout the world." Are we living up to this image? Are we men consumed by the glory of God and who want to share it at every opportunity? Perhaps we are not, and the light within us is a mystery to our friends and family.

Dear God, please make me a priest of the light. Give me the courage to live in the light and share it with those around me rather than letting them reside in darkness.

NOVEMBER 21

INNER DRIVE

Seek more of his strength! Seek more of him! Let's always be seeking the light of his face.
PSALM 105:4 TPT

Men are made to be passionate. They are made to pursue and fight for what's meaningful to them. They are made to achieve and be resilient in light of failure. The psalmist echoes this sentiment and encourages us to push into the life of Christ and "seek more of him." Not a moment should be allowed to slip by in which we do not seek more of him; we should "always be seeking the light of his face." This mindset is one of a content, life-filled believer.

God is not the only thing we can seek. The world is full of distractions that fill our eyes every day and tempt us into pursuing something that leads to death instead of life. We should seek God's strength. Not the weakness of sexual impurity, not the depths of apathy, but the strength of the Lord. Only this will bring us satisfaction through effort.

Lord, give me today the passion to seek more of you. Make me a true believer alive in your life.

NOVEMBER 22

ONCE AND FOREVER

He is able, once and forever, to save those who come to God through him. He lives forever to intercede with God on their behalf.
HEBREWS 7:25 NLT

Christ only had to die once because his sacrifice was perfect and able to cover all sins. That death works forever for every sin we commit. Every time we fail or relapse into old habits, the death of Christ remains satisfactory payment for our forgiveness. As complete as our sinfulness is, his substitutionary death surpasses it in power and breadth. As today's verse declares, "He lives forever to intercede with God on their behalf."

How often do we think about that? Every time we sin, even if it's just a careless word of discouragement, Jesus is interceding for us. He died not just for our greater sins but also for the careless mistakes we make even after knowing we are redeemed. Perhaps we would not take his salvation so lightly if we remembered how often we rely on it.

Holy Jesus, you can save from every mistake. Thank you for being greater than

my immorality and choosing to love me no matter the cost.

NOVEMBER 23

ARE WE WILLING

If we confess our sins, He is faithful and just to forgive us our sins and to cleanse us from all unrighteousness.
1 JOHN 1:9 ESV

Jesus can redeem us in profound and meaningful ways but only if we are willing. He will not draw near to those who will not draw near to him. Even after we are saved, he will not grow us in sanctification if we hide our sins rather than confess them. We need not worry he will be unfaithful, push us away, or despise us for our sin. John explicitly tells us the opposite is true.

Jesus was a man people knew they could trust. Despite his power and might, people knew they could tell the man from Galilee about anything they had done. Is the same true of us? Are we men whom people can confess their sins to, or do they shy away in fear of our disapproval and judgment? If so, we are holding them back from being cleansed of their unrighteousness.

Dear Jesus, thank you for being faithful to forgive. Please teach me to do the same.

I want to be someone others know they can trust and talk to.

NOVEMBER 24

WITHOUT COMPULSION

You must each decide in your heart how much to give.
And don't give reluctantly or in response to pressure.
"For God loves a person who gives cheerfully."
2 CORINTHIANS 9:7 NLT

We can't give cheerfully if we are giving more than we are comfortable with. We also can't give at all if we don't live in gratitude. Jesus gave to us out of his magnificent abundance, and out of this abundance, we give back tokens of generosity. He does not need what we can give; he can raise provisions and blessings out of nothing. He simply wants to transform us into his image, and his image is clothed in generosity.

Paul says, "You must each decide in your heart how much to give." This means we cannot give out of compulsion. If we do not feel like giving or can only bear to give a small fraction of what is ours, perhaps our hearts are not in the right place. Perhaps our unwillingness to give speaks volumes about our character and about how much significance we give to our work rather than acknowledging God does the work.

Dear Lord, please make me a generous man. I am aware of how much I have received; teach me to give willingly as you do.

NOVEMBER 25

MEN OF CONFIDENCE

Do not throw away this confident trust in the Lord.
Remember the great reward it brings you!
HEBREWS 10:35 NLT

The world is confident it can take away our faith and crush us beneath its feet. For this not to be true, we have to be men of confidence who have the utmost trust in the Lord. When a man has confidence in himself, he is misled, but that is not so with God. Our confidence in him is well-founded and will not put us to shame. As Hebrews says, "Remember the great reward it brings you!" We will only be put to shame if we throw away the confidence we have in God's deliverance.

If we are not confident, people around us will know. They will not trust us with leadership or responsibility if we are afraid of the consequences of our actions. Only by walking boldly in God's plans can we step into the roles he has planned for us.

Oh Jesus, teach me to put you first and between me and every challenge I face. Give me confident trust that you can equip me for every good work and help me act without fear of punishment.

NOVEMBER 26

OUT OF SIGHT

Oh, what joy for those whose disobedience is forgiven, whose sin is put out of sight!
PSALM 32:1 NLT

This psalm is a celebration of God's forgiveness. When God chooses to take our wrongdoing, disobedience, and sin and put them out of his sight, what a blessing it is! Having all our wrongs put away is the source of our greatest joy. When someone is a rebel against God, they don't have the ability to ask for forgiveness. Only by God's grace are they moved to a place of repentance, and only by his grace do they come to see how unworthy of his grace they are.

Jesus has put our mistakes out of his sight, but are we still looking at them? Sometimes God forgives us, but we can't do the same. Are we unwilling to forgive ourselves for something? Jesus has forgiven us. Even if the rest of the world does not forgive us, we still have the opportunity to move past our wrongdoing through repentance and forgiveness. Jesus has forgiven our sins and put them out of sight.

Dear Jesus, thank you for removing my sins from sight and mind. I was a man drowning in sin, but now I am a man washed clean by your atoning blood.

NOVEMBER 27

WILLINGLY FOOLISH

The message of the cross is foolishness to those who are perishing, but to us who are being saved it is the power of God.
1 CORINTHIANS 1:18 NKJV

Are we willing to be foolish? Are we willing to look dumb and give up others' respect for the sake of doing what is right? Jesus was mocked and scorned, despised by his own creations, yet he remained strong in his weakness and wise in his foolishness. He was willing to keep his eyes on the cross and do what was right when no one was willing to follow him. Do we have the same resolve, and are we willing to be fools as Jesus was?

The cross was the greatest instrument of suffering the Romans could use. It was despised and considered inhumane. To venerate someone's death on a cross would be foolish to the world, yet the disciples loved this cross with holy enthusiasm and told everyone who would listen about it. Are we willing to be fools in this world for the sake of being spiritually wise?

Dear Jesus, help me let go of the honor and respect men seek and exchange it for true wisdom. May I willingly be a foolish-looking man when others look down on me for it.

NOVEMBER 28

HEART CONTENTS

I have hidden your word in my heart
that I might not sin against you.
PSALM 119:11 NIV

What is contained in your heart? What do you hide in its recesses? Jesus said of the Pharisees, "'These people honor Me with their lips, but their hearts are far from Me" (Matt. 15:8, NIV). The psalmist in today's verse is praising the Lord because, whether or not the world knows it, he knows God is inside of him. He has God's words hidden in his heart, so he won't sin against him.

Faith is both a private and public affair. Men are to share their faith and be active members of their community. They are made to be scaffolding to support others and their growth in faith. But faith, as we see in this verse, is also private. It is the things we think about at night when no one is watching. If we have no faith in private, our faith in public is hypocrisy.

Oh Lord, fill my heart with the right things. Write your words on my heart so I can honor you in small moments when I am alone with my thoughts.

NOVEMBER 29

SURROUNDED BY POWER

May God, the inspiration and fountain of hope, fill you to overflowing with uncontainable joy and perfect peace as you trust in him. And may the power of the Holy Spirit continually surround your life with his super-abundance until you radiate with hope!
ROMANS 15:13 TPT

Paul gave this great blessing to the letter's recipients living in Rome, but it applies to all of us in the faith. He blesses us with peace given by the God of inspiration and hope. More than that, he gives his recipients a mission by saying, "May the power of the Holy Spirit continually surround your life with his super-abundance until you radiate with hope!" By the abundant power of the Holy Spirit, we are to radiate hope in this world lost to cynical hopelessness.

We are surrounded by power greater than ours. Jesus does not expect us to conquer our demons alone or be the men of strength everyone expects us to be. He expects us to walk in trust and rely on the power of the Spirit to live, breathe, and do any task we need to do.

Mighty Jesus, I will put you first in trust and faith. Fill me with your perfect peace and surround me with your power. Give me the support I need to conquer this day.

NOVEMBER 30

BETTER THAN LIVING

Your tender mercies mean more to me than life itself. How I love and praise you, God!
PSALM 63:3 TPT

The psalmist is bold to declare how much he treasures God's "tender mercies." He holds the Lord and his mercy in such high esteem, it means more to him than existence itself. Nothing, absolutely nothing, can replace the love of God. He is more valuable than everything this world has to offer, and in a moment, we could give it all up for him and live without a single regret.

"How I love and praise you," the writer says. His heart is no longer his own; it is given to the Lord in reverence and worship. This is the mind we should have and the reverence we should live. When God is all that matters to us, worldly matters fade. Everything finds its meaning in how God has given it to us and how it is his before it is ours. Yes, the "tender mercies" the Lord showers on us in this life are worth more than life itself.

Dear God, I surrender myself to you in worship. I know my life is nothing without you.

DECEMBER

God is our refuge and strength, an ever-present help in trouble.
PSALM 46:1 NIV

DECEMBER 1

ANCHORED

We have this hope as an anchor for the soul,
firm and secure.
HEBREWS 6:19 NIV

What is the value of hope in a believer's life? How does hope change the way we live our day-to-day lives? According to the writer of Hebrews, hope in the Jesus' salvation acts "as an anchor for the soul" to keep us grounded when the waves of life crash over us. An eternity without God is a terror our wildest fears can't fully comprehend. If our salvation were in question, we would be destroyed by every mistake and trial that threatened us.

We have an anchor, and it is "firm and secure." The waves batter us, but our anchor does not shift. It is not pushed or altered by the wind; it is rooted in the character and the words of God which are unchangeable. No matter the trial, sin, or self-hatred we face, we have this forever-secure fact; Jesus loves us, and he has promised us his salvation.

Oh Lord, thank you for your sacrifice. Thank you for reaching out through the waves to save such a wretched sinner as me. No matter the storm, keep me anchored by your promise.

DECEMBER 2

WITHOUT FATIGUE

You honor me by anointing my head with oil.
My cup overflows with blessings.
PSALM 23:5 NLT

Psalm 23 is David's celebration of God's provision over him. Through every trial and every triumph, David saw the Lord's fatherly hand caring for him. He held onto his God through the valley of the shadow of death and was never found wanting. It's not always easy to look at life optimistically, but in moments of clarity, it becomes undeniably clear that God has been working behind the scenes the whole time.

The mindset of a satisfied man is based on indefatigable gratitude. He will be filled with holy satisfaction when he can say in any circumstance, "My cup overflows with blessings." As long as we have an eternity of God's blessings ahead, what is there to grumble over? The pains of life are great, and the apathy suffocating, but they are nothing compared to God's grace for us.

Oh God, thank you for the honor and blessing you have bestowed on me. Please give me your grace in every circumstance so I can praise you with gratitude.

DECEMBER 3

HIDDEN PERSON

Let your adorning be the hidden person of the heart with the imperishable beauty of a gentle and quiet spirit, which in God's sight is very precious.
1 PETER 3:4 ESV

A man's values are revealed in what he finds attractive in women. If our souls value physical things like "adorning" and charm, that is what we will be attracted to. Once we learn to value character, "imperishable beauty," and aspects that truly matter, we will be drawn toward women who display those qualities. Our sense of attraction will transcend sex and no longer be controlled by it; it will govern itself.

According to the writer of Proverbs, beauty is fleeting, and charm is deceitful. What truly matters is the person we can't see on first glance: the "hidden person of the heart." That determines someone's worth rather than their body or how they carry themselves. That "which in God's sight is very precious" should be just as precious to us. Once it is, our judgment will be like his judgment, and we will see people for who they truly are.

Oh Jesus, sanctify my eyes and soul to see the hidden person of the heart. I can do nothing apart from you, and I need you to reconfigure the person I am. Please help me.

DECEMBER 4

TRUE OVERSEER

In all the work you are doing, work the best you can.
Work as if you were doing it for the Lord, not for people.
COLOSSIANS 3:23 NCV

Against whose standard of conduct are we measuring ourselves? Is our work based on a boss's expectations or God's? We don't work for God as a show and hope to garner his approval by our actions; we work without compulsion. We work from a deep, swelling desire to be in harmony with God's character. We work toward perfection of determination, honesty, and energy.

Paul extends this command over "all the work you are doing." This is more than our nine to five. This is the work of the Lord. It is the way we conduct ourselves from the time we rise to the moment we lay down. This does not mean we live in constant fear of punishment, but rather it is a state of constant, holy dependency. In every moment, we lean on the Lord for strength so we can do his work. Nothing is expected of us apart from the Holy Spirit energizing our limbs.

Holy Spirit, enliven my limbs today. Give me the passion to work as you would work. Give me the strength I can't find on my own.

DECEMBER 5

CONTINUING

Each one of you should continue to live the way God has given you to live—the way you were when God called you.
I CORINTHIANS 7:17 NCV

Paul declares that each of us "should continue." Beginnings, middles, and endings have their unique challenges, and middles are soured by fatigue and apathy. This occurs in our faith journeys too as we undergo years and years of struggles and fights for our faith. Only God can keep the human spirit persevering in those circumstances. Only he can give us the passion we need to last through every high and low.

How should we continue to live? According to Paul, it is "the way God has given you to live—the way you were when God called you." When God reached out and redeemed us, we made a choice to live differently. If we had continued to live the same way, nothing would have changed. It's easy to drift away from what we first saw in God, but his Word is immovable; he does not change his expectations for us in response to our changing behavior. We know his path and need only stay on it through faith.

Oh God, please keep me on the narrow path. Guide me through every year and hold on to me as I push forward toward your kingdom.

DECEMBER 6

BELONG TO HIM

The earth is the LORD's, and everything in it.
The world and all its people belong to him.
PSALM 24:1 NLT

Everything we see is property of the most high God. Everything we judge, reject, or accept is God's. Every person, whether they are boring or enrapturing, repulsive or noble, belongs to God. He loves them and wants them to come home to him. Only the heart of God is big enough to love every individual as if they were the only person in the world. Is there any reason to ignore someone, or anything, without learning about it first?

Men should be inquisitive, teachable image bearers of Jesus. Our Lord did not ignore social outcasts or look down on the work of a carpenter. He was humble and willing to listen despite his omniscience. He never degraded anyone or anything except on moral grounds, and even then, he did so in love. He owned the world and all its people, yet he chose to act humbly and quietly for much of his earthly life.

Oh God, I declare your ownership over this world. Please give me the humility to

appreciate creation and all its people as you do.

DECEMBER 7

BELIEF STRUGGLE

*Let us hold unswervingly to the hope we profess,
for he who promised is faithful.*
HEBREWS 10:23 NIV

We have hope in God's salvation and know he never lies, but when times are tough, it's difficult to keep up that hope. We know in our heads God does not lie, but in our hearts, we stop believing God will actually fulfill his promises. "He who promised is faithful," this verse reminds us. Even when we are clothed in cynicism and distrust, Jesus remains faithful to his promises. Even when we swerve toward sex, work, or relationships for help, the salvation we once hoped in is waiting for us.

"Let us hold unswervingly to the hope we profess," the writer of Hebrews declares. Men are called to give an account of the hope within them. We are called to share our faith with our fellow men, with our families, and especially in the way we act. While sharing what we believe, we must continue to believe it. We must not go through the motions of faith while our souls lie dying. Our actions will also slip, and we will have no testimony and no hope.

> *Oh God, preserve within me the hope of your salvation. Make me tireless on this journey.*

DECEMBER 8

HOPE IN

LORD, where do I put my hope?
My only hope is in you.
PSALM 39:7 NLT

There is no shortage of idols to put our hope in. Careers, friendships, sex, and even working out are ready and willing to take our worship. They are still inherently good and should be enjoyed, but they are unfit to hold hope. God gave men sex drive as an antidote to apathy and to teach them self-control and personal discipline. He gave them careers to magnify their impact in their communities. He gave friendships to men so they would see different parts of the person of God. God even gave men a need for physical exercise to remind them they are embodied and part of a physical world. But he gave them himself to hope in.

"My only hope is in you," the psalmist declares. This is the mind of a man living in the presence of God. When we put our hopes in other things, our loving God will strip away all we have so there is nothing to hope in except him.

Oh Lord, I will hope in you. I praise you for everything you have given me, but I will reserve my hope for you.

DECEMBER 9

CONFLICTING DESIRES

> You open your hand;
> you satisfy the desire of every living thing.
> PSALM 145:16 ESV

The psalmist praises the Lord, saying, "You satisfy the desire of every living thing." That is the glory of natural creation. Every beast, insect, and plant, when in proper balance, lives out what God designed them for and fulfills their role in the natural landscape. The same is true of us. However, we have many conflicting desires, and our sinful nature tries to highjack them.

Our greatest desire is to have meaning. Unless we numb our pain and grow callouses over our hearts, we will feel a deep need for meaning. More than food, water, or even air, men need meaning. Men have started wars over a difference of opinion on the meaning of life. That desire, triumphing over all others, is satisfied only in God and a relationship with him. He is our ultimate satisfaction. Men can rule over every other desire if their desire for meaning is fulfilled in Jesus.

Oh Jesus, please satisfy in me the one desire never meant to be unsatisfied. Show

me the meaning of my existence by giving me yourself.

DECEMBER 10

CLOTHED IN LOVE

Above all, clothe yourselves with love, which binds us all together in perfect harmony.
COLOSSIANS 3:14 NLT

What does it mean to be clothed in love? When someone clothes themselves in love, what does it look like? As the apostle Paul writes, surrounding oneself with love leads to harmony with other believers. Learning to set aside our differences and love each other anyway is the precedent Jesus set for us and the apostles confirmed. Harmony is important to our Savior, and through good love, we can achieve harmony with other believers.

Paul starts with "above all." Love is to have supreme importance. Having love does not mean accepting people's sin or being a doormat for those around us, but it does mean a tremendous amount of sacrifice. To put love first means saying difficult things, helping others when it's inconvenient, and working out solutions instead of ignoring issues.

Dear God, only you can give me true love. Please make me into a man of love who brings harmony to those around him.

DECEMBER 11

HOLY DESIRE

My God, I want to do what you want.
Your teachings are in my heart.
PSALM 40:8 NCV

One of God's greatest designs for our lives is to align our desires with his own. He wants to take our lower desires for affirmation, power, sex, and recognition and transform them into higher desires. He wants us to not just do the right thing but to want to do the right thing with passionate and wholehearted souls. The path is found through meditating and absorbing God's teachings, so they soak into our hearts.

If we only give Jesus half our attention, life will become a hell of our own making. We will be the fighting grounds of a war between God desiring our souls and a world wanting the same. For us to be at peace, we must have Jesus' teachings in our hearts, do what he wants to do, and look at everything through eyes of faith. Every pleasure, enjoyment, and pain has to be understood through God's purpose for it.

Dear Jesus, I put you first today. May I see everything in my life through eyes of faith; I want to see this world as you see it.

DECEMBER 12

CONVICTED LIFE

Don't act thoughtlessly,
but understand what the Lord wants you to do.
EPHESIANS 5:17 NLT

This admonition from Paul is a difficult one to obey. For most men, the mind is a place of automatic sexual thoughts. Even after years of working toward godliness, sexuality fights for control of our minds. Outside sex, there are also larger forces of pride, fear, and insecurity that can falsely inspire our thoughts. Paul tells us to not just think righteously but also understand when our thoughts are coming more from our nervous systems than our spirits.

The Lord finds pleasure in us living righteously. Jesus is gladdened by our righteousness, and he wants us to know how to live like him. This starts and ends with love and knowing how to act with love for both God and our neighbor. Love informs and redeems our thoughts, so acting thoughtlessly is less of a danger, yet the truth of God's Word remains necessary for instruction and guidance.

Dear Lord, convict me of my actions today. Show me where I act out of instinct

rather than thought and change my heart and mind.

DECEMBER 13

STRONG PEACE

The LORD gives his people strength.
The LORD blesses them with peace.
PSALM 29:11 NLT

Have you experienced precarious peace? Whether it was the calm before a loved one passed away or being at home doing menial tasks right before a disaster, we all know worldly peace can't withstand life's storms. Life hurls hurt and pain at us with gale-force strength, and unless we have our lives built on the Rock, we will hurtle into oblivion. Only the peace of the Lord is strong enough to withstand life's attacks.

The Lord's peace is a strong peace. It is not precarious like the peace we feel in passing. His peace is perfect and strong because it carries the promise of eternal life and peace with Jesus. Even when chaos comes and crushes us, eternity with God still awaits. "The LORD blesses them with peace," today's psalm declares. He truly does, and if it is not with us now, it will be with us when we pass from the earth.

Prince of Peace, thank you for your eternal peace. Thank you for the promise of strength and peace this verse gives. Help me live in that promise.

DECEMBER 14

RECONCILING LIFE

> God has made all things new, and reconciled us to himself, and given us the ministry of reconciling others to God.
> 2 CORINTHIANS 5:18 TPT

According to Paul and all the New Testament writers, the gospel is a ministry of reconciliation. Reconciliation is not an easy process and requires a lot of humility and understanding. We need to be able to put ourselves in another person's shoes, understand why they did what they did, and love them in the midst of their wrong choices and mistakes. Reconciliation does not tolerate sin, but it does walk alongside people patiently rather than control their lives and condemn them.

Paul says, "God has made all things new." This is essential for reconciliation because when someone is forgiven, all their past wrongdoing is gone forever. With real repentance, their past is forgiven, and they are reconciled to God. The current way someone treats us is not reason to hate them; it's reason to pray for their redemption. With time, they may treat us as we desire, but it's a slow and long process.

Dear God, I pray for reconciliation in the lives of those around me. Reveal your love to them and free them from bondage.

DECEMBER 15

MAN'S GOOD PRAYER

Let my prayer be as the evening sacrifice that burns like fragrant incense, rising as my offering to you as I lift up my hands in surrendered worship!
PSALM 141:2 TPT

    Do we know how to surrender? Are we willing to give up our plans and offer our lives to God? It's difficult to let go of our lives and give them to God, but it's the only way we can offer a good prayer to God. God does not want a man who only gives token prayers and false sacrifices. He wants a man who gives the good prayers of someone who has rendered their lives entirely to Jesus. Yes, this is the fragrant incense and evening sacrifices God wants to rise to him.
    What a beautiful thing it is to life up our hands in surrendered worship! Joy is only found in freedom, and freedom is only found in liberation from our anxieties and fears by rendering them to God. God also wants us to be freed from our pride and desire for control. We were not made to be prideful or controlling; we were made to live glorious lives of servitude to our Creator.

Oh Jesus, let my prayers be as the evening sacrifice. Let my offering not be token prayers but a life surrendered to you.

DECEMBER 16

MANLY GENTLENESS

Accept one another, then, just as Christ accepted you, in order to bring praise to God.
ROMANS 15:7 NIV

How did Christ accept us? Was it with conditions, judgment, or resentment? Obviously not, but this is often how we accept others. Rather than accepting people wholeheartedly, or even carefully, we accept them without love. Their past sins or the ways they have hurt us stick with us, and we don't forget. It's right to recognize sin in other people and be wary of false redemption stories, but our forgiveness should not be tethered down by our pride.

As men, we are to excel in gentleness. We should be known as people whom others can talk to and be themselves around. If people are afraid of being judged or hurt by us, we are the weakest of men. Our manhood is perfected in strength when we are meek and have the power to restrain our anger and words. A good man accepts his weaker companions without judgment or scorn and thus brings praise to God.

Good Jesus, teach me to excel in gentleness. I want to accept others without

accepting their sins or evil habits but rather for the sake of transformation.

DECEMBER 17

ALWAYS AN ESCAPE

The temptations in your life are no different from what others experience. And God is faithful. He will not allow the temptation to be more than you can stand. When you are tempted, he will show you a way out so that you can endure.
1 CORINTHIANS 10:13 NLT

If something is wrong, Jesus will never require us to do it. There is no condition in which our Savior requires us to sin; he despises the very nature of sin and would never put us in such a situation. This is the case for any addiction or sin we are tempted toward as men. God will not put us in a place where we have to give in. Every time the tempter says there is no way out, we can call him a liar.

As today's verse says, there is always an escape from temptation. We will never be under too much pressure for the strength of God to sustain us. Our temptations are just part of the male experience, and they will pass away and die while we go on to eternity. They have no power over us and don't deserve our attention. Christ is too important of a goal for us to be distracted by the petty antics of the devil.

Oh Jesus, deliver me out of this temptation. Make today a day of faithfulness in which I do not give in to Satan's schemes.

DECEMBER 18

CRUSHED IN GOD

> Weeping may last through the night,
> but joy comes with the morning.
> PSALM 30:5 NLT

Men are expected to be strong and confident. People judge men by how stable they are, and this often breeds a fear of vulnerability. God must not be afraid of our vulnerability, though, because he showers us with tragedies that break and crush us. We do not outlast tragedy by holding ourselves together but by staying in God. We may be crushed, but we will endure as long as we are crushed in God.

The psalmist cries, "Weeping may last through the night." This is followed by a promise of joy, but weeping is not to be scorned because of it. Just because we know we are going to be healed doesn't mean our tears are without meaning. Jesus gives us weeping and pain to lower us. He wants us to be men of humility so others feel safe around us and so we can be like our Savior in gentleness.

Dear Jesus, you are here. In my brokenness, you are near to me. Help me appreciate this moment for what it gives.

DECEMBER 19

UNIQUELY EQUIPPED

God has given each of you a gift from his great variety of spiritual gifts. Use them well to serve one another.
1 PETER 4:10 NLT

God is full of riches. He takes joy in lavishing abundance upon his children, and in this wealth is a variety of spiritual gifts. Each gift holds a piece of the heart of God and reveals his character to those who see the gift at work. Those blessed with hospitable hearts reveal the hospitality of Jesus. Christians blessed with leadership reveal the wisdom and foreknowledge of God. His character is too diverse to be revealed in a single way, so instead, he is revealed among his children in a variety of ways.

It's important to remember we are uniquely equipped for the gospel. We should not expect others to have the same strengths as we do, nor should we be frustrated at the gifts God has given to others but hidden from us. It is his good pleasure to give as he sees fit, and we have no right to judge.

Oh Lord, teach me to serve my fellow man through the gifts you have given me.

Teach me to recognize their gifts as well and rejoice over them.

DECEMBER 20

GLORY TO HIS NAME

Not to us, LORD, not to us but to your name be the glory, because of your love and faithfulness.
PSALM 115:1 NIV

The more passionately we follow the Lord, the more glory will surround us. Solomon and David both fell into the trap of confusing this glory as their own. Both received much blessing and fame by following Yahweh, and both got to a point of forgetting whom that blessing was for. It was for God and his honor and not theirs. This refrain from Psalm 115 is a sweet chorus of humility focused on the love and faithfulness of our incredible Lord and Savior.

The world has a picture for what men should be: achievers and leaders basking in the glory of their work. Turning down fame can almost feel dangerous as if it jeopardizes our reputation. Yet this is the path of the Lord and the path he chose for us. He wants us to be strong in humility and weak in ourselves. He wants children who are not like the children of the world.

Oh God in heaven, remind me of your love and faithfulness. It's why I am here today, and I glorify you for it.

DECEMBER 21

GOD OF DELIVERANCE

He delivered us from such a deadly peril, and he will deliver us. On him we have set our hope that he will deliver us again.
2 CORINTHIANS 1:10 ESV

The Lord God is a god of many qualities. He is the God of justice who lets no sin escape his eye. He is also the God of power and holds the universe's potency in his hands. Even when it's inconvenient to us, the character of God is exact and perfect. He will accept no half-hearted followers; even if it means pain and tribulation for his children, he will make them know his identity and let go of their own. That is the key to the Lord's deliverance.

When we must rise out of peril alone, even deadly peril, God reveals he is our only hope. In humility, we have to give up our strengths and take the hand he stretches out to us. In place of our individuality and pride, he gives us selflessness and love. The more we surrender to God, the more we will be transformed into Christlike men.

Lord God, I give up my strength and pride to you today. Thank you for being the God

of deliverance. Please deliver me from temptations and pride that threaten me.

DECEMBER 22

IN HIS TIME

The LORD will work out his plans for my life—for your faithful love, O LORD, endures forever.
Don't abandon me, for you made me.
PSALM 138:8 NLT

David is desperate as he prays to God in this verse. He pleads, "Don't abandon me, for you made me." He has no other options. He has invested himself fully in God with no backup plans. The more skin we have in the game, the more invested we are in the outcome. When our faith is fully placed in God's plan, we will find ourselves constantly thinking about him. Half-hearted Christians will not have this problem. They will worry about life and focus on themselves and their own plans.

A man should discover how to master his mind through the power of God. He should learn to control his thoughts by reliance on God and not let his emotions rule him. David, in this passage, adeptly fights his anxiety. He reminds himself of God's truth—"your faithful love, O Lord, endures forever"—and uses this truth to view his situation through new eyes. "The Lord will work out his plans for my life."

God, I can trust you with my life. Your plans never fail, and you are worthy of my faith today and every day.

DECEMBER 23

OUR GREATEST SATISFACTION

I have fought the good fight,
I have finished the race,
I have kept the faith.
2 TIMOTHY 4:7 NCV

The harder the fight is, the greater our satisfaction at its completion. Paul considered his faith journey to be his greatest fight and his longest race. Every morning, he put aside himself and put on Christ by living a life of sacrifice and hardship for the sake of the gospel. He was betrayed by friends, beaten and whipped by enemies, and left out in the cold by numerous households. For Paul, though, this was nothing in comparison to what he would receive.

The end of our lives can be filled with our greatest sense of satisfaction. Rather than feelings of loss and regret, we can look back with joy at the way God worked through our pain and trials to further his gospel. We can see how God changed us to be the men we needed to be and how it blessed those around us. We can only do this if we embrace the struggle and deny ourselves each and every day.

Almighty God, I choose today to fight for you. Please be with me. Fill my arms with strength and my mind with hope as I seek your face.

DECEMBER 24

COUNTERFEIT LOVE

Do everything in love.
1 CORINTHIANS 16:14 CSB

Paul's words here are easy to misuse. We easily confuse other emotions with love when they are just counterfeit versions. We convince ourselves we yelled at someone because we love them and are worried about them, but it was just anger. Perhaps we chose to ask someone out because we loved them, but it was just attraction. True love is often inconvenient to us as it is built on sacrifice. To love someone is to put their needs before our own, and this is done by appreciating the love God has shown us.

Paul commands, "Let all that you do be done in love." Not a single selfish action is excused. He is insisting our lives be made complete through putting others first, dealing with them gently, and thinking of how the Lord would like us to treat them. This does not mean resting is wrong, but it means we use our time well in serving others. This service, when done by God's strength, can become our greatest source of joy.

Jesus, please teach me how to act in love. Teach me to reject counterfeit loves and put others first.

DECEMBER 25

CHRIST IS HERALDED

"A child has been born to us; God has given a son to us. He will be responsible for leading the people. His name will be Wonderful Counselor, Powerful God, Father Who Lives Forever, Prince of Peace."
ISAIAH 9:6 NCV

The entire world had waited for the birth of Christ. He was the light for a world lost in darkness, and his birth marked the beginning of the first, and only, perfect earthly life. As God himself, Jesus had no obligation to descend to our level. He could have remained in heaven, but he chose to take on the form of a humble man for the sake of the lost and brokenhearted. Isaiah says, "God has given a son to us." In an instant, the God of the universe gave us the greatest gift we could hope for.

Isaiah heralds Jesus as the ultimate leader perfect in wisdom, power, peace, and fatherliness. Even as a child, Christ was the greatest assurance of salvation the world could have. He gave us his life as an example and his death as an atoning sacrifice. He proved himself for us, though we did not deserve it, and made us children of his kingdom. What other gift is more worthy of celebration?

Baby Jesus, there is no other name more deserving of praise. No one else is suitable to be my leader and Savior. I will celebrate you today for all you have done for me.

DECEMBER 26

HARMONY AND PEACE

Be joyful. Grow to maturity. Encourage each other. Live in harmony and peace. Then the God of love and peace will be with you.
2 CORINTHIANS 13:11 NLT

Harmony and peace are greatly lacking in our world. They are a prize so valuable that most people have given up on ever seeing them. Though it feels too idealistic to be possible, living in harmony and peace is the direct commandment of God. We can even be so bold as to pray for it and wait for God to bring it about. In Christ, we can fulfill the words of Paul by being joyful and experiencing the love and peace of God.

The greatest threat to our peace is us. The more we focus on our development, careers, and everything related to us, the less satisfied we will be. Joy is reserved for those who live their lives for the sake of others. According to Paul, this joy goes hand in hand with peace, and we can't attain one without the other.

Oh Lord, please show me how to be joyful in you. Give me peace that surpasses all understanding. Through your love, teach me to live for those around me.

DECEMBER 27

LONGING FOR DELIVERANCE

*Lord, my every desire is in front of you;
my sighing is not hidden from you.*
PSALM 38:9 CSB

The feelings displayed by King David in this passage are intense and personal. He leans on the Lord tenderly and searches for his mercy amid injustice and persecution. When David pleads with God, he reminds the Lord of his promises and of David's own situation. He says no corner of his own heart is hidden. God knows his longing and his sighing, so why would he leave him in the dust?

God's path toward perfection is not easy, but it does help to be in communication with him. As in any relationship, our relationship to God is at its lowest point when we find ourselves forgetting to talk to him. As men, we need to confess our longings to God, so they do not turn against us and overpower us. Only through leaning on him can we have the strength to fight our demons.

Lord, please search me and know me. I am not the man other people see, but you know who I am and love me all the same. Thank you for this great mercy.

DECEMBER 28

APPROVED WORKER

Make every effort to give yourself to God as the kind of person he will approve. Be a worker who is not ashamed and who uses the true teaching in the right way.
2 TIMOTHY 2:15 NCV

Paul tells Timothy, "Give yourself to God as the kind of person he will approve," and the same admonition applies to us. Our character, reputation, and wisdom must be in line with God so the work we do through his power is not tainted or slandered through our shame. When we advise our brothers and sisters in Christ, we are to be brothers who give "the true teaching in the right way" and not lead any astray through our personal opinions or ulterior motives.

It is important for Christian men to be above reproach, for the world often looks to us to see what Jesus is like. If we don't understand God's Word or speak our personal thoughts as if they were gospel, we slander our Savior's name. A man can be free of these dangers but only through humility and care. We should scrutinize what we say and teach before we say it rather than anyone else pointing it out after we speak.

Dear Jesus, instruct me in the way I should go. Please help me lead others with truth and not empty opinions.

DECEMBER 29

MIMICKING CHRIST'S KINGDOM

Your kingdom is built on what is right and fair. Love and truth are in all you do.
PSALM 89:14 NCV

Every Christian is a small version of Christ's larger kingdom. The virtues Christ wants to see in his kingdom are only possible when they are seen in each of us. If we are not fair and right, and if love and truth is not in all we do, we don't have a part in Christ's kingdom. To be counted with Christ, we have to resemble him, and to resemble him, we need the Holy Spirit working in us. Just trying our best is not good enough; only a holy power can accomplish rightness and fairness in our hearts.

Most men in the world do not have the Holy Spirit working inside of them and have no source of true Christian righteousness. They work out of the desires of their hearts which are deceitful above all other things (Jeremiah 17:9). Putting Jesus and his kingdom first is the only way to not be tossed around by the world and instead lead others to what is right and fair.

God and King, just as you are, may I be right and fair to others. Teach me to put love and truth in every action today so others would know you.

DECEMBER 30

OUR DIFFERENCES

God works in different ways, but it is the same God who does the work in all of us.
1 CORINTHIANS 12:6 NLT

It is natural to think of other people through our understanding. We each have unique experiences, unique personalities, and unique convictions that inform the way we think about the world. This limits us in understanding each other because we only have our human understanding to use. God is unique as the only mind able to understand each and every one of us, and because of this, he "works in different ways" in each of us and matches his methods to our unique personhood.

God, "the same God who does the work in all of us," has the right to cast judgment because he understands everyone completely and perfectly. Because of our uniqueness, however, we cannot. Paul wants us to recognize this inability in ourselves and be careful when judging others. We need to recognize when God is at work and hold back our judgment as finite creatures.

Lord, thank you for giving me and everyone I meet a special, unique imprint of who you are. Please give me an appreciation of this today.

DECEMBER 31

ALWAYS

The LORD will watch over your coming and going both now and forevermore.
PSALM 121:8 NIV

God's promise of provision is eternal. It exists in the current moment, and it exists in our future. Often, one of these two facts eludes us. We understand the abstract idea that God will provide for us, at least ultimately, but we forget he is providing for us here and now. We can trust our current circumstances, inner battles, and daily struggles to him.

It's also easy to forget God will watch over us in the long run. Even if we have food and a roof over our heads today, we can worry about the future. We tend to plan our personal futures and forge as secure of a path as we can. How boldly might we live if we knew that "the LORD will watch over" us both now and in the future?

Lord, you provide for me every day. Even in my old age when I can't provide for myself, you will watch over me. Give me faith for my future today in light of your promises.

www.ingramcontent.com/pod-product-compliance
Lightning Source LLC
Chambersburg PA
CBHW011718220426
43663CB00018B/2912